Francis Bacon

Francis Bacon

*Essays
and
New Atlantis*

Published for the Classics Club ® by

WALTER J. BLACK, INC. · ROSLYN, N. Y.

COPYRIGHT 1942
BY WALTER J. BLACK, INC.

PRINTED IN THE UNITED STATES OF AMERICA

Contents

Introduction	xi
1. *Of Truth*	3
2. *Of Death*	7
3. *Of Unity in Religion*	10
4. *Of Revenge*	17
5. *Of Adversity*	19
6. *Of Simulation and Dissimulation*	21
7. *Of Parents and Children*	26
8. *Of Marriage and Single Life*	29
9. *Of Envy*	32
10. *Of Love*	39
11. *Of Great Place*	42
12. *Of Boldness*	47
13. *Of Goodness, and Goodness of Nature*	50
14. *Of Nobility*	54
15. *Of Seditions and Troubles*	56
16. *Of Atheism*	66
17. *Of Superstition*	71
18. *Of Travel*	74

Contents

19. Of Empire — 77
20. Of Counsel — 84
21. Of Delays — 91
22. Of Cunning — 93
23. Of Wisdom for a Man's Self — 99
24. Of Innovations — 102
25. Of Dispatch — 104
26. Of Seeming Wise — 107
27. Of Friendship — 109
28. Of Expense — 119
29. Of True Greatness of Kingdoms and Estates — 121
30. Of Regimen of Health — 134
31. Of Suspicion — 137
32. Of Discourse — 139
33. Of Plantations — 142
34. Of Riches — 146
35. Of Prophecies — 151
36. Of Ambition — 156
37. Of Masques and Triumphs — 159
38. Of Nature in Men — 162
39. Of Custom and Education — 165
40. Of Fortune — 168
41. Of Usury — 171
42. Of Youth and Age — 177

43. Of Beauty	180
44. Of Deformity	182
45. Of Building	184
46. Of Gardens	190
47. Of Negotiating	199
48. Of Followers and Friends	201
49. Of Suitors	204
50. Of Studies	207
51. Of Faction	210
52. Of Ceremonies and Respects	213
53. Of Praise	216
54. Of Vainglory	219
55. Of Honor and Reputation	222
56. Of Judicature	225
57. Of Anger	232
58 Of Vicissitude of Things	235
New Atlantis	243

Introduction

FRANCIS BACON's reputation has suffered from the world's insistence that a moralist should follow his own advice; having recognized vice and folly, he should avoid them. But in Bacon knowing and doing were as far apart as they are in others. All his life he wooed the Goddess of Getting-on, only to prove that self-seeking ends in disaster.

Bacon was born in London, January 22, 1561. His father, Sir Nicholas Bacon, had been for two years Lord Keeper of the Great Seal and Lord High Chancellor under Queen Elizabeth. His uncle, Sir William Cecil, later Lord Burghley, was Secretary of State. At the age of twelve, according to the custom of the time, Francis was sent to Trinity College, Cambridge. At fifteen he went with the English ambassador to France, where he studied diplomacy at first hand. When his father died in 1579, he returned home and took up the study of law at Gray's Inn. He was admitted to the bar in 1582.

His eminent connections were less helpful than one might expect. As the eighth child, he received nothing from his father's estate. His efforts to secure a place at Court through his uncle, then Lord High Treasurer, failed completely, and he was forced to depend for his living on what he could earn by the practice of law.

By 1591 he had become a close friend and adviser of Queen Elizabeth's favorite, the Earl of Essex, without much improvement in his circumstances. Having failed to get him the post of Attorney General, Essex gave him a valuable piece of land to lighten the burden of his debts. When the brilliant success of the Cadiz expedition made Essex a hero of the people, Bacon urged him to ignore their acclaim and seek only the Queen's favor. But Essex was unwilling or unable to follow this wise advice. He quarreled openly with Elizabeth, and in 1599, after the Irish fiasco, plunged into his foolhardy attempt to seize the government by force. In the ensuing trial for treason Bacon appeared among the Queen's counsel prosecuting his former patron, who was condemned to death and executed in 1601. Perhaps as a lawyer Bacon did no more than his duty, but it is difficult for a layman to avoid feeling that his absence from the case would have been more becoming. His zeal in her behalf did not win him the Queen's favor; no promotion was forthcoming during her reign.

Under King James he fared better. He was knighted in 1603 and in the following year appointed Learned Counsel, a position in which he gave the King valuable advice in the matter of the union with Scotland. His rise was unhindered now. In 1607 he became Solicitor General; in 1613 Attorney General; in 1617, Lord Keeper of the Great Seal; and in 1618, Lord High Chancellor, with the title of Baron Verulam. He had also found a new and

Introduction

powerful patron in the Duke of Buckingham, to whom the third edition of the *Essays* was dedicated.

Though he held the highest office in England, it had not been attained without cost. As he wrote in 1612, "the higher one goeth the fewer true friends he shall have," and he found the pinnacle of success a lonely one. He had not advanced without making enemies, who were only waiting for the proper moment to strike. In 1621, a few months after the King had created him Viscount St. Albans, Bacon was accused of having accepted bribes in cases being tried before him in the Court of Chancery. There was no doubt of the facts, and he soon gave up efforts to defend himself and pleaded guilty. His sentence included imprisonment in the Tower during the King's pleasure, a fine of £40,000, disqualification for any public office, and banishment from the Court. Though these penalties were only partly executed, Bacon's career as a public servant was ended.

Adversity was not without its compensations. For one thing, it gave him time to write. He finished the *History of Henry VII*, which he dedicated in 1622 to Prince Charles, soon to be King. He also prepared a much enlarged Latin translation of the *Advancement of Learning*, of which the first two books had been published in 1605. This was a part of Bacon's great philosophical project, the *Instauratio Magna* (*The Great Restoration*), which he hoped would supersede the work of Aristotle, whose influence, particularly in the natural sciences, was impeding research. Another part of the plan was the *Novum Organum* (*The New Instrument*), a method of inductive reasoning from carefully observed facts to supplant the deductive method of reasoning from abstraction and authority. The *Novum Organum* neglects the method of hypothesis, by which most discoveries are actually made; and Bacon himself ignored the important scientific observations of his age—for example, the astronomy of Copernicus, Kepler, and Galileo, and, in anatomy, the work of Vesalius and the discovery by his own physician, William Harvey, of the circulation of the blood. Still, he pointed the way, if he did not follow it. His zeal for experiment led indirectly to his death. During a snowstorm in the spring of 1626 he decided to try the effect of cold in preventing decay. He bought a fowl and stuffed it with snow. The exposure brought on the illness from which he died April 9, 1626.

There were three editions of Bacon's *Essays* during his life. The first, published in 1597, contained only ten essays: 50, 32, 52, 48, 49, 28, 30, 55, 51, and 47. The second, which appeared in 1612, added twenty-nine new ones: 27, 23, 14, 13, 43, 26, 36, 34, 25, 44, 42, 8, 7, 11, 19, 20, 16, 17, 53, 38, 39, 40, 2, 3, 22, 10, 56, 54, and 29, but omitted 55, "Of Honor and Reputation." The third edition, in 1625, restored 55 and added nineteen more: 1, 4, 5, 6, 9, 12, 15, 18, 21, 24, 31, 33, 35, 37, 41, 45, 46, 57, and 58. This text, the latest and most complete, is the one chosen for the Classics Club edition.

Introduction

The *Essays* deal with many phases of human life—politics, economics, religion, love, marriage, friendship, education, travel; as Bacon said, "they come home to men's business and bosoms." He uses the word *essay* in the literal sense of a *trial* or *weighing*. Readers sometimes feel that both sides of a question are balanced so equally that no conclusion is reached. Others are disturbed by Bacon's tendency to place expediency first as a rule of conduct. But in both cases their resentment springs in part from the realization that what he says is unfortunately true.

In spite of their clear and simple style the *Essays* must be read slowly. They are written in probably the most condensed English prose; they are to be chewed and digested. But they are crammed with a wisdom and experience that well repay the effort. The copious quotations often annoy the modern reader. In spite of his revolt from the medieval traditions, Bacon, like his contemporaries, constantly cites ancient authorities in support of his statements. His pages are spattered with Latin. He did not foresee that this would ever prove a difficulty to readers; in his day to read at all meant primarily to read Latin. The books that he expected to be of permanent interest he wrote in Latin or translated, so that, "being in the universal language," they might last as long as books last.

In an age when the majority of college graduates cannot even read their diplomas, many of the Latin phrases in Bacon's sentences are unintelligible. To make the Classics Club edition of the *Essays* as readable as possible, therefore, the Latin has been transferred to the footnotes and the English translation inserted in its place. The average reader may thus follow Bacon's thought without the intrusion of an unknown language, while the scholar who is curious about the Latin will find it on the same page.

Strictly speaking the *New Atlantis* is not an essay; and yet no apology is needed for including it here. It is one of the famous utopias, those accounts of an ideal world in which authors reveal what is wrong with their own. Though it was probably written some years before his fall, it shows Bacon conscious of the evil of bribery; on his imaginary island of Bensalem an official who takes a reward is regarded with contempt as "twice paid." The happy civilization Bacon pictures has been attained by the application of science to nature. The work is conducted by a learned society called Solomon's House, whose purpose is "the enlarging of the bounds of human empire to the effecting of all things possible." Though it was only a romance, the *New Atlantis* served as the model for the Royal Society, which was unique among academies in taking all knowledge for its province.

Bacon's work was less important in itself than in stimulating the work of others. But he was certainly overmodest in saying that he merely "rang the bell that called the wits together." He is one of the world's great thinkers, and his *Essays*, which contain the distilled essence of his thought, stand as one of the monuments of English literature.

GORDON S. HAIGHT

Essays and New Atlantis

Edited, with Notes and Introduction,
BY GORDON S. HAIGHT, PH.D.

I
Of Truth

WHAT is truth? said jesting Pilate;[1] and would not stay for an answer. Certainly there be that delight in giddiness; and count it a bondage to fix a belief; affecting freewill in thinking as well as in acting. And though the sects of philosophers of that kind be gone, yet there remain certain discoursing wits[2] which are of the same veins, though there be not so much blood in them as was in those of the ancients. But it is not only the difficulty and labor which men take in finding out of truth, nor again that when it is found, it imposeth upon men's thoughts, that doth bring lies in favor; but a natural though corrupt love of the lie itself. One of the later school[3] of the Grecians examineth the matter, and is at a stand to think what should be in it that men should love lies; where neither they make for pleasure, as with poets; nor for advantage, as with the merchant, but for the lie's sake. But I cannot tell; this same truth is a naked and open daylight that doth not show the masks and mummeries and triumphs of the world half so stately and daintily as candle lights. Truth may perhaps come to the price of a pearl that showeth best by day, but it will not rise to the price of a diamond or carbuncle that

[1] John, 18:38. [2] Rambling minds.
[3] Lucian, the Greek satirist, attacked the Skeptics in his *Philopseudes*.

showeth best in varied lights. A mixture of a lie doth ever add pleasure. Doth any man doubt that if there were taken out of men's minds vain opinions, flattering hopes, false valuations, imaginations as one would, and the like, but it would leave the minds of a number of men poor shrunken things, full of melancholy and indisposition, and unpleasing to themselves? One of the fathers, in great severity, called poesy *the wine of evil spirits* [4] because it filleth the imagination, and yet it is but with the shadow of a lie. But it is not the lie that passeth through the mind, but the lie that sinketh in, and settleth in it, that doth the hurt, such as we spake of before. But howsoever these things are thus in men's depraved judgments and affections, yet truth, which only doth judge itself, teacheth that the inquiry of truth, which is the love-making or wooing of it, the knowledge of truth, which is the presence of it, and the belief of truth, which is the enjoying of it, is the sovereign good of human nature. The first creature of God, in the works of the days, was the light of the sense; the last was the light of reason; [5] and his Sabbath work ever since is the illumination of his Spirit. First, he breathed light upon the face of the matter or chaos; then he breathed light into the face of man; and still he breatheth and inspireth light into the face of his chosen. The poet [6] that beautified the

---

[4] Vinum daemonum.   [5] Genesis, 1:3 and 2:7.
[6] Lucretius, the Roman poet and Epicurean philosopher. The passage quoted is paraphrased from the opening lines of the *De Rerum Natura*, book II.

Of Truth

sect,[7] that was otherwise inferior to the rest, saith yet excellently well: *It is a pleasure to stand upon the shore and to see ships tossed upon the sea; a pleasure to stand in the window of a castle and to see a battle and the adventures thereof below; but no pleasure is comparable to the standing upon the vantage-ground of truth* (a hill not to be commanded, and where the air is always clear and serene), *and to see the errors and wanderings and mists and tempests in the vale below;* so always that this prospect be with pity, and not with swelling or pride. Certainly it is heaven upon earth to have a man's mind move in charity, rest in providence, and turn upon the poles of truth.

To pass from theological and philosophical truth to the truth of civil business, it will be acknowledged, even by those that practice it not, that clear and round dealing is the honor of man's nature, and that mixture of falsehood is like alloy in coin of gold and silver, which may make the metal work the better, but it embaseth it. For these winding and crooked courses are the goings of the serpent; which goeth basely upon the belly, and not upon the feet. There is no vice that doth so cover a man with shame as to be found false and perfidious; and therefore Montaigne[8] saith prettily, when he inquired the reason why the word of the lie should be such a disgrace, and such an odious charge; saith he, *If it be well weighed, to say that a man lieth is as much as to say that he is brave*

[7] The followers of Epicurus.
[8] Michel de Montaigne, the French essayist.

towards God and a coward towards men. For a lie faces God and shrinks from man. Surely the wickedness of falsehood and breach of faith cannot possibly be so highly expressed, as in that it shall be the last peal to call the judgments of God upon the generations of men: it being foretold that when *Christ cometh*, he shall not *find faith upon the earth*.[9]

[9] Luke, 18:8.

2
Of Death

MEN fear death as children fear to go in the dark; and as that natural fear in children is increased with tales, so is the other. Certainly, the contemplation of death, as the wages of sin, and passage to another world, is holy and religious; but the fear of it, as a tribute due unto nature, is weak. Yet in religious meditations there is sometimes mixture of vanity and of superstition. You shall read in some of the friars' books of mortification, that a man should think with himself, what the pain is, if he have but his finger's end pressed or tortured; and thereby imagine what the pains of death are, when the whole body is corrupted and dissolved; when many times death passeth with less pain than the torture of a limb, for the most vital parts are not the quickest of sense. And by him that spake only as a philosopher and natural man, it was well said, *The trappings of death are more terrifying than death itself*.[1] Groans and convulsions, and a discolored face, and friends weeping, and blacks and obsequies, and the like, show death terrible. It is worthy the observing that there is no passion in the mind of man so weak but it mates and masters the fear of death; and therefore death is no such ter-

[1] *Pompa mortis magis terret, quam mors ipsa.*

rible enemy when a man hath so many attendants about him that can win the combat of him. Revenge triumphs over death; love slights it; honor aspireth to it; grief flieth to it; fear preoccupateth[2] it; nay, we read, after Otho the Emperor had slain himself, pity (which is the tenderest of affections) provoked many to die out of mere compassion to their sovereign, and as the truest sort of followers. Nay Seneca adds niceness[3] and satiety: *Consider how long you have done the same thing; a man may wish to die not only because he is brave or miserable, but because he is discriminating.*[4] A man would die, though he were neither valiant nor miserable, only upon a weariness to do the same thing so oft over and over. It is no less worthy to observe how little alteration in good spirits the approaches of death make, for they appear to be the same men till the last instant. Augustus Caesar died in a compliment: *Farewell, Livia, forget not the days of our marriage;*[5] Tiberius in dissimulation, as Tacitus saith of him, *His bodily strength was gone, but not his duplicity;*[6] Vespasian in a jest, sitting upon the stool, *It seems I am becoming a god;*[7] Galba with a sentence, *Strike, if it be for*

[2] Anticipates.
[3] Fastidiousness.
[4] *Cogita quamdiu eadem feceris; mori velle, non tantum fortis, aut miser, sed etiam fastidiosus potest.* Epistles, X, 1, 6.
[5] *Livia, conjugii nostri memor, vive et vale.* Suetonius, *Augustus*, XCIX.
[6] *Jam Tiberium vires et corpos, non dissimulatio, deserebant.* Annals, VI, 50.
[7] *Ut puto Deus fio.* Suetonius, *Vespasian*, XXIII.

*the good of the Roman people,*⁸ holding forth his neck, Septimus Severus in dispatch, *Hurry, if there is anything more,*⁹ and the like. Certainly, the Stoics[10] bestowed too much cost upon death, and by their great preparations made it appear more fearful. Better, saith he, *who reckons the close of life as one of the boons of nature.*[11] It is as natural to die as to be born; and to a little infant, perhaps, the one is as painful as the other. He that dies in an earnest pursuit is like one that is wounded in hot blood who, for the time, scarce feels the hurt; and therefore a mind fixed and bent upon somewhat that is good doth avert the dolors of death; but, above all, believe it, the sweetest canticle is *Nunc dimittis,*[12] when a man hath obtained worthy ends and expectations. Death hath this also, that it openeth the gate to good fame, and extinguisheth envy: *When dead, the same man shall be loved.*[13]

---

[8] *Feri, si ex re sit populi Romani.* Suetonius, *Galba,* XX.
[9] *Adeste, si quid mihi restat agendum.* Dion Cassius, LXVII, 17.
[10] The followers of Zeno, who founded the Stoic school. The basis of his doctrines was the duty of making virtue the object of all our researches. According to him, the pleasures of the mind were preferable to those of the body, and his disciples were taught to view with indifference health or sickness, riches or poverty, pain or pleasure.
[11] *Qui finem vitae extremum inter munera ponit naturae.* Juvenal, *Satires,* X, 358.
[12] *Lord, now lettest thou thy servant depart in peace.* Luke, 2:29.
[13] *Extinctus amabitus idem.* Horace, *Epistles,* II, 1, 14.

3
Of Unity in Religion

RELIGION being the chief band of human society, it is a happy thing when itself is well contained within the true band of unity. The quarrels and divisions about religion were evils unknown to the heathen. The reason was because the religion of the heathen consisted rather in rites and ceremonies than in any constant belief; for you may imagine what kind of faith theirs was, when the chief doctors and fathers of their church were the poets. But the true God hath this attribute, that he is a jealous God; and therefore his worship and religion will endure no mixture nor partner. We shall therefore speak a few words concerning the unity of the church; what are the fruits thereof; what the bounds; and what the means.

The fruits of unity (next unto the well-pleasing of God, which is all in all) are two; the one towards those that are without the church, the other towards those that are within. For the former, it is certain that heresies and schisms are, of all others, the greatest scandals, yea, more than corruption of manners; for as in the natural body a wound or solution of continuity is worse than a corrupt humor, so in the spiritual; so that nothing doth so much keep men out of the church, and drive men out of the church, as breach of unity; and therefore, whensoever it

Of Unity in Religion

cometh to that pass that one saith, *Behold, he is in the desert*,[1] another saith, *Behold, he is in the sanctuary*;[2] that is, when some men seek Christ in the conventicles of heretics and others in an outward face of a church, that voice had need continually to sound in men's ears, *Nolite exire, Go not out*. The doctor of the Gentiles[3] (the propriety of whose vocation drew him to have a special care of those without) saith: "If a heathen come in, and hear you speak with several tongues, will he not say that you are mad?" and, certainly, it is little better: when atheists and profane persons do hear of so many discordant and contrary opinions in religion, it doth avert them from the church, and maketh them "to sit down in the chair of the scorners."[4] It is but a light thing to be vouched in so serious a matter, but yet it expresseth well the deformity. There is a master of scoffing, that, in his catalogue of books of a feigned library, sets down this title of a book, *The Morris-Dance of Heretics*;[5] for indeed every sect of them hath a diverse posture or cringe by themselves, which cannot but move derision in worldlings and depraved politicians, who are apt to contemn holy things.

As for the fruit towards those that are within, it is peace, which containeth infinite blessings; it establisheth faith; it kindleth charity; the outward peace of the church distilleth into peace of conscience, and it turneth the labors

---

[1] *Ecce in deserto*. Matthew, 24:26.
[2] *Ecce in penetralibus*.
[3] Paul; I Corinthians, 14:23.
[4] Psalms, 1:1.
[5] Rabelais, *Pantagruel*, II, 7.

of writing and reading of controversies into treatises of mortification and devotion.

Concerning the bounds of unity, the true placing of them importeth exceedingly. There appear to be two extremes; for to certain zealots all speech of pacification is odious. *Is it peace, Jehu?—What hast thou to do with peace? turn thee behind me.*[6] Peace is not the matter, but following, and party. Contrariwise, certain Laodiceans[7] and lukewarm persons think they may accommodate points of religion by middle ways, and taking part of both, and witty reconcilements, as if they would make an arbitrament between God and man. Both these extremes are to be avoided; which will be done if the league of Christians, penned by our Saviour himself, were in the two cross clauses thereof soundly and plainly expounded: *He that is not with us is against us;* and again, *He that is not against us is with us;*[8] that is, if the points fundamental and of substance in religion were truly discerned and distinguished from points not merely of faith, but of opinion, order, or good intention. This is a thing may seem to many a matter trivial, and done already; but if it were done less partially, it would be embraced more generally.

Of this I may give only this advice, according to my small model. Men ought to take heed of rending God's church by two kinds of controversies; the one is, when the matter of the point controverted is too small and light,

[6] II Kings, 9:18. [7] Revelation, 3:14-16.
[8] Matthew, 12:30; Mark, 9:40.

not worth the heat and strife about it, kindled only by contradiction; for, as it is noted by one of the fathers, *Christ's coat indeed had no seam, but the church's vesture was of divers colors;* whereupon he saith, *Let there be variety in the garment, but no division,*⁹ they be two things, unity and uniformity; the other is, when the matter of the point controverted is great, but it is driven to an over-great subtilty and obscurity, so that it becometh a thing rather ingenious than substantial. A man that is of judgment and understanding shall sometimes hear ignorant men differ, and know well within himself that those which so differ mean one thing, and yet they themselves would never agree; and if it come so to pass in that distance of judgment, which is between man and man, shall we not think that God above, that knows the heart, doth not discern that frail men, in some of their contradictions, intend the same thing, and accepteth of both? The nature of such controversies is excellently expressed by St. Paul in the warning and precept that he giveth concerning the same: *Avoid profane and vain babblings, and oppositions of science falsely so called.*¹⁰ Men create oppositions which are not, and put them into new terms, so fixed as, whereas the meaning ought to govern the term, the term in effect governeth the meaning. There be also two false peaces or unities; the one, when the peace is grounded but upon an

⁹ *In veste varietas sit, scissura non sit.*
¹⁰ *Devita profanas vocum novitates, et oppositiones falsi nominis scientiae.* I Timothy, 6:20.

implicit [11] ignorance; for all colors will agree in the dark; the other, when it is pieced up upon a direct admission of contraries in fundamental points; for truth and falsehood, in such things, are like the iron and clay in the toes of Nebuchadnezzar's image; [12] they may cleave, but they will not incorporate.

Concerning the means of procuring unity, men must beware that, in the procuring or muniting of religious unity, they do not dissolve and deface the laws of charity and of human society. There be two swords amongst Christians, the spiritual and temporal, and both have their due office and place in the maintenance of religion; but we may not take up the third sword, which is Mahomet's sword, or like unto it; that is, to propagate religion by wars, or, by sanguinary persecutions, to force consciences; except it be in cases of overt scandal, blasphemy, or intermixture of practice against the state; much less to nourish seditions, to authorize conspiracies and rebellions, to put the sword into the people's hands, and the like, tending to the subversion of all government which is the ordinance of God; for this is but to dash the first table against the second, and so to consider men as Christians, as we forget that they are men. Lucretius the poet, when he beheld the act of Agamemnon, that could endure the sacrificing of his own daughter, exclaimed:

So many evils could religion prompt. [13]

[11] Tangled.   [12] Daniel, 2:33, 41.
[13] *Tantum religio potuit suadere malorom.*

Of Unity in Religion

What would he have said, if he had known of the massacre in France, or the powder treason of England? [14] He would have been seven times more epicure and atheist than he was; for as the temporal sword is to be drawn with great circumspection in cases of religion, so it is a thing monstrous to put it into the hands of the common people; let that be left unto the Anabaptists, and other furies. It was great blasphemy when the devil said, *I will ascend and be like the Highest;* [15] but it is greater blasphemy to personate God, and bring him in saying, *I will descend, and be like the prince of darkness;* and what is it better, to make the cause of religion to descend to the cruel and execrable actions of murdering princes, butchery of people, and subversion of states and governments? Surely this is to bring down the Holy Ghost, instead of the likeness of a dove, in the shape of a vulture or raven; and to set out of the bark of a Christian church a flag of a bark of pirates and assassins; therefore it is most necessary that the church by doctrine and decree, princes by their sword, and all learnings, both Christian and moral, as by their Mercury rod, do damn and send to hell forever those facts and opinions tending to the support of the same, as hath been already in good part done. Surely, in counsels concerning religion, that counsel of the apostle would be prefixed: *The wrath of man worketh not the righteousness of*

---

[14] The massacre of the Huguenots on St. Bartholomew's Day, August 24, 1572; "The Gunpowder Plot," November 5, 1605.
[15] Isaiah, 14:14.

God;[16] and it was a notable observation of a wise father, and no less ingenuously confessed, that those which held and persuaded pressure of consciences were commonly interested therein themselves for their own ends.

[16] *Ira hominis non implet justiciam Dei.* James, 1:20.

4
Of Revenge

REVENGE is a kind of wild justice, which the more man's nature runs to, the more ought law to weed it out; for as for the first wrong, it doth but offend the law, but the revenge of that wrong, putteth the law out of office. Certainly, in taking revenge, a man is but even with his enemy, but in passing it over, he is superior; for it is a prince's part to pardon; and Solomon, I am sure, saith, *It is the glory of a man to pass by an offense*. That which is past is gone and irrevocable, and wise men have enough to do with things present and to come; therefore they do but trifle with themselves that labor in past matters. There is no man doth a wrong for the wrong's sake, but thereby to purchase himself profit, or pleasure, or honor, or the like; therefore, why should I be angry with a man for loving himself better than me? And if any man should do wrong merely out of ill-nature, why, yet it is but like the thorn or briar, which prick and scratch, because they can do no other. The most tolerable sort of revenge is for those wrongs which there is no law to remedy; but then let a man take heed the revenge be such as there is no law to punish, else a man's enemy is still beforehand, and it is two for one. Some, when they take revenge, are desirous the party should know whence it cometh. This is the more generous; for the delight seemeth to be not so much in doing the hurt as in making the party repent; but base and crafty cowards are like the arrow that flieth in the dark. Cosmus, Duke of Florence,[1] had a desperate saying against perfidious or neglecting friends, as if those wrongs were unpardonable. *You shall read*, saith he, *that we are commanded to forgive our enemies; but you never read that we are commanded to forgive our friends*. But yet the spirit of Job was in a better tune: *Shall we*, saith he, *take good at God's hands, and not be content to take evil also?* [2] and so of friends in a proportion. This is certain, that a man that studieth revenge keeps his own wounds green, which otherwise would heal and do well. Public revenges [3] are for the most part fortunate; as that for the death of Caesar; for the death of Pertinax; for the death of Henry the Third of France; [4] and many more. But in private revenges it is not so; nay, rather, vindictive persons live the life of witches, who, as they are mischievous, so end they unfortunate.

---

[1] Cosmo de Medici, or Cosmo I, chief of the Republic of Florence, the encourager of literature and the fine arts.
[2] Job, 2:10.
[3] Punishment awarded by the state with the sanction of the laws.
[4] Caesar was avenged by Antony and Augustus; Pertinax, a Roman emperor, was murdered by the praetorians, who were put to death by Septimius Severus; Jacques Clement, the monk who murdered Henry the Third, was put to death on the spot.

5
Of Adversity

IT WAS a high speech of Seneca (after the manner of the Stoics), that *the good things which belong to prosperity are to be wished, but the good things that belong to adversity are to be admired. (Bona rerum secundarum optabilia, adversarum mirabilia.)* Certainly, if miracles be the command over nature, they appear most in adversity. It is yet a higher speech of his than the other (much too high for a heathen), *It is true greatness to have in one the frailty of a man, and the security of a God. (Vere magnum habere fragilitatem hominis securitatem Dei.)* This would have done better in poesy, where transcendencies are more allowed, and the poets indeed have been busy with it; for it is in effect the thing which is figured in that strange fiction of the ancient poets,[1] which seemeth not to be without mystery; nay, and to have some approach to the state of a Christian, *that Hercules, when he went to unbind Prometheus* (by whom human nature is represented), *sailed the length of the great ocean in an earthen pot or pitcher*, lively describing Christian resolution, that saileth in the frail bark of the flesh through the waves of the world. But to speak in a mean, the virtue of prosperity is

[1] For stealing fire from heaven Prometheus was chained to a rock on Mt. Caucasus.

temperance, the virtue of adversity is fortitude, which in morals is the more heroical virtue. Prosperity is the blessing of the Old Testament, adversity is the blessing of the New, which carrieth the greater benediction, and the clearer revelation of God's favor. Yet even in the Old Testament, if you listen to David's harp, you shall hear as many hearse-like airs as carols; and the pencil of the Holy Ghost hath labored more in describing the afflictions of Job than the felicities of Solomon. Prosperity is not without many fears and distastes; and adversity is not without comforts and hopes. We see, in needleworks and embroideries, it is more pleasing to have a lively work upon a sad and solemn ground, than to have a dark and melancholy work upon a lightsome ground: judge, therefore, of the pleasure of the heart by the pleasure of the eye. Certainly virtue is like precious odors, most fragrant when they are incensed or crushed; for prosperity doth best discover vice, but adversity doth best discover virtue.

6

Of Simulation and Dissimulation

DISSIMULATION is but a faint kind of policy, or wisdom; for it asketh a strong wit and a strong heart to know when to tell truth, and to do it; therefore it is the weaker sort of politicians that are the great dissemblers.

Tacitus saith,[1] *Livia sorted well with the arts of her husband, and dissimulation of her son; attributing arts or policy to Augustus, and dissimulation to Tiberius;* and again, when Mucianus encourageth Vespasian to take arms against Vitellius, he saith, *We rise not against the piercing judgment of Augustus, nor the extreme caution or closeness of Tiberius.*[2] These properties of arts or policy, and dissimulation or closeness, are indeed habits and faculties several, and to be distinguished; for if a man have that penetration of judgment as he can discern what things are to be laid open, and what to be secreted, and what to be showed at half-lights, and to whom and when (which indeed are arts of state, and arts of life, as Tacitus well calleth them), to him a habit of dissimulation is a hinderance and a poorness. But if a man cannot obtain to that judgment, then it is left to him generally to be close, and a dissembler; for where a man cannot choose or vary in partic-

[1] Tacitus, *Annals*, V, 1.   [2] Tacitus, *History*, II, 76.

ulars, there it is good to take the safest and wariest way in general, like the going softly by one that cannot well see. Certainly the ablest men that ever were have had all an openness and frankness of dealing, and a name of certainty and veracity: but then they were like horses well managed, for they could tell passing well when to stop or turn; and at such times, when they thought the case indeed required dissimulation, if then they used it, it came to pass that the former opinion spread abroad, of their good faith and clearness of dealing made them almost invisible.

There be three degrees of this hiding and veiling of a man's self: the first, closeness, reservation, and secrecy; when a man leaveth himself without observation, or without hold to be taken, what he is; the second, dissimulation in the negative, when a man lets fall signs and arguments, that he is not that he is; and the third, simulation in the affirmative, when a man industriously and expressly feigns and pretends to be that he is not.

For the first of these, secrecy, it is indeed the virtue of a confessor; and assuredly the secret man heareth many confessions; for who will open himself to a blab or a babbler? But if a man be thought secret, it inviteth discovery, as the more close air sucketh in the more open; and, as in confession, the revealing is not for worldly use, but for the ease of a man's heart, so secret men come to the knowledge of many things in that kind; while men rather discharge their minds than impart their minds. In few words, mysteries are due to secrecy. Besides (to say truth), naked-

Of Simulation and Dissimulation

ness is uncomely, as well in mind as body; and it addeth no small reverence to men's manners and actions, if they be not altogether open. As for talkers and futile persons, they are commonly vain and credulous withal; for he that talketh what he knoweth, will also talk what he knoweth not; therefore set it down, that a habit of secrecy is both politic and moral. And in this part it is good that a man's face give his tongue leave to speak; for the discovery of a man's self by the tracts[3] of his countenance is a great weakness and betraying, by how much it is many times more marked and believed than a man's words.

For the second, which is dissimulation, it followeth many times upon secrecy by a necessity; so that he that will be secret must be a dissembler in some degree; for men are too cunning to suffer a man to keep an indifferent carriage between both, and to be secret, without swaying the balance on either side. They will so beset a man with questions, and draw him on, and pick it out of him, that without an absurd silence, he must show an inclination one way; or if he do not, they will gather as much by his silence as by his speech. As for equivocations or oraculous speeches, they cannot hold out long: so that no man can be secret, except he give himself a little scope of dissimulation, which is, as it were, but the skirts or train of secrecy.

But for the third degree, which is simulation and false profession, that I hold more culpable and less politic,

[3] Traits or features.

except it be in great and rare matters; and, therefore, a general custom of simulation (which is this last degree) is a vice rising either of a natural falseness, or fearfulness, or of a mind that hath some main faults; which because a man must needs disguise, it maketh him practice simulation in other things, lest his hand should be out of use.

The advantages of simulation and dissimulation are three: first, to lay asleep opposition, and to surprise; for, where a man's intentions are published, it is an alarum to call up all that are against them: the second is, to reserve to a man's self a fair retreat; for if a man engage himself by a manifest declaration, he must go through or take a fall: the third is, the better to discover the mind of another; for to him that opens himself men will hardly show themselves adverse; but will (fair) let him go on, and turn their freedom of speech to freedom of thought; and therefore it is a good shrewd proverb of the Spaniard, *Tell a lie, and find a troth;*[4] as if there were no way of discovery but by simulation. There be also three disadvantages to set it even; the first, that simulation and dissimulation commonly carry with them a show of fearfulness, which, in any business, doth spoil the feathers of round flying up to the mark; the second, that it puzzleth and perplexeth the conceits of many that perhaps would otherwise co-operate with him, and makes a man walk almost alone to his own ends; the third, and greatest, is that it depriveth a man of

[4] Truth.

Of Simulation and Dissimulation

one of the most principal instruments for action, which is trust and belief. The best composition and temperature [5] is to have openness in fame and opinion, secrecy in habit, dissimulation in seasonable use, and a power to feign if there be no remedy.

[5] Temperament.

7
Of Parents and Children

THE joys of parents are secret, and so are their griefs and fears; they cannot utter the one, nor they will not utter the other. Children sweeten labors, but they make misfortunes more bitter; they increase the cares of life, but they mitigate the remembrance of death. The perpetuity by generation is common to beasts; but memory, merit, and noble works, are proper to men: and surely a man shall see the noblest works and foundations have proceeded from childless men, which have sought to express the images of their minds where those of their bodies have failed; so the care of posterity is most in them that have no posterity. They that are the first raisers of their houses are most indulgent towards their children, beholding them as the continuance, not only of their kind, but of their work; and so both children and creatures.

The difference in affection of parents towards their several children is many times unequal, and sometimes unworthy, especially in the mother; as Solomon saith, *A wise son rejoiceth the father, but an ungracious son shames the mother.*[1] A man shall see, where there is a house full of children, one or two of the eldest respected and the young-

[1] Proverbs, 10:1.

Of Parents and Children

est made wantons; but in the midst some that are, as it were, forgotten, who many times, nevertheless, prove the best. The illiberality of parents in allowance towards their children is a harmful error, makes them base, acquaints them with shifts, makes them sort with mean company, and makes them surfeit more when they come to plenty; and, therefore the proof [2] is best when men keep their authority towards their children, but not their purse. Men have a foolish manner (both parents, and schoolmasters, and servants) in creating and breeding an emulation between brothers during childhood, which many times sorteth [3] to discord when they are men, and disturbeth families. The Italians make little difference between children and nephews or near kinsfolk; but so they be of the lump, they care not, though they pass not through their own body; and, to say truth, in nature it is much a like matter; insomuch that we see a nephew sometimes resembleth an uncle or a kinsman more than his own parent, as the blood happens. Let parents choose betimes the vocations and courses they mean their children should take, for then they are most flexible; and let them not too much apply themselves to the disposition of their children, as thinking they will take best to that which they have most mind to. It is true that if the affection or aptness of the children be extraordinary, then it is good not to cross it; but generally the precept is good, *Choose the best course of life;*

[2] Plan or method. [3] Turns.

custom will make it pleasant and easy.[4] Younger brothers are commonly fortunate, but seldom or never where the elder are disinherited.

[4] *Optimum elige, suave et facile illud faciet consuetudo.*

8
Of Marriage and Single Life

HE THAT hath wife and children hath given hostages to fortune; for they are impediments to great enterprises, either of virtue or mischief. Certainly the best works, and of greatest merit for the public, have proceeded from the unmarried or childless men, which, both in affection and means, have married and endowed the public. Yet it were great reason that those that have children should have greatest care of future times, unto which they know they must transmit their dearest pledges. Some there are who, though they lead a single life, yet their thoughts do end with themselves, and account future times impertinences;[1] nay, there are some other that account wife and children but as bills of charges; nay more, there are some foolish, rich, covetous men that take a pride in having no children, because they may be thought so much the richer; for, perhaps they have heard some talk. *Such an one is a great rich man*, and another except to it, *Yea, but he hath a great charge of children*; as if it were an abatement to his riches. But the most ordinary cause of a single life is liberty, especially in certain self-pleasing and humorous[2] minds, which are so sensible of every restraint as they will go near to

[1] Trifles.   [2] Odd.

think their girdles and garters to be bonds and shackles. Unmarried men are best friends, best masters, best servants; but not always best subjects, for they are light to run away, and almost all fugitives are of that condition. A single life doth well with churchmen, for charity will hardly water the ground where it must first fill a pool. It is indifferent for judges and magistrates; for if they be facile and corrupt, you shall have a servant five times worse than a wife. For soldiers, I find the generals commonly in their hortatives put men in mind of their wives and children; and I think the despising of marriage amongst the Turks maketh the vulgar soldier more base. Certainly wife and children are a kind of discipline of humanity; and single men, though they be many times more charitable, because their means are less exhaust,[3] yet, on the other side, they are more cruel and hard-hearted (good to make severe inquisitors), because their tenderness is not so oft called upon. Grave natures, led by custom and therefore constant, are commonly loving husbands, as was said of Ulysses, *He preferred his aged wife Penelope to immortality*.[4] Chaste women are often proud and froward, as presuming upon the merit of their chastity. It is one of the best bonds, both of chastity and obedience, in the wife, if she think her husband wise, which she will never do if she find him jealous. Wives are young men's mistresses, companions for middle age, and old men's nurses, so as a man

[3] Exhausted.   [4] *Vetulam suam praetulit immortalitati.*

may have a quarrel[5] to marry when he will; but yet he was reputed one of the wise men that made answer to the question when a man should marry, *A young man not yet, an older man not at all.*[6] It is often seen that bad husbands have very good wives; whether it be that it raiseth the price of their husbands' kindness when it comes, or that the wives take a pride in their patience; but this never fails, if the bad husbands were of their own choosing, against their friends' consent, for then they will be sure to make good their own folly.

[5] Pretext.
[6] Thales, when urged by his mother to marry, said he was too young; later, when pressed, he replied that he was too old. Plutarch, *Symposiaca*, III, 6; also quoted by Montaigne, *Essays*, II, 8.

9
Of Envy

THERE be none of the affections which have been noted to fascinate or bewitch, but love and envy. They both have vehement wishes; they frame themselves readily into imaginations and suggestions, and they come easily into the eye, especially upon the presence of the objects which are the points that conduce to fascination, if any such thing there be. We see, likewise, the Scripture calleth envy an evil eye;[1] and the astrologers call the evil influences of the stars evil aspects; so that still there seemeth to be acknowledged, in the act of envy, an ejaculation, or irradiation of the eye. Nay, some have been so curious[2] as to note that the times when the stroke or percussion of an envious eye doth most hurt are when the party envied is beheld in glory or triumph, for that sets an edge upon envy; and besides, at such times, the spirits of the person envied do come forth most into the outward parts, and so meet the blow.

But leaving these curiosities (though not unworthy to be thought on in fit place), we will handle what persons are apt to envy others; what persons are most subject to be envied themselves; and what is the difference between public and private envy.

[1] Mark, 7:22.   [2] Observant of detail.

Of Envy

A man that hath no virtue in himself ever envieth virtue in others; for men's minds will either feed upon their own good, or upon others' evil; and who wanteth the one will prey upon the other; and whoso is out of hope to attain to another's virtue will seek to come at even hand³ by depressing another's fortune.

A man that is busy and inquisitive is commonly envious; for to know much of other men's matters cannot be, because all that ado may concern his own estate; therefore, it must needs be that he taketh a kind of play-pleasure in looking upon the fortunes of others; neither can he that mindeth but his own business find much matter for envy; for envy is a gadding passion, and walketh the streets, and doth not keep home: *There is no curious man who is not also malevolent.*⁴

Men of noble birth are noted to be envious towards new men when they rise, for the distance is altered; and it is like a deceit of the eye, that when others come on they think themselves go back.

Deformed persons and eunuchs, and old men and bastards, are envious; for he that cannot possibly mend his own case, will do what he can to impair another's; except these defects light upon a very brave and heroical nature, which thinketh to make his natural wants part of his honor; in that it should be said, *That a eunuch, or a lame man, did such great matters*, affecting the honor of a

---

³ To get even with.
⁴ *Non est curiosus quin idem sit malevolus.* Plautus, *Stichus*, I, 3, 54

miracle; as it was in Narses the eunuch, and Agesilaus and Tamerlane,[5] that were lame men.

The same is the case of men that rise after calamities and misfortunes; for they are as men fallen out with the times, and think other men's harms a redemption of their own sufferings.

They that desire to excel in too many matters, out of levity and vainglory, are ever envious, for they cannot want work; it being impossible but many, in some one of those things, should surpass them; which was the character of Adrian the Emperor, that mortally envied poets and painters, and artificers in works, wherein he had a vein to excel.

Lastly, near kinsfolk and fellows in office, and those that have been bred together, are more apt to envy their equals when they are raised; for it doth upbraid unto them their own fortunes, and pointeth at them, and cometh oftener into their remembrance, and incurreth likewise more into the note of others; and envy ever redoubleth from speech and fame. Cain's envy was the more vile and malignant towards his brother Abel, because when his sacrifice was better accepted there was nobody to look on. Thus much for those that are apt to envy.

Concerning those that are more or less subject to envy:

---

[5] Narses, commander of the Byzantine army which defeated the Goths in Italy in 554; Agesilaus, King of Sparta in the fourth century B.C.; "Timur the Lame," conqueror of Persia, the Near East, and India in the fourteenth century.

Of Envy

First, persons of eminent virtue, when they are advanced, are less envied, for their fortune seemeth but due unto them; and no man envieth the payment of a debt, but rewards and liberality rather. Again, envy is ever joined with the comparing of a man's self; and where there is no comparison, no envy; and therefore kings are not envied but by kings. Nevertheless, it is to be noted that unworthy persons are most envied at their first coming in, and afterwards overcome it better; whereas, contrariwise, persons of worth and merit are most envied when their fortune continueth long; for by that time, though their virtue be the same, yet it hath not the same luster; for fresh men grow up that darken it.

Persons of noble blood are less envied in their rising; for it seemeth but right done to their birth: besides, there seemeth not so much added to their fortune; and envy is as the sunbeams that beat hotter upon a bank or steep rising ground than upon a flat; and, for the same reason, those that are advanced by degrees are less envied than those that are advanced suddenly, and *at a bound*.[6]

Those that have joined with their honor great travels [7] cares, or perils, are less subject to envy; for men think that they earn their honors hardly, and pity them sometimes, and pity ever healeth envy. Wherefore you shall observe, that the more deep and sober sort of politic persons, in their greatness, are ever bemoaning themselves

[6] *Per saltum*. [7] Labors.

what a life they lead, chanting a *quanta patimur;* [8] not that they feel it so, but only to abate the edge of envy; but this is to be understood of business that is laid upon men, and not such as they call unto themselves; for nothing increaseth envy more than an unnecessary and ambitious engrossing of business; and nothing doth extinguish envy more than for a great person to preserve all other inferior officers in their full rights and pre-eminences of their places; for, by that means, there be so many screens between him and envy.

Above all, those are most subject to envy, which carry the greatness of their fortunes in an insolent and proud manner; being never well but while they are showing how great they are, either by outward pomp or by triumphing over all opposition or competition. Whereas wise men will rather do sacrifice to envy in suffering themselves, sometimes of purpose, to be crossed and overborne in things that do not much concern them. Notwithstanding, so much is true, that the carriage of greatness in a plain and open manner (so it be without arrogancy and vainglory), doth draw less envy than if it be in a more crafty and cunning fashion; for in that course a man doth but disavow fortune, and seemeth to be conscious of his own want in worth, and doth but teach others to envy him.

Lastly, to conclude this part, as we said in the beginning that the act of envy had somewhat in it of witchcraft,

[8] *How much we suffer!*

Of Envy

so there is no other cure of envy but the cure of witchcraft; and that is to remove the lot (as they call it), and to lay it upon another; for which purpose the wiser sort of great persons bring in ever upon the stage somebody upon whom to derive [9] the envy that would come upon themselves; sometimes upon ministers and servants, sometimes upon colleagues and associates, and the like; and, for that turn, there are never wanting some persons of violent and undertaking [10] natures, who, so they may have power and business, will take it at any cost.

Now, to speak of public envy: there is yet some good in public envy, whereas in private there is none; for public envy is as an ostracism, that eclipseth men when they grow too great; and therefore it is a bridle also to great ones, to keep them within bounds.

This envy, being in the Latin word *invidia*,[11] goeth in the modern languages by the name of discontentment, of which we shall speak in handling sedition. It is a disease in a state like to infection; for as infection spreadeth upon that which is sound and tainteth it, so, when envy is gotten once into a state, it traduceth even the best actions thereof, and turneth them into an ill odor; and therefore there is little won by intermingling of plausible actions; for that doth argue but a weakness and fear of envy, which hurteth so much the more, as it is likewise usual in infec-

---

[9] Turn aside. [10] Enterprising.
[11] From *in* and *video*, "look upon"; with reference to the so-called "evil eye" of the envious.

tions, which, if you fear them, you call them upon you.

This public envy seemeth to beat chiefly upon principal officers or ministers, rather than upon kings and estates themselves. But this is a sure rule, that if the envy upon the minister be great, when the cause of it in him is small; or if the envy be general in a manner upon all the ministers of an estate, then the envy (though hidden) is truly upon the state itself. And so much of public envy or discontentment, and the difference thereof from private envy, which was handled in the first place.

We will add this in general, touching the affection of envy, that, of all other affections, it is the most importune and continual; for of other affections there is occasion given but now and then; and therefore it was well said, *Envy keeps no holidays;* [12] for it is ever working upon some or other. And it is also noted, that love and envy do make a man pine, which other affections do not, because they are not so continual. It is also the vilest affection, and the most depraved; for which cause it is the proper attribute of the devil, who is called *The envious man, that soweth tares amongst the wheat by night;* [13] as it always cometh to pass that envy worketh subtilely, and in the dark, and to the prejudice of good things, such as is the wheat.

[12] *Invidia festos dies non agit.* [13] Matthew, 13:25.

10
Of Love

THE stage is more beholding [1] to love than the life of man; for as to the stage, love is ever matter of comedies, and now and then of tragedies; but in life it doth much mischief, sometimes like a Siren, sometimes like a Fury. You may observe, that, amongst all the great and worthy persons (whereof the memory remaineth, either ancient or recent), there is not one that hath been transported to the mad degree of love, which shows that great spirits and great business do keep out this weak passion. You must except nevertheless Marcus Antonius, the half partner of the empire of Rome, and Appius Claudius, the decemvir and lawgiver; whereof the former was indeed a voluptuous man, and inordinate, but the latter was an austere and wise man; and therefore it seems (though rarely) that love can find entrance, not only into an open heart, but also into a heart well fortified, if watch be not well kept. It is a poor saying of Epicurus, *We are, to one another, a theater sufficiently large;* [2] as if man, made for the contemplation of heaven and all noble objects, should do nothing but kneel before a little idol, and make himself subject, though not of the mouth (as beasts are) yet of the eye, which was given

[1] Indebted.
[2] *Satis magnum alter alteri theatrum sumus.* Seneca, *Epistles,* 7.

him for higher purposes. It is a strange thing to note the excess of this passion, and how it braves[3] the nature and value of things, by this, that the speaking in a perpetual hyperbole is comely in nothing but in love, neither is it merely in the phrase; for whereas it hath been well said, *That the arch flatterer, with whom all the petty flatterers have intelligence, is a man's self*, certainly, the lover is more; for there was never proud man thought so absurdly well of himself as the lover doth of the person loved; and therefore it was well said, *That it is impossible to love and to be wise*. Neither doth this weakness appear to others only, and not to the party loved, but to the loved most of all, except the love be reciprocal; for it is a true rule, that love is ever rewarded, either with the reciprocal, or with an inward and secret contempt; by how much the more men ought to beware of this passion, which loseth not only other things, but itself. As for the other losses, the poet's relation[4] doth well figure them: *That he that preferred Helena, quitted the gifts of Juno and Pallas;* for whosoever esteemeth too much of amorous affection, quitteth both riches and wisdom. This passion hath his floods in the very times of weakness, which are great prosperity and great adversity, though this latter hath been less observed; both which times kindle love, and make it more fervent, and therefore

---

[3] Insults.
[4] He refers here to the judgment of Paris, mentioned by Ovid in his *Epistles*, of the Goddesses.

Of Love

show it to be the child of folly. They do best who, if they cannot but admit love, yet make it keep quarter, and sever it wholly from their serious affairs and actions of life; for if it check[5] once with business, it troubleth men's fortunes, and maketh men that they can nowise be true to their own ends. I know not how, but martial men are given to love; I think it is but as they are given to wine, for perils commonly ask to be paid in pleasures. There is in man's nature a secret inclination and motion towards love of others, which, if it be not spent upon some one or a few, doth naturally spread itself towards many, and maketh men become humane and charitable, as it is seen sometimes in friars. Nuptial love maketh mankind, friendly love perfecteth it, but wanton love corrupteth and embaseth it.

[5] Interfere.

11

Of Great Place

MEN in great place are thrice servants—servants of the sovereign or state, servants of fame, and servants of business; so as they have no freedom neither in their persons, nor in their actions, nor in their times. It is a strange desire to seek power and to lose liberty; or to seek power over others, and to lose power over a man's self. The rising unto place is laborious, and by pains men come to greater pains; and it is sometimes base, and by indignities men come to dignities. The standing is slippery, and the regress is either a downfall, or at least an eclipse, which is a melancholy thing: *When you are no longer the man you were, there is no reason why you should wish to live*.[1] Nay, retire men cannot when they would, neither will they when it were reason; but are impatient of privateness even in age and sickness, which require the shadow; like old townsmen that will be still sitting at their street door, though thereby they offer age to scorn. Certainly great persons had need to borrow other men's opinions to think themselves happy; for if they judge by their own feeling, they cannot find it; but if they think with themselves what other men think of them, and that other men would fain be as they are, then

[1] *Cum non sis qui fueris, non esse cur velis vivere.* Cicero, *Letters*.

they are happy as it were by report, when, perhaps, they find the contrary within; for they are the first that find their own griefs, though they be the last that find their own faults. Certainly men in great fortunes are strangers to themselves, and while they are in the puzzle of business they have no time to tend their health either of body or mind. *It is a sad fate for a man to die too well known to others, and to himself unknown.*[2]

In place, there is license to do good and evil, whereof the latter is a curse; for in evil, the best condition is not to will, the second not to can.[3] But power to do good is the true and lawful end of aspiring; for good thoughts, though God accept them, yet towards men are little better than good dreams, except they be put in act; and that cannot be without power and place, as the vantage and commanding ground. Merit and good works are the end of man's motion, and conscience of same is the accomplishment of man's rest; if a man can be partaker of God's theater, he shall likewise be partaker of God's rest. *And God saw everything that he had made and, behold, it was very good;*[4] and then the Sabbath.

In the discharge of thy place, set before thee the best examples; for imitation is a globe of precepts, and after a time set before thee thine own example; and examine thy-

---

[2] *Illi mors gravis incubat, qui notus nimis omnibus, ignotus moritur sibi.* Seneca, *Thyestes,* II, 401.

[3] Be able.

[4] *Et conversus Deus, ut aspiceret opera, quae fecerunt manus suae, vidit quod omnia essent bona nimis. Genesis,* 1:31.

self strictly whether thou didst not best at first. Neglect not also the examples of those that have carried themselves ill in the same place; not to set off thyself by taxing their memory, but to direct thyself what to avoid. Reform, therefore, without bravery[5] or scandal of former times and persons; but yet set it down to thyself, as well to create good precedents as to follow them. Reduce things to the first institution, and observe wherein and how they have degenerated; but yet ask counsel of both times—of the ancient time what is best, and of the latter time what is fittest. Seek to make thy course regular, that men may know beforehand what they may expect; but be not too positive and peremptory, and express thyself well when thou digressest from thy rule. Preserve the right of thy place, but stir not questions of jurisdiction; and rather assume thy right in silence, and *as a matter of fact*,[6] than voice it with claims and challenges. Preserve likewise the rights of inferior places; and think it more honor to direct in chief than to be busy in all. Embrace and invite helps and advices touching the execution of thy place; and do not drive away such as bring thee information, as meddlers, but accept of them in good part. The vices of authority are chiefly four: delays, corruption, roughness, and facility. For delays, give easy access, keep times appointed, go through with that which is in hand, and interlace not business but of necessity. For corruption, do not only bind

[5] Boastfulness.   [6] *De facto*.

Of Great Place

thine own hands or thy servant's hands from taking, but bind the hands of suitors also from offering; for integrity used doth the one, but integrity professed, and with a manifest detestation of bribery, doth the other; and avoid not only the fault, but the suspicion. Whosoever is found variable, and changeth manifestly without manifest cause, giveth suspicion of corruption; therefore, always when thou changest thine opinion or course, profess it plainly, and declare it, together with the reasons that move thee to change, and do not think to steal it. A servant or a favorite, if he be inward, and no other apparent cause of esteem, is commonly thought a by-way to close corruption. For roughness is a needless cause of discontent: severity breedeth fear; roughness breedeth hate. Even reproofs from authority ought to be grave, not taunting. Facility [7] is worse than bribery, for bribes come but now and then; if importunity or idle repects [8] lead a man, he shall never be without; as Solomon saith, *To respect persons is not good; for such a man will transgress for a piece of bread.*[9]

It is most true that was anciently spoken: *A place showeth the man; and it showeth some to the better, and some to the worse. A man whom everybody would have thought fit to govern, if he had not governed,*[10] saith Tacitus of Galba; but of Vespasian he

[7] Too great easiness of access.
[8] Personal considerations.
[9] Proverbs, 28:21.
[10] *Omnium consensu capax imperii, nisi imperasset.*

saith, *Vespasian was the only emperor who changed for the better* [after the accession to power],[11] though the one was meant of sufficiency, the other of manners and affection. It is an assured sign of a worthy and generous spirit, whom honor amends; for honor is, or should be, the place of virtue; and as in nature things move violently to their place, and calmly in their place, so virtue in ambition is violent, in authority settled and calm. All rising to great place is by a winding stair; and if there be factions, it is good to side a man's self whilst he is in the rising, and to balance himself when he is placed. Use the memory of thy predecessor fairly and tenderly; for if thou dost not, it is a debt will sure be paid when thou art gone. If thou have colleagues, respect them; and rather call them when they look not for it, than exclude them when they have reason to look to be called. Be not too sensible or too remembering of thy place in conversation and private answers to suitors; but let it rather be said, *When he sits in place, he is another man.*

[11] *Solus imperantium, Vespasianus mutatus in melius.* Tacitus, *History*, I, 49, 50.

12
Of Boldness

IT IS a trivial grammar-school text, but yet worthy a wise man's consideration. Question was asked of Demosthenes, what was the chief part of an orator? He answered, Action. What next?—Action. What next again?—Action.[1] He said it that knew it best, and had, by nature, himself no advantage in that he commended. A strange thing, that that part of an orator which is but superficial, and rather the virtue of a player, should be placed so high above those other noble parts of invention, elocution, and the rest; nay, almost alone, as if it were all in all. But the reason is plain. There is in human nature generally more of the fool than of the wise; and therefore, those faculties by which the foolish part of men's minds is taken are most potent. Wonderful like is the case of boldness in civil business. What first?—Boldness; what second and third?—Boldness. And yet boldness is a child of ignorance and baseness, far inferior to other parts; but, nevertheless, it doth fascinate, and bind hand and foot those that are either shallow in judgment or weak in courage, which are the greatest part, yea, and prevaileth with wise men at weak times; there-

[1] This story is told by Cicero, in *On the Orator;* and by Plutarch, in *Lives of the Ten Orators.*

fore, we see it hath done wonders in popular[2] states, but with senates and princes less, and more, ever upon the first entrance of bold persons into action than soon after; for boldness is an ill keeper of promise. Surely, as there are mountebanks for the natural body, so are there mountebanks for the politic body; men that undertake great cures, and perhaps have been lucky in two or three experiments, but want the grounds of science, and therefore cannot hold out; nay, you shall see a bold fellow many times do Mahomet's miracle. Mahomet made the people believe that he would call a hill to him, and from the top of it offer up his prayers for the observers of his law. The people assembled; Mahomet called the hill to come to him again and again; and when the hill stood still, he was never a whit abashed, but said, *If the hill will not come to Mahomet, Mahomet will go to the hill.* So these men, when they have promised great matters and failed most shamefully, yet if they have the perfection of boldness, they will but slight it over, and make a turn, and no more ado. Certainly to men of great judgment, bold persons are a sport to behold; nay, and to the vulgar also boldness hath somewhat of the ridiculous; for if absurdity be the subject of laughter, doubt you not but great boldness is seldom without some absurdity; especially it is a sport to see when a bold fellow is out of countenance, for that puts his face into a most shrunken and wooden posture, as needs it must;

[2] Democratic.

Of Boldness

for in bashfulness the spirits do a little go and come, but with bold men, upon like occasion, they stand at a stay; like a stale at chess, where it is no mate, but yet the game cannot stir; but this last were fitter for a satire than for a serious observation. This is well to be weighed, that boldness is ever blind, for it seeth not dangers and inconveniences; therefore, it is ill in counsel, good in execution; so that the right use of bold persons is, that they never command in chief, but be seconds and under the direction of others; for in counsel it is good to see dangers; and in execution not to see them except they be very great.

13
Of Goodness, and Goodness of Nature

I TAKE goodness in this sense, the affecting of the weal of men, which is what the Grecians call *philanthropia;* and the word humanity, as it is used, is a little too light to express it. Goodness I call the habit, and goodness of nature the inclination. This, of all virtues and dignities of the mind, is the greatest, being the character of the Deity; and without it man is a busy, mischievous, wretched thing, no better than a kind of vermin. Goodness answers to the theological virtue charity, and admits no excess but error. The desire of power in excess caused the angels to fall; the desire of knowledge in excess caused man to fall; but in charity there is no excess, neither can angel or man come in danger by it. The inclination to goodness is imprinted deeply in the nature of man, insomuch that if it issue not towards men, it will take unto other living creatures; as it is seen in the Turks, a cruel people, who nevertheless are kind to beasts, and give alms to dogs and birds; insomuch, as Busbechius[1] reporteth, a Christian boy in Constantinople had like to have been stoned for gagging in a wag-

[1] Augier Ghislen de Busbec, Flemish scholar and ambassador to Turkey in the sixteenth century.

Of Goodness, and Goodness of Nature 51

gishness a long-billed fowl.[2] Errors, indeed, in this virtue, of goodness or charity, may be committed. The Italians have an ungracious proverb: *So good, that he is good for nothing;*[3] and one of the doctors of Italy, Nicholas Machiavel,[4] had the confidence to put in writing, almost in plain terms, *That the Christian faith had given up good men in prey to those that are tyrannical and unjust;* which he spake, because, indeed, there was never law, or sect, or opinion did so much magnify goodness as the Christian religion doth; therefore, to avoid the scandal and the danger both, it is good to take knowledge of the errors of a habit so excellent. Seek the good of other men, but be not in bondage to their faces or fancies; for that is but facility or softness, which taketh an honest mind prisoner. Neither give thou Aesop's cock a gem, who would be better pleased and happier if he had had a barley-corn. The example of God teacheth the lesson truly: *He sendeth his rain, and maketh his sun to shine upon the just and the unjust;*[5] but he doth not rain wealth, nor shine honor and virtues upon men equally; common benefits are to be communicate with all, but peculiar benefits with choice. And beware how, in making the portraiture, thou breakest the pattern; for divinity maketh the love of ourselves the pattern, the love

---

[2] Stork or crane.
[3] *Tanto buon che val niente.*
[4] Nicolo Machiavelli, Florentine statesman and author; author of *The Prince, History of Florence,* and other works.
[5] Matthew, 5:5.

of our neighbors but the portraiture: *Sell all thou hast, and give it to the poor, and follow me;*[6] but sell not all thou hast, except thou come and follow me; that is, except thou have a vocation wherein thou mayest do as much good with little means as with great; for otherwise, in feeding the streams thou driest the fountain. Neither is there only a habit of goodness directed by right reason, but there is in some men, even in nature, a disposition towards it; as, on the other side, there is a natural malignity, for there be that in their nature do not affect[7] the good of others. The lighter sort of malignity turneth but to a crossness, for forwardness, or aptness to oppose, or difficilness,[8] or the like; but the deeper sort, to envy and mere mischief. Such men in other men's calamities are, as it were, in season, and are ever on the loading part; not so good as the dogs that licked Lazarus's sores,[9] but like flies that are still buzzing upon any thing that is raw; misanthropi, that make it their practice to bring men to the bough, and yet have never a tree for the purpose in their gardens, as Timon[10] had. Such dispositions are the very errors of human nature, and yet they are the fittest timber to make great politics of; like to knee timber,[11] that is good for ships that are ordained to be tossed, but not for building houses that shall

[6] Mark, 10:21.
[7] Desire.
[8] Obstinacy.
[9] Luke, 16:21.
[10] Timon of Athens (so styled by Shakespeare in the play founded on his story) was surnamed the "Misanthrope," from his hatred of mankind.
[11] Timber that has grown crooked.

Of Goodness, and Goodness of Nature

stand firm. The parts and signs of goodness are many. If a man be gracious and courteous to strangers, it shows he is a citizen of the world, and that his heart is no island cut off from other lands, but a continent that joins to them; if he be compassionate towards the afflictions of others, it shows that his heart is like the noble tree that is wounded itself when it gives the balm; [12] if he easily pardons and remits offenses, it shows that his mind is planted above injuries, so that he cannot be shot; if he be thankful for small benefits, it shows that he weighs men's minds, and not their trash; but above all, if he have St. Paul's perfection. that he would wish to be an anathema from Christ for the salvation of his brethren,[13] it shows much of a divine nature, and a kind of conformity with Christ himself.

[12] Incision is the method usually adopted for extracting the resinous and aromatic juices of trees.
[13] Romans, 9:3.

14
Of Nobility

WE WILL speak of nobility first as a portion of an estate,[1] then as a condition of particular persons. A monarchy, where there is no nobility at all, is ever a pure and absolute tyranny as that of the Turks; for nobility attempers sovereignty, and draws the eyes of the people somewhat aside from the line royal: but for democracies they need it not; and they are commonly more quiet and less subject to sedition than where there are stirps[2] of nobles; for men's eyes are upon the business, and not upon the persons; or if upon the persons, it is for the business' sake, as fittest, and not for flags and pedigree. We see the Switzers[3] last well, notwithstanding their diversity of religion and of cantons; for utility is their bond, and not respects.[4] The United Provinces of the Low Countries[5] in their government excel; for where there is an equality the consultations are more indifferent, and the payments and tributes more cheerful. A great and potent nobility addeth majesty to a monarch, but diminisheth power, and putteth life and spirit into the people, but presseth their fortune. It is well when nobles are not too great for sovereignty nor for justice; and yet maintained in that height, as the insolency

[1] State. [2] Families. [3] Swiss. [4] Dignities.
[5] The United Provinces of the Netherlands had then recently emancipated themselves from Spain.

Of Nobility

of inferiors may be broken upon them, before it come on too fast upon the majesty of kings. A numerous nobility causeth poverty and inconvenience in a state; for it is a surcharge of expense; and besides, it being of necessity that many of the nobility fall in time to be weak in fortune, it maketh a kind of disproportion between honor and means.

As for nobility in particular persons, it is a reverend thing to see an ancient castle or building not in decay, or to see a fair timber tree sound and perfect; how much more to behold an ancient noble family, which hath stood against the waves and weathers of time! For new nobility is but the act of power, but ancient nobility is the act of time. Those that are first raised to nobility are commonly more virtuous, but less innocent than their descendants; for there is rarely any rising but by a commixture of good and evil arts; but it is reason the memory of their virtues remain to their posterity, and their faults die with themselves. Nobility of birth commonly abateth industry, and he that is not industrious envieth him that is; besides, noble persons cannot go much higher; and he that standeth at a stay when others rise can hardly avoid motions of envy. On the other side, nobility extinguisheth the passive envy from others towards them, because they are in possession of honor. Certainly kings that have able men of their nobility shall find ease in employing them, and a better slide into their business; for people naturally bend to them, as born in some sort to command.

15

Of Seditions and Troubles

SHEPHERDS of people had need know the calendars of tempests in state, which are commonly greatest when things grow to equality; as natural tempests are greatest about the equinoctia, and as there are certain hollow blasts of wind and secret swellings of seas before a tempest, so are there in states: *He* [the sun] *often warns us that dark uprisings threaten, that treasons and hidden warfare are swelling.*[1] Libels and licentious discourses against the state, when they are frequent and open; and in like sort false news, often running up and down, to the disadvantage of the state, and hastily embraced, are amongst the signs of troubles. Virgil, giving the pedigree of Fame, saith she was sister to the giants: *Mother earth, inflamed with wrath against the gods, brought her forth, they say, the youngest sister of Coeus and Enceladus.*[2]

As if fames were the relics of seditions past; but they are no less indeed the preludes of seditions to come. How-

---

[1] *Ille etiam caecos instare tumultus*
Saepe monet, fraudumque et operta tumescere bella.

Virgil, *Georgics*, I, 464-465.

[2] *Illam Terra parens, irâ irritata deorum,*
Extremam (ut perhibent) Coeo Enceladoque sororem
Progenuit.

Virgil, *Aeneid*, IV, 178-180.

soever, he noteth it right that seditious tumults and seditious fames differ no more but as brother and sister, masculine and feminine; especially if it come to that, that the best actions of a state, and the most plausible, and which ought to give greatest contentment, are taken in ill sense, and traduced; for that shows the envy great, as Tacitus saith, *When great dislike* [of the government] *prevails, both good and bad actions offend*.[3] Neither doth it follow, that because these fames are a sign of troubles, that the suppressing of them with too much severity should be a remedy of troubles; for the despising of them many times checks them best, and the going about to stop them doth but make a wonder long-lived. Also that kind of obedience, which Tacitus speaketh of, is to be held suspected: *They were in office, but disposed to discuss rather than execute the commands of their superiors;*[4] disputing, excusing, cavilling upon mandates and directions, is a kind of shaking off the yoke, and assay of disobedience; especially if, in those disputings, they which are for the direction speak fearfully and tenderly, and those that are against it audaciously.

Also, as Machiavel noteth well, when princes, that ought to be common parents, make themselves as a party, and

---

[3] *Conflatâ magnâ invidiâ, seu bene, seu male, gesta premunt.* Bacon has here quoted incorrectly. Tacitus wrote (*History*, I, 7): "The ruler once detested, his actions, whether good or bad, cause his downfall."
[4] *Erant in officio, sed tamen qui mallent mandata imperantium interpretari. quam exequi. History*, I, 39.

lean to a side; it is as a boat that is overthrown by uneven weight on the one side, as was well seen in the time of Henry the Third of France; for first himself entered league [5] for the extirpation of the Protestants, and presently after the same league was turned upon himself; for when the authority of princes is made but an accessory to a cause, and that there be other bands that tie faster than the band of sovereignty, kings begin to be put almost out of possession.

Also, when discords and quarrels and factions are carried openly and audaciously, it is a sign the reverence of government is lost; for the motions of the greatest persons in a government ought to be as the motions of the planets under *primum mobile*,[6] according to the old opinion, which is, that everyone of them is carried swiftly by the highest motion, and softly in their own motion; and therefore, when great ones in their own particular motion move violently, and as Tacitus expresseth it well, *more freely than was compatible with respect for their rulers*,[7] it is a sign the orbs are out of frame; for reverence is that wherewith princes are girt from God, who threateneth the dissolving thereof: *I will unloose the girdles of kings*.[8]

---

[5] The league which was formed by the Duke de Guise for the extermination of Protestants.

[6] In the Ptolemaic system the *primum mobile* was the outermost sphere, whose motion from east to west made the other spheres, bearing the fixed stars and the planets, revolve about the earth.

[7] *Liberius quam ut imperantium meminissent.* Annals, III, 4.

[8] *Solvam cingula regum.* Isaiah, 45:1.

Of Seditions and Troubles

So when one of the four pillars of government are mainly shaken or weakened (which are religion, justice, counsel, and treasure), men had need to pray for fair weather. But let us pass from this part of predictions (concerning which, nevertheless, more light may be taken from that which followeth), and let us speak first of the materials of seditions; then of the motives of them; and thirdly of the remedies.

Concerning the materials of seditions, it is a thing well to be considered, for the surest way to prevent seditions (if the times do bear it) is to take away the matter of them; for if there be fuel prepared, it is hard to tell whence the spark shall come that shall set it on fire. The matter of seditions is of two kinds, much poverty and much discontentment. It is certain, so many overthrown estates, so many votes for troubles. Lucan noteth well the state of Rome before the civil war: *Hence devouring usury, and interest accumulating rapidly; hence credit shaken, and war profitable to many.*[9] This same *war profitable to many* [10] is an assured and infallible sign of a state disposed to seditions and troubles; and if this poverty and broken estate in the better sort be joined with a want and necessity in the mean people, the danger is imminent and great; for the rebellions of the belly are the worst. As for

---

[9] *Hinc usura vorax, rapidumque in tempore foenus,*
   Hinc concussa fides, et multis utile bellum.

   Pharsalia, I, 181.

[10] *Multis utile bellum.*

discontentments, they are in the politic body like to humors in the natural, which are apt to gather a preternatural heat and to inflame; and let no prince measure the danger of them by this, whether they be just or unjust; for that were to imagine people to be too reasonable, who do often spurn at their own good; nor yet by this, whether the griefs whereupon they rise be in fact great or small; for they are the most dangerous discontentments where the fear is greater than the feeling: *There is a limit to suffering, but none to fear.*[11] Besides, in great oppressions, the same things that provoke the patience do withal mate [12] the courage; but in fears it is not so; neither let any prince or state be secure concerning discontentments, because they have been often or have been long, and yet no peril hath ensued; for as it is true that every vapor or fume doth not turn into a storm, so it is nevertheless true that storms, though they blow over divers times, yet may fall at last; and, as the Spanish proverb noteth well, *The cord breaketh at the last by the weakest pull.*

The causes and motives of seditions are, innovation in religion, taxes, alteration of laws and customs, breaking of privileges, general oppression, advancement of unworthy persons, strangers, dearths, disbanded soldiers, factions grown desperate, and whatsoever in offending people joineth and knitteth them in a common cause.

For the remedies, there may be some general preserva-

---

[11] *Dolendi modus, timendi non item.* Pliny, *Epistles*, VIII, 17.
[12] Stupefy.

Of Seditions and Troubles

tives, whereof we will speak; as for the just cure, it must answer to the particular disease, and so be left to counsel rather than rule.

The first remedy, or prevention, is to remove, by all means possible, that material cause of sedition whereof we spake, which is, want and poverty in the estate;[13] to which purpose serveth the opening and well-balancing of trade, the cherishing of manufacturers; the banishing of idleness; the repressing of waste and excess by sumptuary laws;[14] the improvement and husbanding of the soil; the regulating of prices of things vendible; the moderating of taxes and tributes, and the like. Generally, it is to be foreseen that the population of a kingdom (especially if it be not mown down by wars) do not exceed the stock of the kingdom which should maintain them; neither is the population to be reckoned only by number; for a smaller number, that spend more and earn less, do wear out an estate sooner than a greater number that live lower and gather more. Therefore the multiplying of nobility and other degrees of quality, in an overproportion to the common people, doth speedily bring a state to necessity; and so doth likewise an overgrown clergy, for they bring nothing to the stock;[15] and in like manner, when more are bred scholars than preferments can take off.

[13] The State.
[14] Laws to prevent extravagance in private life by limiting expenditures for clothing, food, etc.
[15] Capital.

It is likewise to be remembered, that, forasmuch as the increase of any estate must be upon the foreigner (for whatsoever is somewhere gotten is somewhere lost), there be but three things which one nation selleth unto another; the commodity, as nature yieldeth it; the manufacture; and the vecture, or carriage; so that, if these three wheels go, wealth will flow as in a spring tide. And it cometh many times to pass, that *materiam superabit opus*,[16] that the work and carriage is more worth than the material, and enricheth a state more; as is notably seen in the Low Countrymen, who have the best mines [17] above ground in the world.

Above all things, good policy is to be used, that the treasure and moneys in a state be not gathered into few hands; for, otherwise, a state may have a great stock, and yet starve. And money is like muck,[18] not good except it be spread. This is done chiefly by suppressing, or, at the least, keeping a strait hand upon the devouring trades of usury, engrossing,[19] great pasturages,[20] and the like.

For removing discontentments, or, at least, the danger of them, there is in every state (as we know) two portions of subjects, the nobles and the commonalty. When one of these is discontent, the danger is not great; for common

---

[16] Ovid, *Metamorphoses*, II, 5.
[17] Bacon refers to the manufactures of the Low Countries.
[18] Manure.
[19] Monopoly.
[20] The demand for wool induced farmers to turn their fields into pastures.

people are of slow motion, if they be not excited by the greater sort; and the greater sort are of small strength, except the multitude be apt and ready to move of themselves; then is the danger, when the greater sort do but wait for the troubling of the waters amongst the meaner, that then they may declare themselves. The poets feign that the rest of the gods would have bound Jupiter, which he hearing of, by the counsel of Pallas, sent for Briareus, with his hundred hands, to come in to his aid; an emblem, no doubt, to show how safe it is for monarchs to make sure of the good will of common people.

To give moderate liberty for griefs and discontentments to evaporate (so it be without too great insolency or bravery), is a safe way; for he that turneth the humors back, and maketh the wound bleed inwards, endangereth malign ulcers and pernicious imposthumations.[21]

The part of Epimetheus[22] might well become Prometheus, in the case of discontentments, for there is not a better provision against them. Epimetheus, when griefs and evils flew abroad, at last shut the lid, and kept Hope in the bottom of the vessel. Certainly the politic and artificial nourishing and entertaining of hopes, and carrying men from hopes to hopes, is one of the best antidotes against the poison of discontentments; and it is a certain sign of a wise government and proceeding, when it can hold men's hearts by hopes, when it cannot by satisfac-

[21] Abscesses.
[22] The myth of Pandora's box is here referred to.

tion; and when it can handle things in such manner as no evil shall appear so peremptory, but that it hath some outlet of hope; which is the less hard to do, because both particular persons and factions are apt enough to flatter themselves, or at least to brave that which they believe not.

Also the foresight and prevention, that there be no likely or fit head whereunto discontented persons may resort, and under whom they may join, is a known but an excellent point of caution. I understand a fit head to be one that hath greatness and reputation, that hath confidence with the discontented party, and upon whom they turn their eyes, and that is thought discontented in his own particular: which kind of persons are either to be won and reconciled to the state, and that in a fast and true manner; or to be fronted with some other of the same party that may oppose them, and so divide the reputation. Generally, the dividing and breaking of all factions and combinations that are adverse to the state, and setting them at distance, or at least distrust amongst themselves, is not one of the worst remedies; for it is a desperate case, if those that hold with the proceeding of the state be full of discord and faction, and those that are against it be entire and united.

I have noted that some witty and sharp speeches which have fallen from princes have given fire to seditions. Caesar did himself infinite hurt in that speech—*Sulla did not know his letters, he could not dictate*,[23] for it did utterly cut off that hope which men had entertained that

[23] *Sulla nescivit literas, non potuit dictare.* Suetonius, *Caesar*, 76-78.

Of Seditions and Troubles

he would, at one time or other, give over his dictatorship. Galba undid himself by that speech, *that his soldiers were levied, not bought;* [24] for it put the soldiers out of hope of the donative. Probus, likewise, by that speech, *If I live, the Roman Empire will have no further need of soldiers,* [25] a speech of great despair for the soldiers, and many the like. Surely princes had need, in tender matters and ticklish times, to beware what they say, especially in these short speeches, which fly abroad like darts and are thought to be shot out of their secret intentions; for as for large discourses, they are flat things and not so much noted.

Lastly, let princes, against all events, not be without some great person, one or rather more, of military valor, near unto them, for the repressing of seditions in their beginnings; for without that, there useth to be more trepidation in court upon the first breaking out of troubles than were fit, and the state runneth the danger of that which Tacitus saith: *And such was the state of mind that a few dared to commit the worst crime, many more would have liked to do so, and all acquiesced;* [26] but let such military persons be assured, and well reputed of, rather than factious and popular; holding also good correspondence with the other great men in the state, or else the remedy is worse than the disease.

[24] *Legi a se militem, non emi.* Tacitus, *History,* I, 5.
[25] *Si vixero, non opus erit amplius Romano imperio militibus.* Flavius Vopiscus, *Probus,* 20.
[26] *Atque is habitus animorum fuit, ut pessimum facinus auderent pauci, plures vellent, omnes paterentur. History,* I, 28.

16
Of Atheism

I HAD rather believe all the fables in the Legend, and the Talmud, and the Alcoran,[1] than that this universal frame is without a mind; and, therefore, God never wrought miracle to convince atheism, because his ordinary works convince it. It is true that a little philosophy inclineth man's mind to atheism, but depth in philosophy bringeth men's minds about to religion; for while the mind of man looketh upon second causes scattered, it may sometimes rest in them, and go no further; but when it beholdeth the chain of them confederate and linked together, it must needs fly to Providence and Deity. Nay, even that school which is most accused of atheism doth most demonstrate religion: that is, the school of Leucippus,[2] and Democritus, and Epicurus; for it is a thousand times more credible that four mutable elements, and one immutable fifth essence,[3] duly and eternally placed, need no God, than that an army

---

[1] *The Golden Legend* is a collection of lives of the saints; the Talmud is the body of Jewish traditional law; the Alcoran or Koran is the sacred book of the followers of Mohammed.

[2] A Greek philosopher who lived about 500 B.C. He founded the atomic philosophy, which was further developed by Democritus.

[3] Aristotle and others held that all matter was composed of four elements, earth, water, fire, and air. The heavenly bodies were composed of a fifth element, the quintessence.

Of Atheism

of infinite small portions, or seeds unplaced, should have produced this order and beauty without a divine marshal. The Scripture saith, *The fool hath said in his heart, there is no God;* it is not said, *The fool hath thought in his heart;*[4] so as he rather saith it by rote to himself, as that he would have, than that he can thoroughly believe it, or be persuaded of it; for none deny there is a God, but those for whom it maketh that there were no God. It appeareth in nothing more, that atheism is rather in the lip than in the heart of man, than by this, that atheists will ever be talking of that their opinion, as if they fainted in it within themselves, and would be glad to be strengthened by the consent of others; nay more, you shall have atheists strive to get disciples, as it fareth with other sects; and, which is most of all, you shall have of them that will suffer for atheism, and not recant; whereas, if they did truly think that there were no such thing as God, why should they trouble themselves? Epicurus is charged that he did but dissemble for his credit's sake, when he affirmed there were blessed natures, but such as enjoyed themselves without having respect to the government of the world. Wherein they say he did temporize, though in secret he thought there was no God; but certainly he is traduced, for his words are noble and divine: *There is no profanity in refusing to believe in the gods of the people; but it is profane to believe of the gods what the people believe of*

[4] Psalm 14:1 and 53:1.

*them.*⁵ Plato could have said no more; and, although he had the confidence to deny the administration, he had not the power to deny the nature. The Indians of the West have names for their particular gods, though they have no name for God; as if the heathens should have had the names Jupiter, Apollo, Mars, etc., but not the word Deus, which shows that even those barbarous people have the notion, though they have not the latitude and extent of it; so that against atheists the very savages take part with the very subtlest philosophers. The contemplative atheist is rare; a Diagoras,⁶ a Bion,⁷ a Lucian,⁸ perhaps, and some others, and yet they seem to be more than they are; for that all that impugn a received religion, or superstition, are, by the adverse part, branded with the name of atheists. But the great atheists indeed are hypocrites, which are ever handling holy things, but without feeling, so as they must needs be cauterized in the end. The causes of atheism are: divisions in religion, if they be many; for any one main division addeth zeal to both sides, but many divisions introduce atheism. Another is, scandal of priests, when it is

---

⁵ *Non Deos vulgi negare profanum; sed vulgi opiniones Diis applicare profanum.* Diogenes Laertius, X, 123.

⁶ Athenian philosopher, who, from the greatest superstition, became an avowed atheist.

⁷ A Greek philosopher, a disciple of Theodorus the atheist, to whose opinions he adhered. His life was said to have been profligate, and his death superstitious.

⁸ Lucian ridiculed the follies and pretensions of some of the ancient philosophers; but though the freedom of his style caused him to be censured for impiety, he hardly deserves to be called an atheist.

come to that which St. Bernard saith: *It is not for us now to say, that the priest is like the people, for the fact is that the people are not even so bad as the priest.*⁹ A third is, custom of profane scoffing in holy matters, which doth by little and little deface the reverence of religion: and lastly, learned times, specially with peace and prosperity; for troubles and adversities do more bow men's minds to religion. They that deny a God destroy a man's nobility, for certainly man is of kin to the beasts by his body; and if he be not of kin to God by his spirit, he is a base and ignoble creature. It destroys likewise magnanimity, and the raising of human nature; for, take an example of a dog, and mark what a generosity and courage he will put on when he finds himself maintained by a man, who, to him, is instead of a God, or *better nature;* ¹⁰ which courage is manifestly such as that creature, without that confidence of a better nature than his own, could never attain. So man, when he resteth and assureth himself upon divine protection and favor, gathereth a force and faith, which human nature in itself could not obtain; therefore, as atheism is in all respects hateful, so in this, that it depriveth human nature of the means to exalt itself above human frailty. As it is in particular persons, so it is in nations: never was there such a state of magnanimity as Rome. Of this state hear what Cicero saith: *Pride ourselves as we may upon our*

---

⁹ *Non est jam dicere, ut populus, sic sacerdos; quia nec sic populus, ut sacerdos.*
¹⁰ *Melior natura.*

country, yet are we not in number superior to the Spaniards, nor in strength to the Gauls, nor in cunning to the Carthaginians, nor to the Greeks in arts, nor to the Italians and Latins themselves in the homely and native sense which belongs to this nation and land; it is in piety only and religion, and the wisdom of regarding the providence of the immortal gods as that which rules and governs all things, that we have surpassed all nations and peoples.[11]

[11] *Quam volumus licet, Patres conscripti, nos amemus, tamen nec numero Hispanos, nec robore Gallos, nec calliditate Poenos, nec artibus Graecos, nec denique hoc ipso hujus gentis et terrae domestico nativoque sensu Italos ipsos et Latinos; sed pietate, ac religione, atque hâc unâ sapientiâ, quod Deorum immortalium numine omnia regi, gubernarique perspeximus, omnes gentes, nationesque superavimus.* On the Responses of the Soothsayers, IX, 19.

17
Of Superstition

IT WERE better to have no opinion of God at all than such an opinion as is unworthy of him; for the one is unbelief, the other is contumely, and certainly superstition is the reproach of the Deity. Plutarch saith well to that purpose: *Surely*, saith he, *I had rather a great deal men should say there was no such man at all as Plutarch, than that they should say that there was one Plutarch that would eat his children as soon as they were born*,[1] as the poets speak of Saturn; and, as the contumely is greater towards God, so the danger is greater towards men. Atheism leaves a man to sense, to philosophy, to natural piety, to laws, to reputation, all which may be guides to an outward moral virtue, though religion were not; but superstition dismounts all these, and erecteth an absolute monarchy in the minds of men. Therefore atheism did never perturb states; for it makes men wary of themselves, as looking no further, and we see the times inclined to atheism (as the time of Augustus Caesar) were civil times; but superstition hath been the confusion of many states, and bringeth in a new *primum mobile*, that ravisheth all the spheres of government. The master of superstition is the people, and in all superstition

[1] Time was personified by Saturn, the Greek Kronos, who devoured all his children. Plutarch, *On Superstition*.

wise men follow fools; and arguments are fitted to practice in a reversed order. It was gravely said by some of the prelates in the Council of Trent, where the doctrine of the schoolmen bare great sway, that the schoolmen were like astronomers, which did feign eccentrics and epicycles,[2] and such engines of orbs to save [3] the phenomena, though they knew there were no such things; and, in like manner, that the schoolmen had framed a number of subtle and intricate axioms and theorems, to save the practice of the Church. The causes of superstition are: pleasing and sensual rites and ceremonies; excess of outward and pharisaical holiness; over-great reverence of traditions, which cannot but load the Church; the stratagems of prelates for their own ambition and lucre; the favoring too much of good intentions, which openeth the gate to conceits and novelties; the taking an aim at divine matters by human, which cannot but breed mixture of imaginations; and lastly, barbarous times, especially joined with calamities and disasters. Superstition, without a veil, is a deformed thing; for, as it addeth deformity to an ape to be so like a man, so the similitude of superstition to religion makes it the more deformed; and as wholesome meat corrupteth to little worms, so good forms and orders corrupt into a number of petty observances. There is a superstition in

[2] The movements of the planets in the Ptolemaic system were explained by assuming that the center of their orbits was at some distance from the earth.
[3] To account for.

avoiding superstition, when men think to do best if they go furthest from the superstition formerly received; therefore care would be had that (as it fareth in ill purgings) the good be not taken away with the bad, which commonly is done when the people is the reformer.

18
Of Travel

TRAVEL, in the younger sort, is a part of education; in the elder, a part of experience. He that travelleth into a country before he hath some entrance into the language, goeth to school, and not to travel. That young men travel under some tutor or grave servant, I allow well, so that he be such a one that hath the language and hath been in the country before; whereby he may be able to tell them what things are worthy to be seen in the country where they go, what acquaintances they are to seek, what exercises or discipline [1] the place yieldeth; for else young men shall go hooded and look abroad little. It is a strange thing that, in sea voyages, where there is nothing to be seen but sky and sea, men should make diaries; but in land travel, wherein so much is to be observed, for the most part they omit it, as if chance were fitter to be registered than observation. Let diaries, therefore, be brought in use. The things to be seen and observed are the courts of princes, especially when they give audience to ambassadors; the courts of justice, while they sit and hear causes; and so of consistories [2] ecclesiastic; the churches and monasteries, with the monuments which are therein extant; the walls and fortifications

[1] Learning.   [2] Synods or councils.

Of Travel

of cities and towns; and so the havens and harbors, antiquities and ruins, libraries, colleges, disputations, and lectures, where any are; shipping and navies; houses and gardens of state and pleasure, near great cities; armories, arsenals, magazines, exchanges, burses,[3] warehouses, exercises of horsemanship, fencing, training of soldiers, and the like; comedies, such whereunto the better sort of persons do resort; treasuries of jewels and robes; cabinets and rarities; and, to conclude, whatsoever is memorable in the places where they go, after all which the tutors or servants ought to make diligent inquiry. As for triumphs, masks, feasts, weddings, funerals, capital executions, and such shows, men need not to be put in mind of them; yet they are not to be neglected. If you will have a young man to put his travel into a little room, and in short time to gather much, this you must do: first, as was said, he must have some entrance into the language before he goeth; then he must have such a servant, or tutor, as knoweth the country, as was likewise said; let him carry with him also some card[4] or book describing the country where he travelleth, which will be a good key to his inquiry; let him keep also a diary; let him not stay long in one city or town, more or less, as the place deserveth, but not long; nay, when he stayeth in one city or town, let him change his lodging from one end and part of the town to another, which is a great adamant[5] of acquaintance; let him sequester himself from

---

[3] Exchanges. [4] Map or chart. [5] Magnet.

the company of his countrymen, and diet in such places where there is good company of the nation where he travelleth; let him, upon his removes from one place to another, procure recommendation to some person of quality residing in the place whither he removeth, that he may use his favor in those things he desireth to see or know. Thus he may abridge his travel with much profit. As for the acquaintance which is to be sought in travel, that which is most of all profitable is acquaintance with the secretaries and employed men of ambassadors, for so in travelling in one country he shall suck the experience of many; let him also see and visit eminent persons in all kinds which are of great name abroad, that he may be able to tell how the life agreeth with the fame. For quarrels, they are with care and discretion to be avoided; they are commonly for mistresses, healths, place, and words; and let a man beware how he keepeth company with choleric and quarrelsome persons, for they will engage him into their own quarrels. When a traveller returneth home, let him not leave the countries where he hath travelled altogether behind him, but maintain a correspondence by letters with those of his acquaintance which are of most worth; and let his travel appear rather in his discourse than in his apparel or gesture, and in his discourse let him be rather advised in his answers, than forward to tell stories; and let it appear that he doth not change his country manners for those of foreign parts, but only prick in some flowers of that he hath learned abroad into the customs of his own country.

19
Of Empire

IT IS a miserable state of mind to have few things to desire, and many things to fear; and yet that commonly is the case of kings, who, being, at the highest, want matter of desire,[1] which makes their minds more languishing; and have many representations of perils and shadows, which makes their minds the less clear; and this is one reason, also, of that effect which the Scripture speaketh of, *that the king's heart is inscrutable;*[2] for multitude of jealousies, and lack of some predominant desire, that should marshal and put in order all the rest, maketh any man's heart hard to find or sound. Hence it comes, likewise, that princes many times make themselves desires, and set their hearts upon toys: sometimes upon a building; sometimes upon erecting of an order; sometimes upon the advancing of a person; sometimes upon obtaining excellency in some art or feat of the hand, as Nero for playing on the harp; Domitian for certainty of the hand with the arrow; Commodus for playing at fence; Caracalla for driving chariots, and the like. This seemeth incredible unto those that know not the principle, that the mind of man is more cheered and refreshed by profiting in small things than by standing at

[1] Something to create excitement. [2] Proverbs, 25:33.

a stay³ in great. We see, also, that kings that have been fortunate conquerors in their first years, it being not possible for them to go forward infinitely, but that they must have some check or arrest in their fortunes, turn in their latter years to be superstitious and melancholy; as did Alexander the Great, Diocletian,⁴ and, in our memory, Charles the Fifth,⁵ and others; for he that is used to go forward, and findeth a stop, falleth out of his own favor, and is not the thing he was.

To speak now of the true temper of empire, it is a thing rare and hard to keep, for both temper and distemper consist of contraries; but it is one thing to mingle contraries, another to interchange them. The answer of Apollonius to Vespasian is full of excellent instruction. Vespasian asked him, *What was Nero's overthrow?* He answered, *Nero could touch and tune the harp well; but in government sometimes he used to wind the pins too high, sometimes to let them down too low.* And certain it is, that nothing destroyeth authority so much as the unequal and untimely interchange of power pressed too far and relaxed too much.

This is true, that the wisdom of all these latter times in princes' affairs is rather fine deliveries and shiftings of

---

³ Making a stop at.

⁴ After a prosperous reign of twenty-one years, Diocletian abdicated the throne and retired.

⁵ After having reigned thirty-five years, he abdicated the thrones of Spain and Germany, and passed the last two years of his life in retirement.

Of Empire

dangers and mischiefs, when they are near, than solid and grounded courses to keep them aloof; but this is but to try masteries with fortune, and let men beware how they neglect and suffer matter of trouble to be prepared. For no man can forbid the spark nor tell whence it may come. The difficulties in princes' business are many and great; but the greatest difficulty is often in their own mind. For it is common with princes (saith Tacitus) to will contradictories: *The desires of princes are generally violent and incompatible with each other;*[6] for it is the solecism of power to think to command the end, and yet not to endure the mean.

Kings have to deal with their neighbors, their wives, their children, their prelates or clergy, their nobles, their second nobles or gentlemen, their merchants, their commons, and their men of war; and from all these arise dangers, if care and circumspection be not used.

First, for their neighbors, there can no general rule be given (the occasions are so variable), save one which ever holdeth; which is, that princes do keep due sentinel, that none of their neighbors do overgrow so (by increase of territory, by embracing of trade, by approaches, or the like), as they become more able to annoy them than they were; and this is generally the work of standing counsels to foresee and to hinder it. During that triumvirate of kings, King Henry the Eighth of England, Francis the

---

[6] *Sunt plerumque regum voluntates vehementes, et inter se contrariae.* Not Tacitus but Sallust, *Jugurthine War.*

First, King of France, and Charles the Fifth, Emperor, there was such a watch kept that none of the three could win a palm of ground, but the other two would straightways balance it, either by confederation, or, if need were, by a war; and would not in any wise take up peace at interest; and the like was done by that league (which Guicciardini [7] saith was the security of Italy) made between Ferdinando, King of Naples, Lorenzius Medicis, and Ludovicus Sforza, potentates, the one of Florence, the other of Milan. Neither is the opinion of some of the schoolmen to be received, that a war cannot justly be made, but upon a precedent injury or provocation; for there is no question but a just fear of an imminent danger, though there be no blow given, is a lawful cause of war.

For their wives, there are cruel examples of them. Livia is infamed [8] for the poisoning of her husband; Roxolana, Solyman's wife,[9] was the destruction of that renowned prince, Sultan Mustapha, and otherwise troubled his house and succession; Edward the Second of England's Queen [10] had the principal hand in the deposing and murder of her husband.

This kind of danger is then to be feared chiefly when

[7] Florentine historian of the sixteenth century.
[8] Spoken badly of. Livia was said to have hastened the death of Augustus, to prepare the accession of her son Tiberius to the throne.
[9] Roxalana, wife of Solyman the Magnificent, conspired against the life of his son Mustapha in order to secure the throne for her own son.
[10] The infamous Isabella of Anjou.

the wives have plots for the raising of their own children, or else that they be advoutresses.[11]

For their children, the tragedies likewise of dangers from them have been many; and generally the entering of fathers into suspicion of their children hath been ever unfortunate. The destruction of Mustapha (that we named before) was so fatal to Solyman's line, as the succession of the Turks from Solyman until this day is suspected to be untrue and of strange blood; for that Selymus the Second was thought to be supposititious. The destruction of Crispus, a young prince of rare towardness, by Constantinus the Great, his father, was in like manner fatal to his house; for both Constantinus and Constance, his sons, died violent deaths; and Constantius, his other son, did little better, who died indeed of sickness, but after that Julianus had taken arms against him. The destruction of Demetrius,[12] son to Philip the Second of Macedon, turned upon the father, who died of repentance. And many like examples there are; but few or none where the fathers had good by such distrust, except it were where the sons were up in open arms against them; as was Selymus the First against Bajazet, and the three sons of Henry the Second, King of England.

For their prelates, when they are proud and great, there is also danger from them; as it was in the times of Ansel-

---
[11] Adulteresses.
[12] He was falsely accused by his brother Perseus of attempting to dethrone his father, on which he was put to death by the order of Philip.

mus [18] and Thomas Becket, Archbishops of Canterbury, who, with their crosiers, did almost try it with the king's sword; and yet they had to deal with stout and haughty kings; William Rufus, Henry the First, and Henry the Second. The danger is not from that state, but where it hath a dependence of foreign authority; or where the churchmen come in and are elected, not by the collation of the King or particular patrons, but by the people.

For their nobles, to keep them at a distance it is not amiss; but to depress them may make a king more absolute but less safe, and less able to perform anything that he desires. I have noted it in my History of King Henry the Seventh of England, who depressed his nobility, whereupon it came to pass that his times were full of difficulties and troubles; for the nobility, though they continued loyal unto him, yet did they not co-operate with him in his business; so that, in effect, he was fain to do all things himself.

For their second nobles, there is not much danger from them, being a body dispersed. They may sometimes discourse high, but that doth little hurt; besides, they are a counterpoise to the higher nobility, that they grow not too potent; and, lastly, being the most immediate in authority with the common people, they do best temper popular commotions.

---

[18] Anselm was Archbishop of Canterbury in the time of William Rufus and Henry the First. Through his rigid assertion of the rights of the clergy he was continually embroiled with his sovereign.

Of Empire

For their merchants, they are *vena porta:* [14] and if they flourish not, a kingdom may have good limbs, but will have empty veins, and nourish little. Taxes and imposts upon them do seldom good to the king's revenue, for that which he wins in the hundred [15] he loseth in the shire; the particular rates being increased, but the total bulk of trading rather decreased.

For their commons, there is little danger from them, except it be where they have great and potent heads; or where you meddle with the point of religion, or their customs, or means of life.

For their men of war, it is a dangerous state where they live and remain in a body, and are used to donatives; whereof we see examples in the Janizaries [16] and Praetorian bands of Rome; but trainings of men, and arming them in several places, and under several commanders, and without donatives, are things of defense and no danger.

Princes are like to heavenly bodies, which cause good or evil times; and which have much veneration, but no rest. All precepts concerning kings are in effect comprehended in those two remembrances, *Remember that thou art a man* and *Remember that thou art a God* or *a representative of God;* [17] the one bridleth their power and the other their will.

---

[14] The great vessel that conveys the blood to the liver.
[15] A subdivision of the shire.
[16] The Janizaries were the bodyguards of the Turkish sultans.
[17] *Memento quod es homo;* and *Memento quod es Deus,* or *vice Dei.*

20

Of Counsel

THE greatest trust between man and man is the trust of giving counsel; for in other confidences men commit the parts of life, their lands, their goods, their children, their credit, some particular affair; but to such as they make their counsellors they commit the whole; by how much the more they are obliged to all faith and integrity. The wisest princes need not think it any diminution to their greatness, or derogation to their sufficiency to rely upon counsel. God himself is not without, but hath made it one of the great names of his blessed Son, *The Counsellor*.[1] Solomon hath pronounced that, *in counsel is stability*.[2] Things will have their first or second agitation: if they be not tossed upon the arguments of counsel, they will be tossed upon the waves of fortune, and be full of inconstancy, doing and undoing, like the reeling of a drunken man. Solomon's son[3] found the force of counsel, as his father saw the necessity of it; for the beloved kingdom of God was first rent and broken by ill counsel; upon which counsel there are set for our instruction the two marks whereby bad counsel is forever best discerned, that it was

---

[1] Isaiah, 9:6.   [2] Proverbs, 20:18.
[3] Rehoboam, from whom the ten tribes of Israel revolted, and elected Jeroboam their king. See I Kings, 12.

young counsel for the persons, and violent counsel for the matter.

The ancient times do set forth in figure both the incorporation and inseparable conjunction of counsel with kings, and the wise and politic use of counsel by kings; the one, in that they say Jupiter did marry Metis, which signifieth counsel; whereby they intend that sovereignty is married to counsel; the other in that which followeth, which was thus: they say, after Jupiter was married to Metis, she conceived by him and was with child; but Jupiter suffered her not to stay till she brought forth, but eat her up; whereby he became himself with child, and was delivered of Pallas armed, out of his head. Which monstrous fable containeth a secret of empire, how kings are to make use of their council of state; that first, they ought to refer matters unto them, which is the first begetting or impregnation; but when they are elaborate, molded, and shaped in the womb of their counsel, and grow ripe and ready to be brought forth, that then they suffer not their council to go through with the resolution and direction, as if it depended on them; but take the matter back into their own hands, and make it appear to the world that the decrees and final directions (which, because they come forth with prudence and power, are resembled to Pallas armed), proceeded from themselves; and not only from their authority, but (the more to add reputation to themselves) from their head and device.

Let us now speak of the inconveniences of counsel, and

of the remedies. The inconveniences that have been noted in calling and using counsel are three: first, the revealing of affairs, whereby they become less secret; secondly, the weakening of the authority of princes, as if they were less of themselves; thirdly, the danger of being unfaithfully counselled, and more for the good of them that counsel than of him that is counselled; for which inconveniences, the doctrine of Italy, and practice of France, in some kings' times, hath introduced cabinet councils; a remedy worse than the disease.

As to secrecy, princes are not bound to communicate all matters with all counsellors, but may extract and select; neither is it necessary that he that consulteth what he should do, should declare what he will do; but let princes beware that the unsecreting of their affairs comes not from themselves; and, as for cabinet councils, it may be their motto, *I am full of leaks;*[4] one futile person, that maketh it his glory to tell, will do more hurt than many that know it their duty to conceal. It is true, there be some affairs which require extreme secrecy, which will hardly go beyond one or two persons besides the king. Neither are those counsels unprosperous; for, besides the secrecy, they commonly go on constantly in one spirit of direction without distraction; but then it must be a prudent king, such as is able to grind with a handmill;[5] and those inward counsellors had need also to be wise men, and especially

---

[4] *Plenus rimarum sum.* Terence, *Eunuchus*, I, ii, 25.
[5] That is, without complicated machinery of government.

true and trusty to the king's ends; as it was with King Henry the Seventh of England, who, in his greatest business, imparted himself to none, except it were to Morton[6] and Fox.[7]

For weakening of authority, the fable[8] showeth the remedy; nay, the majesty of kings is rather exalted than diminished when they are in the chair of council; neither was there ever prince bereaved of his dependencies by his council, except where there hath been either an over-greatness in one counsellor, or an over-strict combination in divers, which are things soon found and holpen.[9]

For the last inconvenience, that men will counsel with an eye to themselves; certainly, *he shall not find faith upon the earth*,[10] is meant of the nature of times, and not of all particular persons. There be that are in nature faithful and sincere, and plain and direct, not crafty and involved: let princes, above all, draw to themselves such natures. Besides, counsellors are not commonly so united, but that one counsellor keepeth sentinel over another; so that if any do counsel out of faction or private ends, it commonly comes to the king's ear; but the best remedy is, if princes

---

[6] John Morton, Archbishop of Canterbury.
[7] Richard Fox, Bishop of Winchester.
[8] Before mentioned, relative to Jupiter and Metis.
[9] Remedied.
[10] *Non inveniet fidem super terram.* Bacon probably alludes to the words of Jesus, "When the son of Man cometh, shall he find faith upon the earth?" Luke, 18:8.

know their counsellors, as well as their counsellors know them: *The greatest virtue of a prince is to know his own.*[11] And on the other side, counsellors should not be too speculative into their sovereign's person. The true composition of a counsellor is, rather to be skillful in their master's business than in his nature; for then he is like to advise him, and not to feed his humor. It is of singular use to princes, if they take the opinions of their council both separately and together; for private opinion is more free, but opinion before others is more reverend. In private, men are more bold in their own humors; and in consort, men are more obnoxious[12] to others' humors; therefore it is good to take both; and of the inferior sort rather in private, to preserve freedom; of the greater, rather in consort, to preserve respect. It is in vain for princes to take counsel concerning matters, if they take no counsel likewise concerning persons; for all matters are as dead images; and the life of the execution of affairs resteth in the good choice of persons. Neither is it enough to consult concerning persons, *according to classes,*[13] as in an idea or mathematical description, what the kind and character of the person should be; for the greatest errors are committed, and the most judgment is shown, in the choice of individuals. It was truly said, *The best counsellors are the dead;*[14] *books will speak plain when counsellors blanch;* therefore it is

---

[11] *Principis est virtus maxima nosse suos.* Martial, *Epigrams*, VIII, 15, 8.
[12] Subject to or exposed to.
[13] *Secundum genera.*
[14] *Optimi consiliarii mortui.*

Of Counsel

good to be conversant in them, specially the books of such as themselves have been actors upon the stage.

The councils at this day in most places are but familiar meetings, where matters are rather talked on than debated; and they run too swift to the order or act of council. It were better that in causes of weight, the matter were propounded one day and not spoken to till the next day; *Night is the season for counsel;* [15] so was it done in the commission of union [16] between England and Scotland, which was a grave and orderly assembly. I commend set days for petitions; for both it gives the suitors more certainty for their attendance, and it frees the meetings for matters of estate, that they may *attend to the business in hand.*[17] In choice of committees for ripening business for the council, it is better to choose indifferent persons, than to make an indifferency by putting in those that are strong on both sides. I commend, also, standing commissions; as for trade, for treasure, for war, for suits, for some provinces; for where there be divers particular councils, and but one council of estate (as it is in Spain), they are in effect no more than standing commissions, save that they have greater authority. Let such as are to inform councils out of their particular professions (as lawyers, seamen, mintmen, and the like) be first heard before committees; and

---

[15] *In nocte consilium.*
[16] On the accession of James VI of Scotland to the throne of England in 1603.
[17] *Hoc agere.*

then, as occasion serves, before the council; and let them not come in multitudes, or in a tribunitious [18] manner; for that is to clamor councils, not to inform them. A long table and a square table, or seats about the walls, seem things of form, but are things of substance; for at a long table a few at the upper end, in effect, sway all the business; but in the other form there is more use of the counsellors' opinions that sit lower. A king, when he presides in council, let him beware how he opens his own inclination too much in that which he propoundeth; for else counsellors will but take the wind of him, and, instead of giving free counsel, will sing him a song of *I shall please.*[19]

[18] Declamatory.
[19] Quoted in jest from Psalm 114:9 in the Vulgate: *Placebo Domino in regione vivotum.*

21
Of Delays

FORTUNE is like the market, where, many times, if you can stay a little, the price will fall; and again, it is sometimes like Sibylla's offer,[1] which at first offereth the commodity at full, then consumeth part and part, and still holdeth up the price; for occasion (as it is in the common verse) *turneth a bald noddle,*[2] *after she hath presented her locks in front, and no hold taken;* or, at least, turneth the handle of the bottle first to be received, and after the belly, which is hard to clasp. There is surely no greater wisdom than well to time the beginnings and onsets of things. Dangers are no more light, if they once seem light; and more dangers have deceived men than forced them; nay, it were better to meet some dangers halfway, though they come nothing near, than to keep too long a watch upon their approaches; for if a man watch too long, it is odds he will fall asleep. On the other side, to be deceived with

[1] The Cumaean Sibyl, who offered to sell nine of the Sibylline Books to the Roman king, Tarquin the Proud; when he declined, she burned three of the books, and asked the same price for the remaining six; then she burned three more, and asked the original price for the three. The king was advised by his augur that the books were invaluable, and the Sibyl was paid the sum she demanded.

[2] Bald head. Bacon alludes to the common saying: "Take time by the forelock."

too long shadows (as some have been when the moon was low and shone on their enemies' back), and so to shoot off before the time; or to teach dangers to come on by over early buckling towards them, is another extreme. The ripeness or unripeness of the occasion (as we said) must ever be well weighed; and generally it is good to commit the beginnings of all great actions to Argus with his hundred eyes, and the ends to Briareus[3] with his hundred hands, first to watch and then to speed; for the helmet of Pluto, which maketh the politic man go invisible, is secrecy in the council, and celerity in the execution; for when things are once come to the execution, there is no secrecy comparable to celerity; like the motion of a bullet in the air, which flieth so swift as it outruns the eye.

[3] Son of Uranus (Heaven) and Gaea (Earth), who with his brothers conquered the Titans when they made war upon the gods.

22

Of Cunning

WE TAKE cunning for a sinister or crooked wisdom; and certainly there is great difference between a cunning man and a wise man, not only in point of honesty, but in point of ability. There be that can pack the cards, and yet cannot play well; so there are some that are good in canvasses and factions, that are otherwise weak men. Again, it is one thing to understand persons, and another thing to understand matters; for many are perfect in men's humors that are not greatly capable of the real part of business, which is the constitution of one that hath studied men more than books. Such men are fitter for practice than for counsel, and they are good but in their own alley.[1] Turn them to new men, and they have lost their aim; so as the old rule, to know a fool from a wise man, *Send them both naked among strangers, and then you will see,*[2] doth scarce hold for them; and, because these cunning men are like haberdashers of small wares, it is not amiss to set forth their shop.

It is a point of cunning to wait upon[3] him with whom you speak with your eye, as the Jesuits give it in precept; for there be many wise men that have secret hearts and

---

[1] Bowling alley.
[2] *Mitte ambos nudos ad ignotos, et videbis.*
[3] To watch.

transparent countenances; yet this would be done with a demure abasing of your eye sometimes, as the Jesuits also do use.

Another is that when you have anything to obtain of present dispatch, you entertain and amuse the party with whom you deal with some other discourse, that he be not too much awake to make objections. I knew a counsellor and secretary that never came to Queen Elizabeth of England with bills to sign, but he would always first put her into some discourse of estate,[4] that she might the less mind the bills.

The like surprise may be made by moving things when the party is in haste, and cannot stay to consider advisedly of that is moved.

If a man would cross a business that he doubts some other would handsomely and effectually move, let him pretend to wish it well, and move it himself in such sort as may foil it.

The breaking off in the midst of that one was about to say, as if he took himself up, breeds a greater appetite in him with whom you confer to know more.

And because it works better when anything seemeth to be gotten from you by question than if you offer it of yourself, you may lay a bait for a question, by showing another visage and countenance than you are wont; to the end to give occasion for the party to ask what the

[4] State.

Of Cunning

matter is of the change, as Nehemiah[5] did: *And I had not, before that time, been sad before the king.*

In things that are tender and unpleasing, it is good to break the ice by some whose words are of less weight, and to reserve the more weighty voice to come in as by chance, so that he may be asked the question upon the other's speech; as Narcissus did, in relating to Claudius the marriage of Messalina and Silius.

In things that a man would not be seen in himself, it is a point of cunning to borrow the name of the world, as to say, *The world says,* or *There is a speech abroad.*

I knew one that, when he wrote a letter, he would put that which was most material in a postscript, as if it had been a by-matter.

I knew another that, when he came to have speech, he would pass over that that he intended most; and go forth and come back again, and speak of it as a thing that he had almost forgot.

Some procure themselves to be surprised at such times as it is like the party that they work upon will suddenly come upon them, and to be found with a letter in their hand, or doing somewhat which they are not accustomed, to the end they may be apposed of [6] those things which of themselves they are desirous to utter.

It is a point of cunning to let fall those words in a man's own name, which he would have another man learn and

---

[5] Nehemiah, 2:1. [6] Be questioned upon.

use, and thereupon take advantage. I knew two that were competitors for the secretary's place in Queen Elizabeth's time, and yet kept good quarter[7] between themselves, and would confer one with another upon the business; and the one of them said, that to be a secretary in the declination of a monarchy was a ticklish thing, and that he did not affect[8] it; the other straight caught up those words, and discoursed with divers of his friends that he had no reason to desire to be secretary in the declination of a monarchy. The first man took hold of it, and found means it was told the Queen, who, hearing of a declination of a monarchy, took it so ill, as she would never after hear of the other's suit.

There is a cunning, which we in England call *the turning of the cat in the pan;* which is, when that which a man says to another, he lays it as if another had said it to him; and, to say truth, it is not easy, when such a matter passed between two, to make it appear from which of them it first moved and began.

It is a way that some men have, to glance and dart at others by justifying themselves by negatives; as to say, *This I do not;* as Tigellinus did towards Burrhus: *He had no other hope but to see to the safety of the emperor.*[9]

Some have in readiness so many tales and stories, as there is nothing they would insinuate, but they can wrap it into

[7] On good terms.   [8] Desire it.
[9] *Se non diversas spes, sed incolumitatem imperatoris simpliciter spectare.* Tacitus, *Annals*, XIV, 57.

Of Cunning

a tale, which serveth both to keep themselves more in guard, and to make others carry it with more pleasure.

It is a good point of cunning for a man to shape the answer he would have in his own words and propositions; for it makes the other party stick the less.

It is strange how long some men will lie in wait to speak somewhat they desire to say; and how far about they will fetch, and how many other matters they will beat over to come near it. It is a thing of great patience, but yet of much use.

A sudden, bold, and unexpected question doth many times surprise a man, and lay him open. Like to him that, having changed his name, and walking in Paul's,[10] another suddenly came behind him and called him by his true name, whereat straightways he looked back.

But these small wares and petty points of cunning are infinite, and it were a good deed to make a list of them; for that nothing doth more hurt in a state than that cunning men pass for wise.

But certainly, some there are that know the resorts[11] and falls[12] of business that cannot sink into the main of it;[13] like a house that hath convenient stairs and entries, but never a fair room. Therefore you shall see them find out pretty looses[14] in the conclusion, but are noways able to examine or debate matters; and yet commonly they take

---

[10] St. Paul's Cathedral in London.
[11] Movements, or springs.
[12] Chances, or vicissitudes.
[13] Enter deeply into.
[14] Lucky shots.

advantage of their inability, and would be thought wits of direction. Some build rather upon the abusing of others, and (as we now say) putting tricks upon them, than upon soundness of their own proceedings; but Solomon saith: *The wise men looks where he is walking; the fool strays into the snare.*[15]

[15] *Prudens advertit ad gressus suos, stultus divertit ad dolos.*

23
Of Wisdom for a Man's Self

An ant is a wise creature for itself, but it is a shrewd[1] thing in an orchard or garden; and certainly, men that are great lovers of themselves waste the public. Divide with reason between self-love and society; and be so true to thyself as thou be not false to others, especially to thy king and country. It is a poor center of a man's actions, himself. It is right earth;[2] for that only stands fast upon his own center; whereas all things that have affinity with the heavens move upon the center of another, which they benefit. The referring of all to a man's self is more tolerable in a sovereign prince, because themselves are not only themselves, but their good and evil is at the peril of the public fortune; but it is a desperate evil in a servant to a prince, or a citizen in a republic; for whatsoever affairs pass such a man's hands, he crooketh them to his own ends, which must needs be often eccentric[3] to the ends of his master or state. Therefore, let princes or states choose such servants as have not this mark; except they mean their service should be made but the accessory. That which maketh the effect more pernicious is that all proportion is

---

[1] Mischievous.   [2] Exactly like the earth.
[3] Having a different center. Bacon did not believe in the Copernican system.

lost. It were disproportion enough for the servant's good to be preferred before the master's; but yet it is a greater extreme, when a little good of the servant shall carry things against a great good of the master. And yet that is the case of bad officers, treasurers, ambassadors, generals, and other false and corrupt servants; which set a bias [4] upon their bowl, of their own petty ends and envies, to the overthrow of their master's great and important affairs; and, for the most part, the good such servants receive is after the model of their own fortune; but the hurt they sell for that good is after the model of their master's fortune. And certainly, it is the nature of extreme self-lovers, as they will set a house on fire, and it were but to roast their eggs; and yet these men many times hold credit with their masters, because their study is but to please them, and profit themselves; and for either respect they will abandon the good of their affairs.

Wisdom for a man's self is, in many branches thereof, a depraved thing. It is the wisdom of rats, that will be sure to leave a house somewhat before it fall; it is the wisdom of the fox, that thrusts out the badger who digged and made room for him; it is the wisdom of crocodiles, that shed tears when they would devour. But that which is specially to be noted is that those which (as Cicero says of Pompey) are *lovers of themselves, without a rival*,[5] are many times un-

---

[4] The lopsided weight of the ball used in bowling, which makes it swerve from a straight course.
[5] *Sui amantes, sine rivali.* Cicero, *Letters*, III, 8.

fortunate; and whereas they have all their times sacrificed to themselves, they become in the end themselves sacrifices to the inconstancy of fortune, whose wings they thought by their self-wisdom to have pinioned.

24
Of Innovations

As the births of living creatures at first are ill-shapen, so are all innovations, which are the births of time; yet notwithstanding, as those that first bring honor into their family are commonly more worthy than most that succeed, so the first precedent (if it be good) is seldom attained by imitation; for ill, to man's nature as it stands perverted, hath a natural motion strongest in continuance, but good, as a forced motion, strongest at first. Surely every medicine is an innovation, and he that will not apply new remedies must expect new evils, for time is the greatest innovator; and if time, of course, alter things to the worse, and wisdom and counsel shall not alter them to the better, what shall be the end? It is true, that what is settled by custom, though it be not good, yet at least it is fit; and those things which have long gone together, are, as it were, confederate within themselves;[1] whereas new things piece not so well; but, though they help by their utility, yet they trouble by their inconformity; besides, they are like strangers, more admired and less favored. All this is true, if time stood still, which, contrariwise, moveth so round,[2] that a froward retention of custom is as turbulent a thing as

[1] Adapted to each other.   [2] Fast.

an innovation; and they that reverence too much old times are but a scorn to the new. It were good, therefore, that men in their innovations would follow the example of time itself, which indeed innovateth greatly, but quietly, and by degrees scarce to be perceived; for otherwise, whatsoever is new is unlooked for, and ever it mends some and pairs[3] other; and he that is holpen, takes it for a fortune, and thanks the time; and he that is hurt, for a wrong, and imputeth it to the author. It is good also not to try experiments in states, except the necessity be urgent, or the utility evident; and well to beware that it be the reformation that draweth on the change, and not the desired change that pretendeth the reformation; and lastly, that the novelty, though it be not rejected, yet be held for a suspect,[4] and, as the Scripture saith, *That we make a stand upon the ancient way, and then look about us, and discover what is the straight and right way, and so to walk in it.*[5]

[3] Injures or impairs.   [4] A thing suspected.
[5] He probably alludes to Jeremiah, 6:16.

25
Of Dispatch

AFFECTED dispatch is one of the most dangerous things to business that can be; it is like that which the physicians call predigestion, or hasty digestion, which is sure to fill the body full of crudities, and secret seeds of diseases. Therefore, measure not dispatch by the times of sitting, but by the advancement of the business; and as in races, it is not the large stride, or high lift, that makes the speed, so in business, the keeping close to the matter, and not taking of it too much at once, procureth dispatch. It is the care of some only to come off speedily for the time, or to contrive some false periods of business, because they may seem men of dispatch; but it is one thing to abbreviate by contracting,[1] another by cutting off; and business so handled at several sittings, or meetings, goeth commonly backward and forward in an unsteady manner. I knew a wise man that had it for a byword, when he saw men hasten to a conclusion, *Stay a little, that we may make an end the sooner*.

On the other side, true dispatch is a rich thing; for time is the measure of business, as money is of wares; and business is bought at a dear hand where there is small dispatch. The Spartans and Spaniards have been noted to be of small

---

[1] By means of good management.

Of Dispatch

dispatch: *Let my death come from Spain;*[2] for then it will be sure to be long in coming.

Give good hearing to those that give the first information in business, and rather direct them in the beginning, than interrupt them in the continuance of their speeches; for he that is put out of his own order will go forward and backward, and be more tedious while he waits upon his memory, than he could have been if he had gone on in his own course; but sometimes it is seen that the moderator is more troublesome than the actor.

Iterations[3] are commonly loss of time; but there is no such gain of time as to iterate often the state of the question; for it chaseth away many a frivolous speech as it is coming forth. Long and curious speeches are as fit for dispatch as a robe or mantle with a long train is for a race. Prefaces, and passages,[4] and excusations,[5] and other speeches of reference to the person, are great wastes of time; and though they seem to proceed of modesty, they are bravery.[6] Yet beware of being too material when there is any impediment, or obstruction in men's wills; for preoccupation of mind[7] ever requireth preface of speech, like a fomentation to make the unguent enter.

Above all things, order and distribution, and singling out of parts, is the life of dispatch, so as the distribution be not too subtile; for he that doth not divide will never enter

---

[2] *Mi venga la muerte de Spagna.*
[3] Repetitions.
[4] Transitions.
[5] Apologies.
[6] Boasting.
[7] Prejudice.

well into business; and he that divideth too much will never come out of it clearly. To choose time is to save time; and an unseasonable motion is but beating the air. There be three parts of business: the preparation, the debate, or examination, and the perfection. Whereof, if you look for dispatch, let the middle only be the work of many, and the first and last the work of few. The proceeding, upon somewhat conceived in writing, doth for the most part facilitate dispatch; for though it should be wholly rejected, yet that negative is more pregnant of direction [8] than an indefinite, as ashes are more generative than dust.

[8] Stimulating.

26
Of Seeming Wise

IT HATH been an opinion that the French are wiser than they seem, and the Spaniards seem wiser than they are; but howsoever it be between nations, certainly it is so between man and man; for, as the apostle saith of godliness, *Having a show of godliness, but denying the power thereof*,[1] so certainly there are, in points of wisdom and sufficiency, that do nothing, or little very solemnly—*trifles, with great effort*.[2] It is a ridiculous thing, and fit for a satire to persons of judgment, to see what shifts these formalists have, and what prospectives to make superficies to seem body, that hath depth and bulk. Some are so close and reserved as they will not show their wares but by a dark light, and seem always to keep back somewhat; and when they know within themselves they speak of that they do not well know, would nevertheless seem to others to know of that which they may not well speak. Some help themselves with countenance and gesture, and are wise by signs; as Cicero saith of Piso, that when he answered him he fetched one of his brows up to his forehead, and bent the other down to his chin: *With one brow raised to your forehead, the other bent downward to your chin, you reply that cruelty de-*

[1] II Timothy, 3:5.
[2] *Magno conatu nugas.* Terence, *The Self-Tormentor*, III, v, 8.

lights you not.[3] Some think to bear it by speaking a great word and being peremptory; and go on, and take by admittance that which they cannot make good. Some, whatsoever is beyond their reach, will seem to despise or make light of it as impertinent or curious, and so would have their ignorance seem judgment. Some are never without a difference, and commonly by amusing men with a subtlety, blanch the matter; of whom A. Gellius saith, *A senseless man, who disrupts weighty matters by verbal subtleties.*[4] Of which kind also Plato, in his Protagoras, bringeth in Prodicus in scorn, and maketh him make a speech that consisteth of distinctions from the beginning to the end. Generally such men, in all deliberations, find ease to be of the negative side, and affect a credit to object and foretell difficulties; for when propositions are denied, there is an end of them, but if they be allowed, it requireth a new work; which false point of wisdom is the bane of business. To conclude, there is no decaying merchant, or inward beggar,[5] hath so many tricks to uphold the credit of their wealth as these empty persons have to maintain the credit of their sufficiency. Seeming wise men may make shift to get opinion, but let no man choose them for employment; for certainly you were better take for business a man somewhat absurd than overformal.

[3] *Respondes, altero ad frontem sublato, altero ad mentum depresso supercilio; crudelitatem tibi non placere. Against Piso*, VI.
[4] *Hominem delirum, qui verborum minutiis rerum frangit pondera.* Quintilian, X, 1.
[5] One really insolvent, though to the world he does not appear so.

27
Of Friendship

IT HAD been hard for him that spake it [1] to have put more truth and untruth together in few words than in that speech: *Whosoever is delighted in solitude, is either a wild beast or a god:* for it is most true that a natural and secret hatred and aversion towards society in any man hath somewhat of the savage beast; but it is most untrue that it should have any character at all of the divine nature, except it proceed, not out of a pleasure in solitude, but out of a love and desire to sequester a man's self for a higher conversation; such as is found to have been falsely and feignedly in some of the heathen; as Epimenides, the Candian; Numa, the Roman; Empedocles, the Sicilian; and Apollonius, of Tyana; [2] and truly and really in divers of the ancient hermits and holy fathers of the church. But little do men perceive what solitude is and how far it extendeth; for a crowd is not company, and faces are but a gallery of pictures, and

[1] Aristotle, *Politics*, I, 2.
[2] Epimenides, a poet of Crete, is said by Pliny to have fallen into a sleep which lasted 57 years. Numa, legendary Roman King, pretended that he was instructed in the art of legislation by the divine nymph Egeria, who dwelt in the Arician grove. Empedocles, the Sicilian philosopher, is said to have thrown himself into the crater of Mount Aetna so that his disappearance might make people think him a god. Apollonius of Tyana, the Pythagorean philosopher, pretended to miraculous powers.

talk but a tinkling cymbal, where there is no love. The Latin adage meeteth with it a little, *A great city is a great solitude;* [3] because in a great town friends are scattered, so that there is not that fellowship, for the most part, which is in less neighborhoods: but we may go further, and affirm most truly, that it is a mere and miserable solitude to want true friends, without which the world is but a wilderness; and even in this sense also of solitude, whosoever in the frame of his nature and affections is unfit for friendship, he taketh it of the beasts, and not from humanity.

A principal fruit of friendship is the ease and discharge of the fullness and swellings of the heart, which passions of all kinds do cause and induce. We know diseases of stoppings and suffocations are the most dangerous in the body, and it is not much otherwise in the mind. You may take sarza [4] to open the liver, steel to open the spleen, flower of sulphur for the lungs, castoreum [5] for the brain, but no receipt openeth the heart but a true friend, to whom you may impart griefs, joys, fears, hopes, suspicions, counsels, and whatsoever lieth upon the heart to oppress it, in a kind of civil shrift or confession.

It is a strange thing to observe how high a rate great kings and monarchs do set upon this fruit of friendship whereof we speak; so great, as they purchase it many times at the hazard of their own safety and greatness; for princes, in regard of the distance of their fortune from that of their

[3] *Magna civitas, magna solitudo.* [4] Sarsaparilla.
[5] A medicinal substance obtained from the beaver.

subjects and servants, cannot gather this fruit, except (to make themselves capable thereof) they raise some persons to be as it were companions and almost equals to themselves, which many times sorteth to inconvenience. The modern languages give unto such persons the name of favorites, or privadoes, as if it were matter of grace or conversation; but the Roman name attaineth the true use and cause thereof, naming them *Sharers of troubles;*[6] for it is that which tieth the knot. And we see plainly that this hath been done, not by weak and passionate princes only, but by the wisest and most politic that ever reigned, who have oftentimes joined to themselves some of their servants, whom both themselves have called friends, and allowed others likewise to call them in the same manner, using the word received between private men.

L. Sulla, when he commanded Rome, raised Pompey (after surnamed the Great) to that height, that Pompey vaunted himself for Sulla's overmatch; for when he had carried the consulship for a friend of his, against the pursuit of Sulla, and that Sulla did a little resent thereat, and began to speak great, Pompey turned upon him again, and, in effect, bade him be quiet; for that more men adored the sun rising than the sun setting. With Julius Caesar, Decimus Brutus had obtained that interest, as he set him down in his testament for heir in remainder after his nephew; and this was the man that had power with him to draw him

[6] *Participes curarum.*

forth to his death; for when Caesar would have discharged the senate, in regard of some ill presages, and specially a dream of Calpurnia, this man lifted him gently by the arm out of his chair, telling him he hoped he would not dismiss the senate till his wife had dreamt a better dream;[7] and it seemeth his favor was so great, as Antonius, in a letter which is recited verbatim in one of Cicero's Philippics, calleth him *venefica, witch*, as if he had enchanted Caesar. Augustus raised Agrippa (though of mean birth) to that height, as, when he consulted with Maecenas about the marriage of his daughter Julia, Maecenas took the liberty to tell him that he must either marry his daughter to Agrippa, or take away his life; there was no third way, he had made him so great. With Tiberius Caesar, Sejanus had ascended to that height, as they two were termed and reckoned as a pair of friends. Tiberius, in a letter to him, saith, *Because of our friendship, I have not concealed these things from you.*[8] And the whole senate dedicated an altar to Friendship, as to a goddess, in respect of the great dearness of friendship between them two. The like, or more, was between Septimius Severus and Plautianus; for he forced his eldest son to marry the daughter of Plautianus, and would often maintain Plautianus in doing affronts to his son; and did write also in a letter to the senate, by these words: *I love the man so well, as I wish he may over-live*

---

[7] Plutarch, *Lives*, V, 65.
[8] *Haec pro amicitiâ nostrâ non occultavi.* Tacitus, *Annals*, IV, 40.

me.[9] Now if these princes had been as a Trajan, or a Marcus Aurelius, a man might have thought that this had proceeded of an abundant goodness of nature; but being men so wise, of such strength and severity of mind, and so extreme lovers of themselves, as all these were, it proveth most plainly that they found their own felicity (though as great as ever happened to mortal men) but as an half-piece, except they might have a friend to make it entire; and yet, which is more, they were princes that had wives, sons, nephews; and yet all these could not supply the comfort of friendship.

It is not to be forgotten what Comineus [10] observeth of his first master, Duke Charles the Hardy,[11] namely, that he would communicate his secrets with none, and, least of all, those secrets which troubled him most. Whereupon he goeth on, and saith, that towards his latter time that closeness did impair and a little perish his understanding. Surely, Comineus might have made the same judgment, also, if it had pleased him, of his second master, Louis the Eleventh, whose closeness was indeed his tormentor. The parable of Pythagoras is dark, but true: *Cor ne edito, Eat not the heart.* Certainly, if a man would give it a hard phrase, those that want friends to open themselves unto are cannibals of their own hearts; but one thing is most admirable (wherewith I will conclude this first fruit of friendship), which is,

---

[9] Dion Cassius, LXXV, 6.
[10] Philip de Comines, a noted French historian and statesman.
[11] Charles the Bold, Duke of Burgundy.

that this communicating of a man's self to his friend works two contrary effects, for it redoubleth joys and cutteth griefs in halves; for there is no man that imparteth his joys to his friend, but he joyeth the more; and no man that imparteth his griefs to his friend, but he grieveth the less. So that it is, in truth, of operation upon a man's mind of like virtue as the alchemists used to attribute to their stone for man's body, that it worketh all contrary effects, but still to the good and benefit of nature. But yet, without praying in aid [12] of alchemists, there is a manifest image of this in the ordinary course of nature; for in bodies union strengtheneth and cherisheth any natural action; and on the other side weakeneth and dulleth any violent impression; and even so it is of minds.

The second fruit of friendship is healthful and sovereign for the understanding, as the first is for the affections; for friendship maketh indeed a fair day in the affections from storm and tempests, but it maketh daylight in the understanding, out of darkness and confusion of thoughts. Neither is this to be understood only of faithful counsel, which a man receiveth from his friend; but before you come to that, certain it is, that whosoever hath his mind fraught with many thoughts, his wits and understanding do clarify and break up in the communicating and discoursing with another; he tosseth his thoughts more easily; he marshalleth them more orderly; he seeth how they look

---

[12] Becoming an advocate.

Of Friendship

when they are turned into words; finally, he waxeth wiser than himself; and that more by an hour's discourse than by a day's meditation. It was well said by Themistocles to the king of Persia: *That speech was like cloth of Arras, opened and put abroad, whereby the imagery doth appear in figure; whereas in thoughts they lie but as in packs.*[13] Neither is this second fruit of friendship, in opening the understanding, restrained only to such friends as are able to give a man counsel (they indeed are best), but even without that a man learneth of himself, and bringeth his own thoughts to light, and whetteth his wits as against a stone, which itself cuts not. In a word, a man were better relate himself to a statue or picture, than to suffer his thoughts to pass in smother.

Add now, to make this second fruit of friendship complete, that other point which lieth more open and falleth within vulgar observation; which is faithful counsel from a friend. Heraclitus [14] saith well, in one of his enigmas, *Dry light is ever the best;* and certain it is that the light that a man receiveth by counsel from another is drier and purer than that which cometh from his own understanding and judgment, which is ever infused and drenched in his affections and customs. So, as there is as much difference between the counsel that a friend giveth, and that a man giveth himself, as there is between the counsel of a friend and of a flatterer; for there is no such flatterer as is a man's self,

---

[13] Plutarch, *Lives*, I, 315.
[14] Heraclitus, a celebrated Greek philosopher.

and there is no such remedy against flattery of a man's self, as the liberty of a friend. Counsel is of two sorts, the one concerning manners, the other concerning business; for the first, the best preservative to keep the mind in health is the faithful admonition of a friend. The calling of a man's self to a strict account is a medicine sometimes too piercing and corrosive; reading good books of morality is a little flat and dead; observing our faults in others is sometimes improper for our case; but the best receipt (best, I say, to work, and best to take) is the admonition of a friend. It is a strange thing to behold what gross errors and extreme absurdities many (especially of the greater sort) do commit for want of a friend to tell them of them, to the great damage both of their fame and fortune; for, as St. James saith, they are as men *that look sometimes into a glass, and presently forget their own shape and favor*.[15] As for business, a man may think, if he will, that two eyes see no more than one; or, that a gamester seeth always more than a looker-on; or, that a man in anger is as wise as he that has said over the four and twenty letters, or, that a musket may be shot off as well upon the arm as upon a rest; and such other fond and high imaginations, to think himself all in all; but when all is done, the help of good counsel is that which setteth business straight. And if any man think that he will take counsel, but it shall be by pieces, asking counsel in one business of one man, and in another business of an-

---

[15] James, 1:23.

other man; it is well (that is to say, better, perhaps, than if he asked none at all); but he runneth two dangers: one, that he shall not be faithfully counselled; for it is a rare thing, except it be from a perfect and entire friend, to have counsel given, but such as shall be bowed and crooked to some ends which he hath that giveth it; the other that he shall have counsel given, hurtful and unsafe (though with good meaning), and mixed partly of mischief and partly of remedy; even as if you would call a physician that is thought good for the cure of the disease you complain of, but is unacquainted with your body; and therefore, may put you in a way for a present cure, but overthroweth your health in some other kind, and so cure the disease and kill the patient. But a friend, wholly acquainted with a man's estate, will beware, by furthering present business, how he dasheth upon other inconvenience. And therefore, rest not upon scattered counsels; they will rather distract and mislead, than settle and direct.

After these two noble fruits of friendship (peace in the affections and support of the judgment), followeth the last fruit, which is like the pomegranate, full of many kernels; I mean aid, and bearing a part in all actions and occasions. Here the best way to represent to life and manifold use of friendship is to cast and see how many things there are which a man cannot do himself; and then it will appear that it was a sparing speech of the ancients to say, *that a friend is another himself*, for that a friend is far more than himself. Men have their time, and die many times in desire of some things which they principally take to heart; the bestowing of a child, the finishing of a work, or the like. If a man have a true friend, he may rest almost secure that the care of those things will continue after him; so that a man hath, as it were, two lives in his desires. A man hath a body, and that body is confined to a place; but where friendship is, all offices of life are, as it were, granted to him and his deputy, for he may exercise them by his friend. How many things are there, which a man cannot, with any face or comeliness, say or do himself? A man can scarce allege his own merits with modesty, much less extol them; a man cannot sometimes brook to supplicate, or beg, and a number of the like; but all these things are graceful in a friend's mouth, which are blushing in a man's own. So, again, a man's person hath many proper [16] relations which he cannot put off. A man cannot speak to his son but as a father; to his wife but as a husband; to his enemy but upon terms; whereas a friend may speak as the case requires, and not as it sorteth with [17] the person. But to enumerate these things were endless. I have given the rule, where a man cannot fitly play his own part: if he have not a friend, he may quit the stage.

[16] Personal, private.   [17] Suits.

28
Of Expense

RICHES are for spending, and spending for honor and good actions; therefore, extraordinary expense must be limited by the worth of the occasion; for voluntary undoing may be as well for a man's country as for the kingdom of heaven; but ordinary expense ought to be limited by a man's estate, and governed with such regard, as it be within his compass, and not subject to deceit and abuse of servants, and ordered to the best show, that the bills may be less than the estimation abroad. Certainly if a man will keep but of even hand, his ordinary expenses ought to be but to the half of his receipts; and, if he think to wax rich, but to the third part. It is no baseness for the greatest to descend and look into their own estate. Some forbear it, not upon negligence alone, but doubting [1] to bring themselves into melancholy, in respect they shall find it broken; but wounds cannot be cured without searching. He that cannot look into his own estate at all, had need both choose well those whom he employeth, and change them often; for new are more timorous, and less subtle. He that can look into his estate but seldom, it behooveth him to turn all to certainties. A man had need, if he be plentiful in some

[1] Fearing.

kind of expense, to be as saving again in some other: as, if he be plentiful in diet, to be saving in apparel; if he be plentiful in the hall, to be saving in the stable; and the like. For he that is plentiful in expenses of all kinds will hardly be preserved from decay. In clearing [2] of a man's estate, he may as well hurt himself in being too sudden, as in letting it run on too long; for hasty selling is commonly as disadvantageable as interest. Besides, he that clears at once will relapse; for, finding himself out of straits, he will revert to his customs; but he that cleareth by degrees induceth a habit of frugality, and gaineth as well upon his mind as upon his estate. Certainly, who hath a state to repair, may not despise small things; and, commonly, it is less dishonorable to abridge petty charges, than to stoop to petty gettings. A man ought warily to begin charges which once begun will continue; but in matters that return not, he may be more magnificent.

[2] From debts and incumbrances.

29

Of the True Greatness of Kingdoms and Estates

THE speech of Themistocles, the Athenian, which was haughty and arrogant, in taking so much to himself, had been a grave and wise observation and censure, applied at large to others. Desired at a feast to touch a lute, he said, *He could not fiddle, but yet he could make a small town a great city*.[1] These words (holpen a little with a metaphor) may express two different abilities in those that deal in business of estate; for if a true survey be taken of counsellors and statesmen, there may be found (though rarely) those which can make a small state great, and yet cannot fiddle: as, on the other side there will be found a great many that can fiddle very cunningly, but yet are so far from being able to make a small state great, as their gift lieth the other way—to bring a great and flourishing estate to ruin and decay. And certainly those degenerate arts and shifts, whereby many counsellors and governors gain both favor with their masters and estimation with the vulgar, deserve no better name than fiddling; being things rather pleasing for the time, and graceful to themselves only, than

[1] Plutarch, *Lives*, I, 283.

tending to the weal and advancement of the state which they serve. There are also (no doubt) counsellors and governors which may be held sufficient, *negotiis pares*, able to manage affairs, and to keep them from precipices and manifest inconveniences; which, nevertheless, are far from the ability to raise and amplify an estate in power, means, and fortune. But be the workmen what they may be, let us speak of the work; that is, the true greatness of kingdoms and estates, and the means thereof. An argument fit for great and mighty princes to have in their hand; to the end, that neither by overmeasuring their forces, they lose themselves in vain enterprises, nor, on the other side, by undervaluing them, they descend to fearful and pusillanimous counsels.

The greatness of an estate, in bulk and territory, doth fall under measure; and the greatness of finances and revenue doth fall under computation. The population may appear by musters, and the number and greatness of cities and towns by cards and maps; but yet there is not anything amongst civil affairs more subject to error than the right valuation and true judgment concerning the power and forces of an estate. The kingdom of heaven is compared, not to any great kernel, or nut, but to a grain of mustard-seed;[2] which is one of the least grains, but hath in it a property and spirit hastily to get up and spread. So are there states great in territory, and yet not apt to enlarge

[2] He alludes to Matthew, 13:31.

Of the True Greatness of Kingdoms, Estates

or command; and some that have but a small dimension of stem, and yet apt to be the foundations of great monarchies.

Walled towns, stored arsenals and armories, goodly races of horse, chariots of war, elephants, ordnance, artillery, and the like; all this is but a sheep in a lion's skin, except the breed and disposition of the people be stout and warlike. Nay, number itself in armies importeth not much, where the people is of weak courage; for, as Virgil saith, *It never troubles a wolf how many the sheep be.*[3] The army of the Persians in the plains of Arbela was such a vast sea of people as it did somewhat astonish the commanders in Alexander's army, who came to him, therefore, and wished him to set upon them by night; but he answered, *He would not pilfer the victory;* and the defeat was easy.[4] When Tigranes,[5] the Armenian, being encamped upon a hill with four hundred thousand men, discovered the army of the Romans, being not above fourteen thousand, marching towards him, he made himself merry with it, and said, *Yonder men are too many for an ambassage, and too few for a fight;* but before the sun set, he found them enow to give him the chase with infinite slaughter. Many are the examples of the great odds between number and courage; so that a man may truly make a judgment, that the principal point of greatness in any state is to have a race of military

---

[3] Virgil, *Eclogues*, VII, 52.   [4] Plutarch, *Lives*, IV, 336.
[5] King of Armenia, who was vanquished by Lucullus, and finally submitted to Pompey.

men. Neither is money the sinews of war (as it is trivially said), where the sinews of men's arms, in base and effeminate people, are failing: for Solon said well to Croesus (when in ostentation he showed him his gold), *Sir, if any other come that hath better iron than you, he will be master of all this gold.* Therefore, let any prince or state think soberly of his forces, except his militia of natives be of good and valiant soldiers; and let princes, on the other side, that have subjects of martial disposition, know their own strength unless they be otherwise wanting unto themselves. As for mercenary forces (which is the help in this case) all examples show that, whatsoever estate or prince doth rest upon them, he may spread his feathers for a time, but he will mew [6] them soon after.

The blessing of Judah and Issachar [7] will never meet; that the same people, or nation, should be both the lion's whelp and the ass between burdens; neither will it be, that a people overlaid with taxes should ever become valiant and martial. It is true that taxes levied by consent of the estate do abate men's courage less; as it hath been seen notably in the excises of the Low Countries, and, in some degree, in the subsidies of England; for you must note that we speak now of the heart, and not of the purse; so that, although the same tribute and tax, laid by consent or by imposing, be all one to the purse, yet it works di-

[6] Moult.
[7] The allusion is to the prophetic words of Jacob on his death-bed. Genesis, 49:9, 14, 15.

Of the True Greatness of Kingdoms, Estates 125

versely upon courage. So that you may conclude, that no people overcharged with tribute is fit for empire.

Let states that aim at greatness take heed how their nobility and gentlemen do multiply too fast; for that maketh the common subject grow to be a peasant and base swain, driven out of heart, and, in effect, but the gentleman's laborer. Even as you may see in coppice woods; if you leave your staddles [8] too thick, you shall never have clean underwood, but shrubs and bushes. So in countries, if the gentlemen be too many, the commons will be base; and you will bring it to that, that not the hundred poll will be fit for a helmet, especially as to the infantry, which is the nerve of an army; and so there will be great population and little strength. This which I speak of hath been nowhere better seen than by comparing of England and France; whereof England, though far less in territory and population, hath been, nevertheless, an overmatch; in regard, the middle people of England make good soldiers, which the peasants of France do not. And herein the device of King Henry the Seventh (whereof I have spoken largely in the history of his life) was profound and admirable; in making farms and houses of husbandry of a standard, that is, maintained with such a proportion of land unto them as may breed a subject to live in convenient plenty, and no servile condition, and to keep the plough in the hands of the owners, and not mere hirelings; and

[8] Young trees.

thus, indeed, you shall attain to Virgil's character, which he gives to ancient Italy: *A land mighty in arms and fertile in soil.*[9]

Neither is that state (which, for anything I know, is almost peculiar to England, and hardly to be found anywhere else, except it be, perhaps, in Poland) to be passed over; I mean the state of free servants and attendants upon noblemen and gentlemen, which are noways inferior unto the yeomanry for arms; and, therefore, out of all question, the splendor and magnificence, and great retinues, and hospitality of noblemen and gentlemen received into custom, do much conduce unto martial greatness; whereas, contrariwise, the close and reserved living of noblemen and gentlemen causeth a penury of military forces.

By all means, it is to be procured that the trunk of Nebuchadnezzar's tree of monarchy[10] be great enough to bear the branches and the boughs; that is, that the natural subjects of the crown, or state, bear a sufficient proportion to the stranger subjects that they govern. Therefore, all states that are liberal of naturalization towards strangers are fit for empire; for to think that a handful of people can, with the greatest courage and policy in the world, embrace too large extent of dominion, it may hold for a time, but it will fail suddenly. The Spartans were a nice[11] people in point of naturalization; whereby, while they kept their compass, they stood firm;

---

[9] *Terra potens armis atque ubere glebae.* Virgil, *Aeneid*, I, 531.
[10] See Daniel, 4:10.
[11] Discriminating.

Of the True Greatness of Kingdoms, Estates

but when they did spread, and their boughs were becoming too great for their stem, they became a windfall upon the sudden. Never any state was, in this point, so open to receive strangers into their body as were the Romans; therefore, it sorted with them accordingly, for they grew to the greatest monarchy. Their manner was to grant naturalization (which they called *jus civitatis*), and to grant it in the highest degree, that is, not only *right of trade, right of marriage, right of inheritance*, but also *right of suffrage* and *right of honor*;[12] and this not to singular persons alone, but likewise to whole families; yea, to cities and sometimes to nations. Add to this their custom of plantation of colonies, whereby the Roman plant was removed into the soil of other nations, and, putting both constitutions together, you will say that it was not the Romans that spread upon the world, but it was the world that spread upon the Romans; and that was the sure way of greatness. I have marvelled sometimes at Spain, how they clasp and contain so large dominions with so few natural Spaniards; but sure the whole compass of Spain is a very great body of a tree, far above Rome and Sparta at the first; and, besides, though they have not had that usage to naturalize liberally, yet they have that which is next to it; that is, to employ, almost indifferently, all nations in their militia of ordinary soldiers; yea, and sometimes in their highest commands; nay, it seemeth at this instant

[12] *Jus commercii, jus connubii, jus haereditatis, jus suffragii, jus honorum.*

they are sensible of this want of natives, as by the Pragmatical Sanction,[13] now published, appeareth.

It is certain that sedentary and within-door arts, and delicate manufactures (that require rather the finger than the arm), have in their nature a contrariety to a military disposition; and, generally, all warlike people are a little idle, and love danger better than travail; neither must they be too much broken of it, if they shall be preserved in vigor. Therefore, it was great advantage in the ancient states of Sparta, Athens, Rome, and others, that they had the use of slaves, which commonly did rid those manufactures; but that is abolished, in greatest part, by the Christian law. That which cometh nearest to it is to leave those arts chiefly to strangers (which, for that purpose, are the more easily to be received), and to contain the principal bulk of the vulgar natives within those three kinds, tillers of the ground, free servants, and handicraftsmen of strong and manly arts; as smiths, masons, carpenters, etc., not reckoning professed soldiers.

But, above all, for empire and greatness, it importeth most, that a nation do profess arms as their principal honor, study, and occupation; for the things which we formerly have spoken of are but habilitations [14] towards arms; and what is habilitation without intention and act? Romulus, after his death (as they report or feign), sent

---

[13] Spanish law which gave certain privileges to married persons and further immunities to those having six children.
[14] Qualifications.

a present to the Romans, that, above all, they should intend [15] arms, and then they should prove the greatest empire of the world. The fabric of the state of Sparta was wholly (though not wisely) framed and composed to that scope and end; the Persians and Macedonians had it for a flash; [16] the Gauls, Germans, Goths, Saxons, Normans, and others, had it for a time; the Turks have it at this day, though in great declination. Of Christian Europe, they that have it are in effect only the Spaniards; but it is so plain that every man profiteth in that he most intendeth, that it needeth not to be stood upon. It is enough to point at it, that no nation which doth not directly profess arms may look to have greatness fall into their mouths; and, on the other side, it is a most certain oracle of time that those states that continue long in that profession (as the Romans and Turks principally have done) do wonders; and those that have professed arms but for an age have, notwithstanding, commonly attained that greatness in that age which maintained them long after, when their profession and exercise of arms had grown to decay.

Incident to this point is for a state to have those laws or customs which may reach forth unto them just occasions (as may be pretended) of war; for there is that justice imprinted in the nature of men, that they enter not upon wars (whereof so many calamities do ensue), but upon some, at the least specious, grounds and quarrels. The Turk

[15] Attend to.   [16] For a short period.

hath at hand, for cause of war, the propagation of his law or sect, a quarrel that he may always command. The Romans, though they esteemed the extending the limits of their empire to be great honor to their generals when it was done, yet they never rested upon that alone to begin a war. First, therefore, let nations that pretend to greatness have this, that they be sensible of wrongs, either upon borderers, merchants, or politic ministers; and that they sit not too long upon a provocation: secondly, let them be pressed, and ready to give aids and succors to their confederates, as it ever was with the Romans; insomuch, as if the confederate had leagues defensive with divers other states, and, upon invasion offered, did implore their aids severally, yet the Romans would ever be the foremost, and leave it to none other to have the honor. As for the wars, which were anciently made on the behalf of a kind of party, or tacit conformity of estate, I do not see how they may be well justified: as when the Romans made a war for the liberty of Graecia; or, when the Lacedaemonians and Athenians made wars to set up or pull down democracies and oligarchies; or when wars were made by foreigners, under the pretense of justice or protection, to deliver the subjects of others from tyranny and oppression, and the like. Let it suffice that no estate expect to be great that is not awake upon any just occasion of arming.

Nobody can be healthful without exercise, neither natural body nor politic; and certainly to a kingdom, or estate, a just and honorable war is the true exercise. A civil war, indeed, is like the heat of a fever; but a foreign war is like the heat of exercise, and serveth to keep the body in health; for, in a slothful peace, both courages will effeminate and manners corrupt. But, howsoever it be for happiness, without all question for greatness, it maketh to be still, for the most part, in arms; and the strength of a veteran army (though it be a chargeable business) always on foot, is that which commonly giveth the law, or, at least, the reputation amongst all neighbor states, as may well be seen in Spain, which hath had, in one part or other, a veteran army, almost continually, now by the space of sixscore years.

To be master of the sea is an abridgement of a monarchy. Cicero, writing to Atticus, of Pompey's preparation against Caesar, saith, *Pompey's plan is clearly that of Themistocles; for he believes that whoever is master of the sea is matser of all things*,[17] and, without doubt Pompey had tired out Caesar, if upon vain confidence he had not left that way. We see the great effects of battles by sea. The battle of Actium decided the empire of the world: the battle of Lepanto arrested the greatness of the Turk. There be many examples where sea fights have been final to the war; but this is when princes, or states, have set up their rest upon the battles. But thus much is certain, that he that commands the sea is at great liberty, and may take as much and as little of the war as he will; whereas,

[17] *Consilium Pompeii plane Themistocleum est; putat enim, qui mari potitur, eum rerum potiri. Ad Atticus*, X, 8.

those that be strongest by land are many times, nevertheless, in great straits. Surely, at this day, with us of Europe the vantage of strength at sea (which is one of the principal dowries of this kingdom of Great Britain) is great; both because most of the kingdoms of Europe are not merely inland, but girt with the sea most part of their compass; and because the wealth of both Indies seems, in great part, but an accessory to the command of the seas.

The wars of latter ages seem to be made in the dark, in respect of the glory and honor which reflected upon men from the wars in ancient time. There be now, for martial encouragement, some degrees and orders of chivalry, which, nevertheless, are conferred promiscuously upon soldiers and no soldiers; and some remembrance, perhaps, upon the escutcheon, and some hospitals for maimed soldiers, and such like things; but in ancient times, the trophies erected upon the place of the victory; the funeral laudatives,[18] and monuments for those that died in the wars; the crowns and garlands personal; the style of emperor which the great kings of the world after borrowed; the triumphs of the generals upon their return; the great donatives and largesses upon the disbanding of the armies; were things able to inflame all men's courages. But, above all, that of the triumph amongst the Romans was not pageants or gaudery, but one of the wisest and noblest institutions that ever was; for it contained three things:

[18] Formal praise.

honor to the general, riches to the treasury out of the spoils, and donatives to the army. But that honor, perhaps, were not fit for monarchies, except it be in the person of the monarch himself, or his sons; as it came to pass in times of Roman emperors who did impropriate the triumphs to themselves and their sons, for such wars as they did achieve in person, and left only for wars achieved by subjects, some triumphal garments and ensigns to the general.

To conclude: No man can by care-taking (as the Scripture saith) *add a cubit to his stature*,[19] in this little model of a man's body; but in the great frame of kingdoms and commonwealths, it is in the power of princes or estates to add amplitude and greatness to their kingdom; for by introducing such ordinances, constitutions, and customs, as we have now touched, they may sow greatness to their posterity and succession: but these things are commonly not observed, but left to take their chance.

[19] Matthew, 6:2; Luke, 12:25.

30
Of Regimen of Health

THERE is a wisdom in this beyond the rules of physic. A man's own observation, what he finds good of, and what he finds hurt of, is the best physic to preserve health; but it is a safer conclusion to say, *This agreeth not well with me, therefore I will not continue it;* than this, *I find no offense of this, therefore I may use it:* for strength of nature in youth passeth over many excesses which are owing a man till his age.[1] Discern of the coming on of years, and think not to do the same things still; for age will not be defied. Beware of sudden change in any great point of diet, and, if necessity enforce it, fit the rest to it; for it is a secret both in nature and state, that it is safer to change many things than one. Examine thy customs of diet, sleep, exercise, apparel, and the like; and try, in any thing thou shalt judge hurtful, to discontinue it by little and little; but so, as if thou dost find any inconvenience by the change, thou come back to it again; for it is hard to distinguish that which is generally held good and wholesome from that which is good particularly and fit for thine own body. To be free-minded and cheerfully disposed at hours of meat, and of sleep, and of exercise, is one of the best precepts

[1] The effects of which are not felt till old age.

of long lasting. As for the passions and studies of the mind, avoid envy, anxious fears, anger fretting inwards, subtle and knotty inquisitions, joys and exhilarations in excess, sadness not communicated. Entertain hopes, mirth rather than joy, variety of delights, rather than surfeit of them; wonder and admiration, and therefore novelties; studies that fill the mind with splendid and illustrious objects, as histories, fables, and contemplations of nature. If you fly physic in health altogether, it will be too strange for your body when you shall need it; if you make it too familiar, it will work no extraordinary effect when sickness cometh. I commend rather some diet, for certain seasons, than frequent use of physic, except it be grown into a custom; for those diets alter the body more and trouble it less. Despise no new accident in your body, but ask opinion [2] of it. In sickness, respect health principally; and in health, action; for those that put their bodies to endure in health, may, in most sicknesses which are not very sharp, be cured only with diet and tendering. Celsus [3] could never have spoken it as a physician, had he not been a wise man withal, when he giveth it for one of the great precepts of health and lasting, that a man do vary and interchange contraries, but with an inclination to the more benign extreme. Use fasting and full eating, but rather full eating; watching and sleep, but rather sleep; sitting and exercise, but rather exercise, and the like; so shall nature be

[2] Take medical advice.
[3] Famous Roman physician of the first century.

cherished, and yet taught masteries. Physicians are some of them so pleasing and conformable to the humor of the patient, as they press not the true cure of the disease; and some other are so regular in proceeding according to art for the disease, as they respect not sufficiently the condition of the patient. Take one of a middle temper; or, if it may not be found in one man, combine two of either sort; and forget not to call as well the best acquainted with your body, as the best reputed of for his faculty.

31
Of Suspicion

SUSPICIONS amongst thoughts are like bats amongst birds, they ever fly by twilight. Certainly they are to be repressed, or at the least well guarded; for they cloud the mind, they lose friends, and they check with business, whereby business cannot go on currently and constantly. They dispose kings to tyranny, husbands to jealousy, wise men to irresolution and melancholy. They are defects, not in the heart but in the brain; for they take place in the stoutest natures, as in the example of Henry the Seventh of England. There was not a more suspicious man, nor a more stout, and in such a composition they do small hurt; for commonly they are not admitted, but with examination, whether they be likely or no; but in fearful natures they gain ground too fast. There is nothing makes a man suspect much, more than to know little; and, therefore, men should remedy suspicion by procuring to know more, and not to keep their suspicions in smother. What would men have? Do they think those they employ and deal with are saints? Do they not think they will have their own ends, and be truer to themselves than to them? Therefore, there is no better way to moderate suspicions than to account upon such suspicions as true, and yet to bridle them as false: for so far a man ought to make use of suspicions as to provide, as if that should be true that he suspects, yet it may do him no hurt. Suspicions that the mind of itself gathers are but buzzes; but suspicions that are artificially nourished, and put into men's heads by the tales and whisperings of others, have stings. Certainly the best mean to clear the way in this same wood of suspicions is frankly to communicate them with the party that he suspects: for thereby he shall be sure to know more of the truth of them than he did before; and withal, shall make that party more circumspect, not to give further cause of suspicion. But this would not be done to men of base natures; for they, if they find themselves once suspected, will never be true. The Italian says, *Suspicion is the passport to faith;*[1] as if suspicion did give a passport to faith; but it ought rather to kindle it to discharge itself.

[1] *Sospetto licentia fede.*

32
Of Discourse

SOME in their discourse desire rather commendation of wit in being able to hold all arguments, than of judgment in discerning what is true; as if it were a praise to know what might be said and not what should be thought. Some have certain commonplaces and themes, wherein they are good, and want variety, which kind of poverty is for the most part tedious, and, when it is once perceived, ridiculous. The honorablest part of talk is to give the occasion,[1] and again to moderate and pass to somewhat else; for then a man leads the dance. It is good in discourse and speech of conversation to vary and intermingle speech of the present occasion with arguments, tales with reasons, asking of questions with telling of opinions, and jest with earnest; for it is a dull thing to tire, and, as we say now, to jade anything too far. As for jest, there be certain things which ought to be privileged from it; namely, religion, matters of state, great persons, any man's present business of importance, and any case that deserveth pity; yet there be some that think their wits have been asleep, except they dart out somewhat that is piquant, and to the quick; that is a vein which would be bridled:—

[1] To introduce the subject.

Boy, spare the whip, and tighter hold the reins.[2]

And, generally, men ought to find the difference between saltness and bitterness. Certainly, he that hath a satirical vein, as he maketh others afraid of his wit, so he had need be afraid of others' memory. He that questioneth much, shall learn much, and content much, but especially if he apply his questions to the skill of the persons whom he asketh: for he shall give them occasion to please themselves in speaking, and himself shall continually gather knowledge; but let his questions not be troublesome, for that is fit for a poser.[3] And let him be sure to leave other men their turns to speak; nay, if there be any that would reign and take up all the time, let him find means to take them off, and to bring others on, as musicians used to do with those that dance too long galliards.[4] If you dissemble sometimes your knowledge of that you are thought to know, you shall be thought, another time, to know that you know not. Speech of a man's self ought to be seldom, and well chosen. I knew one was wont to say in scorn, *He must needs be a wise man, he speaks so much of himself;* and there is but one case wherein a man may commend himself with good grace, and that is in commending virtue in another, especially if it be such a virtue whereunto

[2] *Parce, puer, stimulis, et fortius utere loris.* Ovid, *Metamorphoses*, II, 127.
[3] One who tests or examines.
[4] The galliard was a dance fashionable in the time of Queen Elizabeth.

Of Discourse

himself pretendeth. Speech of touch[5] towards others should be sparingly used; for discourse ought to be as a field, without coming home to any man. I knew two noblemen, of the west part of England, whereof the one was given to scoff, but kept ever royal cheer in his house; the other would ask of those that had been at the other's table, *Tell, truly, was there never a flout or dry blow*[6] *given?* To which the guest would answer, *Such and such a thing passed.* The lord would say, *I thought he would mar a good dinner.* Discretion of speech is more than eloquence; and to speak agreeably to him with whom we deal is more than to speak in good words or in good order. A good continued speech, without a good speech of interlocution, shows slowness; and a good reply, or second speech, without a good settled speech, showeth shallowness and weakness. As we see in beasts that those that are weakest in the course are yet nimblest in the turn; as it is betwixt the greyhound and the hare. To use too many circumstances, ere one come to the matter, is wearisome; to use none at all, is blunt.

[5] Remarks about particular individuals.
[6] Insult or a sarcastic remark.

33
Of Plantations[1]

PLANTATIONS are amongst ancient, primitive, and heroical works. When the world was young, it begat more children; but now it is old, it begets fewer; for I may justly account new plantations to be the children of former kingdoms. I like a plantation in a pure soil; that is, where people are not displanted to the end to plant in others; for else it is rather an extirpation than a plantation. Planting of countries is like planting of woods, for you must make account to lose almost twenty years' profit and expect your recompense in the end; for the principal thing that hath been the destruction of most plantations hath been the base and hasty drawing of profit in the first years. It is true, speedy profit is not to be neglected, as far as may stand[2] with the good of the plantation, but no further. It is a shameful and unblessed thing to take the scum of people and wicked condemned men to be the people with whom you plant; and not only so, but it spoileth the plantation; for they will ever live like rogues, and not fall to work; but be lazy, and do mischief, and spend victuals, and be quickly weary, and then certify over to their country to the discredit of the plantation. The people wherewith you plant ought to be gardeners, ploughmen, labor-

[1] Colonies.   [2] Be consistent.

Of Plantations   143

ers, smiths, carpenters, joiners, fishermen, fowlers, with some few apothecaries, surgeons, cooks, and bakers. In a country of plantations, first look about what kind of victual the country yields of itself to hand; as chestnuts, walnuts, pineapples, olives, dates, plums, cherries, wild honey, and the like, and make use of them. Then consider what victual, or esculent things there are, which grow speedily, and within the year; as parsnips, carrots, turnips, onions, radish, artichokes of Jerusalem, maize, and the like. For wheat, barley, and oats, they ask too much labor; but with pease and beans you may begin, both because they ask less labor, and because they serve for meat as well as for bread; and of rice, likewise, cometh a great increase, and it is a kind of meat. Above all, there ought to be brought store of biscuit, oatmeal, flour, meal, and the like, in the beginning, till bread may be had. For beasts, or birds, take chiefly such as are least subject to diseases, and multiply fastest; as swine, goats, cocks, hens, turkeys, geese, house-doves, and the like. The victual in plantations ought to be expended almost as in a besieged town, that is, with certain allowance; and let the main part of the ground employed to gardens or corn be to a common stock; and to be laid in, and stored up, and then delivered out in proportion; besides some spots of ground that any particular person will manure for his own private use. Consider, likewise, what commodities the soil where the plantation is doth naturally yield, that they may some way help to defray the charge of the plantation; so it be not, as was said, to the untimely prejudice of the main business, as it hath fared with tobacco in Virginia. Wood commonly aboundeth but too much; and therefore timber is fit to be one. If there be iron ore and streams whereupon to set the mills, iron is a brave commodity where wood aboundeth. Making of bay-salt, if the climate be proper for it, would be put in experience; growing silk,[3] likewise, if any be, is a likely commodity; pitch and tar, where store of firs and pines are, will not fail; so drugs and sweet woods, where they are, cannot but yield great profit; soap-ashes, likewise, and other things that may be thought of; but moil[4] not too much under ground, for the hope of mines is very uncertain, and useth to make the planters lazy in other things. For government, let it be in the hands of one, assisted with some counsel, and let them have commission to exercise martial laws, with some limitation; and, above all, let men make that profit of being in the wilderness, as they have God always, and his service, before their eyes. Let not the government of the plantation depend upon too many counsellors and undertakers in the country that planteth, but upon a temperate number; and let those be rather noblemen and gentlemen than merchants, for they look ever to the present gain. Let there be freedoms from custom, till the plantation be of strength; and not only freedom from custom, but freedom to carry their commodities where they may make their best of them, except

[3] Vegetable silk. Hakluyt speaks of it as "silk of grass" (III, 324).
[4] To labor hard.

Of Plantations

there be some special cause of caution. Cram not in people, by sending too fast company after company; but rather hearken how they waste, and send supplies proportionably; but so as the number may live well in the plantation, and not by surcharge be in penury. It hath been a great endangering to the health of some plantations that they have built along the sea and rivers, in marish[5] and unwholesome grounds; therefore, though you begin there, to avoid carriage and other like discommodities, yet build still rather upwards from the streams than along. It concerneth, likewise, the health of the plantation, that they have good store of salt with them, that they may use it in their victuals when it shall be necessary. If you plant where savages are, do not only entertain them with trifles and gingles,[6] but use them justly and graciously, with sufficient guard, nevertheless; and do not win their favor by helping them to invade their enemies, but for their defense it is not amiss; and send oft of them over to the country that plants that they may see a better condition than their own, and commend it when they return. When the plantation grows to strength, then it is time to plant with women as well as with men; that the plantation may spread into generations, and not be ever pieced from without. It is the sinfullest thing in the world, to forsake or destitute a plantation once in forwardness; for, besides the dishonor, it is the guiltiness of blood of many commiserable persons.

[5] Marshy.   [6] Gewgaws, or rattles.

34
Of Riches

I CANNOT call riches better than the baggage of virtue; the Roman word is better, *impedimenta;* for as the baggage is to an army, so is riches to virtue; it cannot be spared nor left behind, but it hindereth the march; yea, and the care of it sometimes loseth or disturbeth the victory. Of great riches there is no real use, except it be in the distribution; the rest is but conceit.[1] So saith Solomon: *Where much is, there are many to consume it; and what hath the owner, but the sight of it with his eyes?*[2] The personal fruition in any man cannot reach to feel great riches: there is a custody of them, or a power of dole and donative of them, or a fame of them, but no solid use to the owner. Do you not see what feigned prices are set upon little stones and rarities? and what works of ostentation are undertaken, because there might seem to be some use of great riches? But then you will say, they may be of use to buy men out of dangers or troubles; as Solomon saith: *Riches are as a stronghold in the imagination of the rich man;* but this is excellently expressed, that it is in imagination, and not always in fact; for, certainly, great riches have sold more men than they have bought out. Seek not proud riches,

[1] Imagination.   [2] Ecclesiastes, 5:11.

Of Riches

but such as thou mayest get justly, use soberly, distribute cheerfully, and leave contentedly; yet have no abstract nor friarly contempt of them, but distinguish, as Cicero saith well of Rabirius Posthumus: *In seeking to increase his fortune it was apparent that he sought not the gratification of avarice, but the means of doing good.*[3] Hearken also to Solomon, and beware of hasty gathering of riches: *He who maketh haste to be rich shall not be innocent.*[4] The poets feign, that when Plutus (which is riches) is sent from Jupiter, he limps, and goes slowly; but when he is sent from Pluto,[5] he runs, and is swift of foot; meaning, that riches gotten by good means and just labor pace slowly; but when they come by the death of others (as by the course of inheritance, testaments, and the like), they come tumbling upon a man. But it might be applied likewise to Pluto, taking him for the devil; for when riches come from the devil (as by fraud and oppression, and unjust means), they come upon speed. The ways to enrich are many, and most of them foul: parsimony is one of the best, and yet is not innocent; for it withholdeth men from works of liberality and charity. The improvement of the ground is the most natural obtaining of riches; for it is our great mother's blessing, the earth's, but it is slow; and yet, where men of great wealth do stoop to husbandry, it mul-

---

[3] *In studio rei amplificandae apparebat, non avaritiae praedam, sed instrumentum bonitati quaeri.*
[4] *Qui festinat ad divitias, non erit insons.* Proverbs, 28:20.
[5] The king of the infernal regions.

tiplieth riches exceedingly. I knew a nobleman in England that had the greatest audits[6] of any man in my time, a great grazier, a great sheep-master, a great timber-man, a great collier, a great corn-master, a great leadman, and so of iron, and a number of the like points of husbandry; so as the earth seemed a sea to him in respect of the perpetual importation. It was truly observed by one, *That himself came very hardly to a little riches, and very easily to great riches;* for when a man's stock is come to that, that he can expect the prime of markets,[7] and overcome those bargains, which for their greatness are few men's money, and be partner in the industries of younger men, he cannot but increase mainly.[8] The gains of ordinary trades and vocations are honest, and furthered by two things, chiefly: by diligence, and by a good name for good and fair dealing; but the gains of bargains are of a more doubtful nature, when men shall wait upon others' necessity: broke by[9] servants and instruments to draw them on; put off others cunningly that would be better chapmen; and the like practices, which are crafty and naught. As for the chopping of bargains, when a man buys not to hold, but to sell over again, that commonly grindeth double, both upon the seller and upon the buyer. Sharings do greatly enrich, if the hands be well chosen that are trusted. Usury is the certainest means of gain, though one of the worst; as that

---

[6] Rent-roll, or account taken of income.
[7] Wait till prices have risen.
[8] Greatly.   [9] Deal with.

Of Riches

whereby a man doth eat his bread, *in the sweat of another's brow;* [10] and, besides, doth plough upon Sundays; but yet certain though it be, it hath flaws, for that the scriveners and brokers do value [11] unsound men to serve their own turn. The fortune, in being the first in an invention, or in a privilege, doth cause sometimes a wonderful overgrowth in riches, as it was with the first sugar-man in the Canaries; therefore, if a man can play the true logician, to have as well judgment as invention, he may do great matters, especially if the times be fit. He that resteth upon gains certain, shall hardly grow to great riches; and he that puts all upon adventures, doth oftentimes break and come to poverty; it is good, therefore, to guard adventures with certainties that may uphold losses. Monopolies, and coemption [12] of wares for resale, where they are not restrained, are great means to enrich; especially if the party have intelligence what things are like to come into request, and so store himself beforehand. Riches gotten by service, though it be of the best rise, yet when they are gotten by flattery, feeding humors, and other servile conditions, they may be placed amongst the worst. As for fishing for testaments and executorships (as Tacitus saith of Seneca, *He collected wills and orphans as with a net*) [13] it is yet worse, by how much men submit themselves to meaner persons than in service. Believe not much them that seem

---

[10] *In sudore vultûs alieni.*   [11] Vouch for the credit of.
[12] Cornering.
[13] *Testamenta et orbos tamquam indagine capi. Annals,* XIII, 42.

to despise riches, for they despise them that despair of them; and none worse when they come to them. Be not penny-wise; riches have wings, and sometimes they fly away of themselves, sometimes they must be set flying to bring in more. Men leave their riches either to their kindred, or to the public; and moderate portions prosper best in both. A great state left to an heir is as a lure to all the birds of prey round about to seize on him, if he be not the better stablished in years and judgment; likewise, glorious [14] gifts and foundations are like sacrifices without salt, and but the painted sepulchers of alms, which soon will putrefy and corrupt inwardly. Therefore, measure not thine advancements by quantity, but frame them by measure, and defer not charities till death; for, certainly, if a man weigh it rightly, he that doth so is rather liberal of another man's than of his own.

[14] Ostentatious.

35
Of Prophecies

I MEAN not to speak of divine prophecies, nor of heathen oracles, nor of natural predictions; but only of prophecies that have been of certain memory, and from hidden causes. Saith the Pythonissa [1] to Saul, *Tomorrow thou and thy sons shall be with me.* Virgil hath these verses from Homer: *But the house of Aeneas shall reign over all lands, even his children's children, and their generations.*[2] A prophecy, as it seems, of the Roman empire. Seneca the tragedian hath these verses: *There shall come a time when Oceanus shall loosen the chains of the world and the vast earth shall be laid open; another Tiphys shall disclose new worlds, nor shall Thule be the farthest land.*[3] A prophecy of the discovery of America. The daughter of Polycrates dreamed that Jupiter bathed her father, and Apollo

---

[1] Pythoness, used in the sense of "witch." I Samuel, 28:19.

[2] *At domus Aeneae cunctis dominabitur oris,*
Et nati natorum, et qui nascentur ab illis.
                                    Aeneid, III, 97-98.

[3] *Venient annis*
Saecula seris, quibus Oceanus
Vincula rerum laxet, and ingens
Pateat Tellus, Tiphysque novos
Detegat orbes; nec sit terris
Ultima Thule.
                                    Medea, II, 374-378.

anointed him; and it came to pass that he was crucified in an open place, where the sun made his body run with sweat, and the rain washed it.[4] Philip of Macedon dreamed he sealed up his wife's belly, whereby he did expound it, that his wife should be barren; but Aristander the soothsayer told him his wife was with child, because men do not use to seal vessels that are empty.[5] A phantasm that appeared to M. Brutus in his tent, said to him, *Thou shalt see me again at Philippi*.[6] Tiberius said to Galba, *Thou too shalt taste of empire*.[7] In Vespasian's time, there went a prophecy in the East, that those that should come forth of Judea should reign over the world; which, though it may be was meant of our Saviour, yet Tacitus expounds it of Vespasian.[8] Domitian dreamed, the night before he was slain, that a golden head was growing out of the nape of his neck;[9] and, indeed, the succession that followed him, for many years, made golden times. Henry the Sixth of England said of Henry the Seventh, when he was a lad, and gave him water, *This is the lad that shall enjoy the crown for which we strive*. When I was in France, I heard from one Dr. Pena that the queen mother,[10] who was given to curious arts, caused the king her husband's nativity

---

[4] Herodotus, III, 124, 125.
[5] Plutarch, *Lives*, IV, 299.
[6] *Philippis iterum me videbis*. Plutarch, *Lives*, VI, 217.
[7] *Degustabis imperium*. Suetonius, *Galba*, IV.
[8] *History*, V, 13.
[9] Suetonius, *Domitian*, 23.
[10] Catherine de Medici, the wife of Henry II of France.

to be calculated under a false name; and the astrologer gave a judgment that he should be killed in a duel; at which the queen laughed, thinking her husband to be above challenges and duels; but he was slain upon a course at tilt, the splinters of the staff of Montgomery going in at his beaver. The trivial prophecy which I heard when I was a child, and Queen Elizabeth was in the flower of her years, was,

> *When hempe is spunne,*
> *England's done;*

whereby it was generally conceived that after the princes had reigned which had the principal letters of that word hempe (which were Henry, Edward, Mary, Philip, and Elizabeth), England should come to utter confusion; which, thanks be to God, is verified only in the change of the name; for that the king's style is now no more of England, but of Britain.[11] There was also another prophecy before the year of eighty-eight, which I do not well understand.

> *There shall be seen upon a day,*
> *Between the Baugh and the May,*
> *The black fleet of Norway.*
> *When that that is come and gone,*
> *England build houses of lime and stone,*
> *For after wars you shall have none.*

[11] James I was the first king of Great Britain, Scotland having been united with England when he came to the throne in 1603.

It was generally conceived to be meant of the Spanish fleet that came in eighty-eight; for that the king of Spain's surname, as they say, is Norway. The prediction of Regiomontanus,[12] *Eighty-eight will be a year of wonders*,[13] was thought likewise accomplished in the sending of that great fleet, being the greatest in strength, though not in number, of all that ever swam upon the sea. As for Cleon's dream,[14] I think it was a jest; it was that he was devoured of a long dragon; and it was expounded of [15] a maker of sausages that troubled him exceedingly. There are numbers of the like kind, especially if you include dreams and predictions of astrology; but I have set down these few only of certain credit, for example. My judgment is that they ought all to be despised, and ought to serve but for winter talk by the fireside; though, when I say despised, I mean it as for belief; for otherwise, the spreading or publishing of them is in no sort to be despised, for they have done much mischief; and I see many severe laws made to suppress them. That that hath given them grace and some credit consisteth in three things. First, that men mark when they hit, and never mark when they miss; as they do, generally, also of dreams. The second is that probable conjectures or obscure traditions many times turn them-

---

[12] Regiomontanus (Johann Müller) was an astronomer of Königsberg.
[13] *Octogesimus octavus mirabilis annus.*
[14] Aristophanes satirizes the Athenian demagogue Cleon in *The Knights*, 197-201.
[15] By.

Of Prophecies

selves into prophecies; while the nature of man, which covereth divination, thinks it no peril to foretell that which indeed they do but collect, as that of Seneca's verse; for so much was then subject to demonstration, that the globe of the earth had great parts beyond the Atlantic, which might be probably conceived not to be all sea; and adding thereto the tradition in Plato's Timaeus, and his Atlanticus,[16] it might encourage one to turn it to a prediction. The third and last (which is the great one) is that almost all of them, being infinite in number, have been impostures, and, by idle and crafty brains, merely contrived and feigned, after the event past.

[16] An illusion to the *Critias* of Plato, in which a mythical lost continent is spoken of as "Atlantis."

36
Of Ambition

AMBITION is like choler, which is a humor [1] that maketh men active, earnest, full of alacrity, and stirring, if it be not stopped; but if it be stopped, and cannot have its way, it becometh adust,[2] and thereby malign and venomous. So ambitious men, if they find the way open for their rising, and still get forward, they are rather busy than dangerous; but if they be checked in their desires, they become secretly discontent, and look upon men and matters with an evil eye, and are best pleased when things go backward; which is the worst property in a servant of a prince or state. Therefore, it is good for princes, if they use ambitious men, to handle it so, as they be still progressive, and not retrograde; which, because it cannot be without inconvenience, it is good not to use such natures at all; for if they rise not with their service, they will take order to make their service fall with them. But since we have said, it were good not to use men of ambitious natures, except it be upon necessity, it is fit we speak in what cases they are of necessity. Good commanders in the wars must be taken, be they never so ambitious; for the use of their

[1] The four humors thought to compose the human body were blood, phlegm, choler (bile), and melancholy (black bile).
[2] Fiery.

Of Ambition

service dispenseth with the rest; and to take a soldier without ambition, is to pull off his spurs. There is also great use of ambitious men in being screens to princes in matters of danger and envy; for no man will take that part, except he be like a seeled [3] dove, that mounts and mounts, because he cannot see about him. There is use, also, of ambitious men, in pulling down the greatness of any subject that overtops; as Tiberius used Macro [4] in the pulling down of Sejanus. Since, therefore, they must be used in such cases, there resteth to speak how they are to be bridled, that they may be less dangerous. There is less danger of them if they be of mean birth than if they be noble; and if they be rather harsh of nature, than gracious and popular; and if they be rather new raised than grown cunning and fortified in their greatness. It is counted by some a weakness in princes to have favorites; but it is, of all others, the best remedy against ambitious great ones; for when the way of pleasuring and displeasuring lieth by the favorite, it is impossible any other should be overgreat. Another means to curb them is to balance them by others as proud as they; but then there must be some middle counsellors, to keep things steady, for without that ballast the ship will roll too much. At the least, a prince may animate and inure some meaner persons to be, as it were, scourges to ambitious men. As for the having of them obnoxious to [5] ruin, if they

[3] Blindfolded.
[4] A favorite of Tiberius, whose murder by Nero he helped instigate. Dion Cassius, LVIII, 9.   [5] Liable to.

be of fearful natures, it may do well; but if they be stout and daring, it may precipitate their designs, and prove dangerous. As for the pulling of them down, if the affairs require it, and that it may not be done with safety suddenly, the only way is the interchange continually of favors and disgraces, whereby they may not know what to expect, and be, as it were, in a wood. Of ambitions, it is less harmful the ambition to prevail in great things than that other to appear in every thing; for that breeds confusion and mars business; but yet, it is less danger to have an ambitious man stirring in business than great in dependencies. He that seeketh to be eminent amongst able men, hath a great task, but that is ever good for the public; but he that plots to be the only figure amongst ciphers is the decay of a whole age. Honor hath three things in it: the vantage-ground to do good; the approach to kings and principal persons; and the raising of a man's own fortunes. He that hath the best of these intentions, when he aspireth, is an honest man; and that prince that can discern of these intentions in another that aspireth is a wise prince. Generally, let princes and states choose such ministers as are more sensible of duty than of rising, and such as love business rather upon conscience than upon bravery;[6] and let them discern a busy nature from a willing mind.

[6] Show.

37
Of Masques and Triumphs

THESE things are but toys to come amongst such serious observations; but yet, since princes will have such things, it is better they should be graced with elegancy, than daubed with cost. Dancing to song is a thing of great state and pleasure. I understand it that the song be in choir, placed aloft, and accompanied with some broken music,[1] and the ditty fitted to the device. Acting in song, especially in dialogues, hath an extreme good grace; I say acting, not dancing (for that is a mean and vulgar thing); and the voices of the dialogue would be strong and manly (a base and a tenor, no treble), and the ditty high and tragical, not nice or dainty. Several choirs, placed one over against another, and taking the voices by catches anthem-wise, give great pleasure. Turning dances into figure[2] is a childish curiosity; and, generally, let it be noted, that those things which I here set down are such as to naturally take the sense, and not respect petty wonderments. It is true, the alterations of scenes, so it be quietly and without noise, are things of great beauty and pleasure for they feed and relieve the eye before it be full of the same object. Let the scenes abound with light, specially colored and

[1] Part-music, for different kinds of instruments.
[2] That is, into letters spelling out the name of the person honored.

varied; and let the masquers, or any other that are to come down from the scene, have some motions upon the scene itself before their coming down; for it draws the eye strangely, and makes it with great pleasure to desire to see that it cannot perfectly discern. Let the songs be loud and cheerful, and not chirpings or pulings; let the music, likewise, be sharp and loud, and well placed. The colors that show best by candlelight are white, carnation, and a kind of sea-water green; and oes or sprangs,[3] as they are of no great cost, so they are of most glory. As for rich embroidery, it is lost and not discerned. Let the suits of the masquers be graceful, and such as become the person when the vizors are off; not after examples of known attires, Turks, soldiers, mariners, and the like. Let anti-masques[4] not be long; they have been commonly of fools, satyrs, baboons, wild men, antics, beasts, sprites, witches, Ethiopes, pigmies, turquets,[5] nymphs, rustics, Cupids, statues moving, and the like. As for angels, it is not comical enough to put them in anti-masques; and any thing that is hideous, as devils, giants, is, on the other side, as unfit; but, chiefly, let the music of them be recreative, and with some strange changes. Some sweet odors suddenly coming forth, without any drops falling, are, in such a company as there is steam and heat, things of great pleasure and re-

[3] Spangles shaped like the letter O.
[4] Or anti-masques. These were interludes dividing the acts of the more serious masque, performed by professional actors, while the masque was played by ladies and gentlemen.
[5] Turklets; Turkish dwarfs.

freshment. Double masques, one of men, another of ladies, addeth state and variety; but all is nothing, except the room be kept clear and neat.

For justs, and tourneys, and barriers, the glories of them are chiefly in the chariots, wherein the challengers make their entry; especially if they be drawn with strange beasts, as lions, bears, camels, and the like; or in the devices of their entrance, or in the bravery of their liveries, or in the goodly furniture of their horses and armor. But enough of these toys.

38
Of Nature in Men

NATURE is often hidden, sometimes overcome, seldom extinguished. Force maketh nature more violent in the return; doctrine and discourse maketh nature less importune, but custom only doth alter and subdue nature. He that seeketh victory over his nature, let him not set himself too great nor too small tasks; for the first will make him dejected by often failings, and the second will make him a small proceeder, though by often prevailings. And at the first, let him practice with helps, as swimmers do with bladders, or rushes; but, after a time, let him practice with disadvantages, as dancers do with thick shoes; for it breeds great perfection, if the practice be harder than the use. Where nature is mighty, and therefore the victory hard, the degrees had need be, first, to stay and arrest nature in time; like to him that would say over the four and twenty letters when he was angry; then to go less in quantity: as if one should, in forbearing wine, come from drinking healths to a draught at a meal; and, lastly, to discontinue altogether; but if a man have the fortitude and resolution to enfranchise himself at once, that is the best: *He best vindicates the freedom of his mind who bursts the chains*

that gall his breast and ceases once for all to suffer.[1]
Neither is the ancient rule amiss, to bend nature as a wand to a contrary extreme, whereby to set it right; understanding it where the contrary extreme is no vice. Let not a man force a habit upon himself with a perpetual continuance, but with some intermission, for both the pause reinforceth the new onset; and if a man that is not perfect be ever in practice, he shall as well practice his errors as his abilities, and induce one habit of both; and there is no means to help this but by seasonable intermissions. But let not a man trust his victory over his nature too far; for nature will lie buried a great time, and yet revive upon the occasion or temptation; like as it was with Aesop's damsel, turned from a cat to a woman, who sat very demurely at the board's end till a mouse ran before her. Therefore let a man either avoid the occasion altogether, or put himself often to it, that he may be little moved with it. A man's nature is best perceived in privateness, for there is no affectation; in passion, for that putteth a man out of his precepts; and in a new case or experiment, for there custom leaveth him. They are happy men whose natures sort with their vocations; otherwise they may say, *My soul has long been a sojourner,*[2] when they converse in those things they do not affect.[3] In studies, whatsoever a man com-

---

[1] *Optimus ille animi vindex laedentia pectus*
Vincula qui rupit, dedoluitque semel.
                    Ovid, *Remedy of Love*, 293-294.
[2] *Multum incola fuit anima mea.*   [3] Like.

mandeth upon himself, let him set hours for it: but whatsoever is agreeable to his nature, let him take no care for any set times; for his thoughts will fly to it of themselves, so as the spaces of other business or studies will suffice. A man's nature runs either to herbs or weeds; therefore let him seasonably water the one and destroy the other.

39
Of Custom and Education

MEN's thoughts are much according to their inclination; their discourse and speeches according to their learning and infused opinions; but their deeds are, after, as they have been accustomed; and, therefore, as Machiavel well noteth (though in an evil-favored instance), there is no trusting to the force of nature, nor to the bravery of words, except it be corroborate by custom. His instance is, that, for the achieving of a desperate conspiracy, a man should not rest upon the fierceness of any man's nature, or his resolute undertakings, but take such a one as hath had his hands formerly in blood; but Machiavel knew not of a Friar Clement, nor a Ravaillac, nor a Jaureguy, nor a Baltazar Gerard;[1] yet his rule holdeth still, that nature, nor the engagement of words, are not so forcible as custom. Only superstition is now so well advanced that men of the first blood are as firm as butchers by occupation; and votary[2] resolution is made equipollent to custom, even in matter of blood. In other things, the predominancy of custom is everywhere visible, insomuch as a man would

[1] Clement killed Henry III of France in 1589; Ravaillac murdered Henry IV in 1610. Jaureguy in 1582 attempted to assassinate William, Prince of Orange, who was killed by Baltazar Gerard in 1584.
[2] A resolution taken with a vow.

wonder to hear men profess, protest, engage, give great words, and then do just as they have done before, as if they were dead images and engines, moved only by the wheels of custom. We see, also, the reign or tyranny of custom, what it is.

The Indians (I mean the sect[3] of their wise men) lay themselves quietly upon a stack of wood, and so sacrifice themselves by fire; nay, the wives strive to be burned with the corpses of their husbands. The lads of Sparta, of ancient time, were wont to be scourged upon the altar of Diana, without so much as quecking.[4] I remember, in the beginning of Queen Elizabeth's time of England, an Irish rebel[5] condemned put up a petition to the deputy that he might be hanged in a withe, and not in a halter, because it had been so used with former rebels. There be monks in Russia for penance that will sit a whole night in a vessels of water, till they be engaged with hard ice. Many examples may be put of the force of custom, both upon mind and body; therefore, since custom is the principal magistrate of man's life, let men, by all means, endeavor to obtain good customs. Certainly custom is most perfect when it beginneth in young years: this we call education, which is, in effect, but an early custom. So we see in languages the tongue is more pliant to all expressions and sounds, the joints are more supple to all feats of activity

---

[3] Plutarch tells of the Hindu sect, the Gymnosophistae or naked philosophers, who ended their lives in this fashion.
[4] Flinching.   [5] Brian O'Rourke, executed in 1597.

Of Custom and Education

and motions in youth than afterwards; for it is true that late learners cannot so well take the ply, except it be in some minds that have not suffered themselves to fix, but have kept themselves open and prepared to receive continual amendment, which is exceeding rare. But if the force of custom, simple and separate, be great, the force of custom, copulate and conjoined and collegiate, is far greater; for there example teacheth, company comforteth, emulation quickeneth, glory raiseth; so as in such places the force of custom is in his exaltation.[6] Certainly, the great multiplication of virtues upon human nature resteth upon societies well ordained and disciplined; for commonwealths and good governments do nourish virtue grown, but do not much mend the seeds; but the misery is that the most effectual means are now applied to the ends least to be desired.

[6] An astrological term signifying that position of a planet in which its influence was greatest.

40
Of Fortune

It cannot be denied, but outward accidents conduce much to fortune; favor, opportunity, death of others, occasion fitting virtue; but, chiefly, the mold of a man's fortune is in his own hands: *Every man is the architect of his own fortune*,[1] saith the poet; and the most frequent of external causes is that the folly of one man is the fortune of another; for no man prospers so suddenly as by others' errors. *A serpent must eat another serpent before he can become a dragon.*[2] Overt and apparent virtues bring forth praise: but there be secret and hidden virtues that bring forth fortune; certain deliveries of a man's self, which have no name. The Spanish name, *disemboltura*,[3] partly expresseth them, when there be not stonds[4] nor restiveness in a man's nature, but that the wheels of his mind keep way with the wheels of his fortune; for so Livy (after he had described Cato Major in these words, *Such was this man's strength of body and mind that wherever he had been born, he could have made him-*

---

[1] *Faber quisque fortunae suae.*
[2] *Serpens nisi serpentem comederit non fit draco.*
[3] Adaptability.
[4] Impediments, causes for hesitation.

Of Fortune

self a fortune,)[5] falleth upon that, that he had *a versatile mind:*[6] therefore, if a man look sharply and attentively, he shall see Fortune; for though she be blind, yet she is not invisible. The way of Fortune is like the milky way in the sky; which is a meeting, or knot, of a number of small stars, not seen asunder, but giving light together; so are there a number of little and scarce discerned virtues, or rather faculties and customs, that make men fortunate. The Italians note some of them, such as a man would little think. When they speak of one that cannot do amiss, they will throw in into his other conditions, that he hath *a little of the fool;*[7] and, certainly, there be not two more fortunate properties than to have a little of the fool, and not too much of the honest; therefore, extreme lovers of their country, or masters, were never fortunate; neither can they be, for when a man placeth his thoughts without himself, he goeth not his own way. A hasty fortune maketh an enterpriser and remover (the French hath it better, *entreprenant*, or *remuant*); but the exercised fortune maketh the able man. Fortune is to be honored and respected, and it be but for her daughters, Confidence and Reputation; for those two Felicity breedeth; the first within a man's self, the latter in others towards him. All wise men, to decline the envy of their own virtues, use to ascribe them to Providence and Fortune; for so they may

---

[5] *In illo viro, tantum robur corporis et animi fuit, ut quocunque loco natus esset fortunam sibi facturus videretur.* History, XXXIX, 40.
[6] *Versatile ingenium.*   [7] *Poco di matto.*

the better assume them; and, besides, it is greatness in a man to be the care of the higher powers. So Caesar said to the pilot in the tempest, *You carry Caesar and his fortune*.[8] So Sulla chose the name of *Felix*, and not of *Magnus*;[9] and it hath been noted, that those who ascribe openly too much to their own wisdom and policy, end unfortunate. It is written that Timotheus the Athenian,[10] after he had, in the account he gave to the state of his government, often interlaced his speech, *and in this Fortune had no part*, never prospered in anything he undertook afterwards. Certainly there be whose fortunes are like Homer's verses, that have a slide and easiness more than the verses of other poets; as Plutarch saith of Timoleon's fortune in respect of that of Agesilaus or Epaminondas;[11] and that this should be, no doubt it is much in a man's self.

---

[8] *Caesarem portas, et fortunam ejus.* Plutarch, *Lives*, V, 41.

[9] *Fortunate* rather than *Great*. Plutarch, *Lives*, III, 315.

[10] An Athenian naval commander in the fourth century B.C. *Ibid.*, III, 272.

[11] Timoleon was a celebrated Corinthian general; Agesilaus, King of Sparta; Epaminondas, a Theban general, all of the fourth century, B.C.

41
Of Usury[1]

MANY have made witty invectives against usury. They say it is pity the devil should have God's part, which is the tithe;[2] that the usurer is the greatest Sabbath-breaker, because his plough goeth every Sunday; that the usurer is the drone that Virgil speaketh of:

Drive from their hives the drones, a lazy herd;[3]

that the usurer breaketh the first law that was made for mankind after the fall, which was, *in the sweat of thy face shalt thou eat thy bread;*[4] not, *in the sweat of another's face;*[5] that usurers should have orangetawny[6] bonnets, because they do Judaize; that it is against nature for money to beget money,[7] and the like. I say this only, that usury is a *concession to the hardness of men's hearts;*[8] for, since

---

[1] Bacon uses the word in the general sense of "lending money upon interest," not "exorbitant interest."

[2] The maximum rate of interest was limited by a statute of Henry VIII to 10 percent.

[3] *Ignavum fucos pecus a praesibus arcent.* Georgics, IV, 168.

[4] *In sudore vultûs tui comedes panem tuum.* Genesis, 3:19.

[5] *In sudore vultûs alieni.*

[6] Yellow was the color Jews were commonly required to wear.

[7] Aristotle's fanciful doctrine of increase of money was taken quite seriously in Bacon's time.

[8] *Concessum propter duritiem cordis.*

there must be borrowing and lending, and men are so hard of heart as they will not lend freely, usury must be permitted. Some others have made suspicious and cunning propositions of banks, discovery [9] of men's estates, and other inventions; but few have spoken of usury usefully. It is good to set before us the incommodities and commodities of usury, that the good may be either weighed out, or culled out; and warily to provide, that, while we make forth to that which is better, we meet not with that which is worse.

The discommodities of usury are, first, that it makes fewer merchants; for were it not for this lazy trade of usury, money would not lie still, but would, in great part, be employed upon merchandising, which is the *vena porta* of wealth in a state. The second, that it makes poor merchants; for as a farmer cannot husband his ground so well if he sit at [10] a great rent, so the merchant cannot drive his trade so well if he sit at great usury. The third is incident to the other two; and that is, the decay of customs of kings, or states, which ebb or flow with merchandising. The fourth, that it bringeth the treasure of a realm or state into a few hands; for the usurer being at certainties, and others at uncertainties, at the end of the game most of the money will be in the box; and ever a state flourisheth when wealth is more equally spread. The fifth, that it beats down the price of land; for the employment of money is chiefly

[9] Requiring men to declare their incomes.
[10] Has to pay.

Of Usury

either merchandising or purchasing, and usury waylays both. The sixth, that it doth dull and damp all industries, improvements, and new inventions, wherein money would be stirring, if it were not for this slug. The last, that it is the canker and ruin of many men's estates, which, in process of time, breeds a public poverty.

On the other side, the commodities of usury are, first, that, howsoever usury in some respect hindereth merchandising, yet in some other it advanceth it; for it is certain that the greatest part of trade is driven by young merchants upon borrowing at interest; so as if the usurer either call in, or keep back his money, there will ensue presently a great stand of trade. The second is, that, were it not for this easy borrowing upon interest, men's necessities would draw upon them a most sudden undoing, in that they would be forced to sell their means (be it lands or goods), far under foot;[11] and so, whereas usury doth but gnaw upon them, bad markets would swallow them quite up. As for mortgaging or pawning, it will little mend the matter; for either men will not take pawns without use, or, if they do, they will look precisely for the forfeiture. I remember a cruel moneyed man in the country that would say, *The devil take this usury, it keeps us from forfeitures of mortgages and bonds*. The third and last is, that it is a vanity to conceive that there would be ordinary borrowing without profit; and it is impossible to conceive the

[11] At too low a price.

number of inconveniences that will ensue, if borrowing be cramped. Therefore, to speak of the abolishing of usury is idle; all states have ever had it in one kind or rate, or other; so as that opinion must be sent to Utopia.[12]

To speak now of the reformation and reglement [13] of usury, how the discommodities of it may be best avoided, and the commodities retained. It appears, by the balance of commodities and discommodities of usury, two things are to be reconciled; the one, that the tooth of usury be grinded, that it bite not too much; the other, that there be left open a means to invite moneyed men to lend to the merchants for the continuing and quickening of trade. This cannot be done, except you introduce two several sorts of usury, a less and a greater; for if you reduce usury to one low rate, it will ease the common borrower, but the merchant will be to seek for money; and it is to be noted that the trade of merchandise, being the most lucrative, may bear usury at a good rate; other contracts not so.

To serve both intentions, the way would be briefly thus: that there be two rates of usury; the one free and general for all; the other under license only to certain persons, and in certain places of merchandising. First, therefore, let usury in general be reduced to five in the hundred, and let that rate be proclaimed to be free and current; and let the state shut itself out to take any penalty for the same.

[12] The imaginary country described in Sir Thomas More's political romance of that name.
[13] Regulation.

Of Usury

This will preserve borrowing from any general stop or dryness; this will ease infinite borrowers in the country; this will, in good part, raise the price of land, because land purchased at sixteen years' purchase will yield six in the hundred, and somewhat more, whereas this rate of interest yields but five. This, by like reason, will encourage and edge industrious and profitable improvements, because many will rather venture in that kind, than take five in the hundred, especially having been used to greater profit. Secondly, let there be certain persons licensed to lend to known merchants upon usury at a higher rate, and let it be with the cautions following: Let the rate be, even with the merchant himself, somewhat more easy than that he used formerly to pay; for, by that means, all borrowers shall have some ease by this reformation, be he merchant, or whosoever; let it be no bank or common stock, but every man be master of his own money; not that I altogether mislike banks, but they will hardly be brooked, in regard of certain suspicions. Let the state be answered [14] some small matter for the license, and the rest left to the lender; for if the abatement be but small, it will no whit discourage the lender; for he, for example, that took before ten or nine in the hundred, will sooner descend to eight in the hundred, than give over his trade of usury, and go from certain gains to gains of hazard. Let these licensed lenders be in number indefinite, but restrained to certain

[14] Paid.

principal cities and towns of merchandising; for then they will be hardly able to color [15] other men's moneys in the country, so as the license of nine will not suck away the current rate of five; for no man will send his moneys far off, nor put them into unknown hands.

If it be objected that this doth in a sort authorize usury, which before was in some places but permissive; the answer is, that it is better to mitigate usury by declaration, than to suffer it to rage by connivance.

[15] Use as their own.

42
Of Youth and Age

A MAN that is young in years may be old in hours, if he have lost no time; but that happeneth rarely. Generally, youth is like the first cogitations, not so wise as the second; for there is a youth in thoughts as well as in ages; and yet the invention of young men is more lively than that of old, and imaginations stream into their minds better, and, as it were, more divinely. Natures that have much heat, and great and violent desires and perturbations, are not ripe for action till they have passed the meridian of their years: as it was with Julius Caesar and Septimius Severus; of the latter of whom it is said, *He passed his youth full of errors, of madness, even;*[1] and yet he was the ablest emperor, almost, of all the list; but reposed natures may do well in youth, as it is seen in Augustus Caesar, Cosmus Duke of Florence, Gaston de Foix,[2] and others. On the other side, heat and vivacity in age is an excellent composition[3] for business. Young men are fitter to invent than to judge, fitter for execution than for counsel, and fitter for new

---

[1] *Juventutem egit erroribus, imo furoribus plenam.* Spartianus, *Life of Severus*, II.
[2] He was a nephew of Louis XII of France and a commander of the French Army.
[3] Temperament.

projects than for settled business; for the experience of age, in things that fall within the compass of it, directeth them; but in new things abuseth them. The errors of young men are the ruin of business; but the errors of aged men amount but to this, that more might have been done, or sooner.

Young men, in the conduct and manage of actions, embrace more than they can hold; stir more than they can quiet; fly to the end, without consideration of the means and degrees; pursue some few principles which they have chanced upon absurdly; care not to innovate, which draws unknown inconveniences; use extreme remedies at first; and that, which doubleth all errors, will not acknowledge or retract them, like an unready horse, that will neither stop nor turn. Men of age object too much, consult too long, adventure too little, repent too soon, and seldom drive business home to the full period, but content themselves with a mediocrity of success. Certainly it is good to compound employments of both; for that will be good for the present, because the virtues of either age may correct the defects of both; and good for succession, that young men may be learners, while men in age are actors; and, lastly, good for externe accidents, because authority followeth old men, and favor and popularity youth; but, for the moral part, perhaps, youth will have the pre-eminence, as age hath for the politic. A certain rabbin, upon the text, *Your young men shall see visions, and your old men shall*

Of Youth and Age

dream dreams,[4] inferreth that young men are admitted nearer to God than old, because vision is a clearer revelation than a dream; and, certainly, the more a man drinketh of the world, the more it intoxicateth; and age doth profit rather in the powers of understanding than in the virtues of the will and affections. There be some have an over-early ripeness in their years, which fadeth betimes; these are, first, such as have brittle wits, the edge whereof is soon turned; such as was Hermogenes [5] the rhetorician, whose books are exceedingly subtle; who afterwards waxed stupid. A second sort is of those that have some natural dispositions, which have better grace in youth than in age; such as is a fluent and luxuriant speech, which becomes youth well, but not age; so Tully saith of Hortensius: [6] *He remained the same, though it was no longer becoming.*[7] The third is of such as take too high a strain at the first, and are magnanimous more than tract of years can uphold; as was Scipio Africanus, of whom Livy saith, in effect, *His last deeds did not equal his first.*[8]

---

[4] Isaac Abrabanel, a distinguished expounder of the Bible, on Joel, 2:28.
[5] He lived in the second century A.D., and is said to have lost his memory at the age of 25.
[6] A well-known Roman orator, at one time a rival of Cicero (Tully).
[7] *Idem manebat, neque idem decebat.* Cicero, *Brutus*, 95.
[8] *Ultima primis cedebant. History*, XXXVIII, 53.

43
Of Beauty

VIRTUE is like a rich stone, best plain set; and surely virtue is best in a body that is comely, though not of delicate features, and that hath rather dignity of presence than beauty of aspect; neither is it always most seen, that very beautiful persons are otherwise of great virtue; as if nature were rather busy not to err, than in labor to produce excellency; and therefore they prove accomplished, but not of great spirit, and study rather behavior than virtue. But this holds not always; for Augustus Caesar, Titus Vespasianus, Philip le Bel of France, Edward the Fourth of England, Alcibiades of Athens, Ismael the Sophy of Persia, were all high and great spirits, and yet the most beautiful men of their times. In beauty, that of favor is more than that of color; and that of decent and gracious motion, more than that of favor.[1] That is the best part of beauty, which a picture cannot express; no, nor the first sight of the life. There is no excellent beauty that hath not some strangeness in the proportion. A man cannot tell whether Apelles,[2] or Albert Dürer, were the more trifler; whereof the one would make a personage by geometrical proportions; the other, by taking the best parts out of divers faces

[1] Face.
[2] A famous Greek painter, contemporary with Alexander the Great.

Of Beauty

to make one excellent. Such personages, I think, would please nobody but the painter that made them: not but I think a painter may make a better face than ever was; but he must do it by a kind of felicity (as a musician that maketh an excellent air in music), and not by rule. A man shall see faces, that, if you examine them part by part, you shall find never a good, and yet altogether do well. If it be true that the principal part of beauty is in decent motion, certainly it is no marvel, though persons in years seem many times more amiable; *The autumn of beautiful persons is beautiful;*[3] for no youth can be comely but by pardon,[4] and considering the youth as to make up the comeliness. Beauty is as summer fruits, which are easy to corrupt, and cannot last; and, for the most part, it makes a dissolute youth, and an age a little out of countenance; but yet certainly again, if it light well, it maketh virtues shine, and vices blush.

[3] *Pulchrorum autumnus pulcher*. Plutarch, *Lives*, II, 90.
[4] By making allowances.

44
Of Deformity

DEFORMED persons are commonly even with nature; for, as nature hath done ill by them, so do they by nature, being for the most part (as the Scripture saith) *void of natural affection;*[1] and so they have their revenge of nature. Certainly, there is a consent[2] between the body and the mind, and where nature erreth in the one, she ventureth in the other: *Ubi peccat in uno, periclitatur in altero.* But because there is in man an election, touching the frame of his mind, and a necessity in the frame of his body, the stars of natural inclination are sometimes obscured by the sun of discipline and virtue; therefore, it is good to consider of deformity, not as a sign which is more deceivable, but as a cause which seldom faileth of the effect. Whosoever hath anything fixed in his person that doth induce contempt, hath also a perpetual spur in himself to rescue and deliver himself from scorn; therefore, all deformed persons are extreme bold; first, as in their own defense, as being exposed to scorn, but, in process of time, by a general habit. Also, it stirreth in them industry, and especially of this kind, to watch and observe the weakness of others, that they may have somewhat to repay. Again,

[1] Romans, 1:31; Timothy, 3:3.   [2] Agreement, harmony.

Of Deformity

in their superiors, it quencheth jealousy towards them, as persons that they think they may at pleasure despise; and it layeth their competitors and emulators asleep, as never believing they should be in possibility of advancement till they see them in possession; so that upon the matter, in a great wit, deformity is an advantage to rising. Kings in ancient times (and at this present in some countries) were wont to put great trust in eunuchs, because they that are envious towards all are more obnoxious and officious[3] towards one; but yet their trust towards them hath rather been as to good spials,[4] and good whisperers, than good magistrates and officers; and much like is the reason of deformed persons. Still the ground is, they will, if they be of spirit, seek to free themselves from scorn, which must be either by virtue or malice; and, therefore, let it not be marvelled, if sometimes they prove excellent persons; as was Agesilaüs, Zanger, the son of Solyman, Aesop, Gasca, president of Peru; and Socrates may go likewise amongst them, with others.[5]

---

[3] Humble and dutiful.   [4] Spies.
[5] Agesilaus, King of Sparta, was born lame; Zanger was called "the Crooked"; Aesop is said to have been hideously deformed; Pedro de la Gasca had a small body and very long legs; Socrates had a very homely face.

45
Of Building

HOUSES are built to live in, and not to look on, therefore, let use be preferred before uniformity, except where both may be had. Leave the goodly fabrics of houses, for beauty only, to the enchanted palaces of the poets, who build them with small cost. He that builds a fair house upon an ill seat[1] committeth himself to prison; neither do I reckon it an ill seat only where the air is unwholesome, but likewise where the air is unequal. As you shall see many fine seats set upon a knap[2] of ground environed with higher hills round about it, whereby the heat of the sun is pent in, and the wind gathereth as in troughs; so as you shall have, and that suddenly, as great diversity of heat and cold as if you dwelt in several places. Neither is it ill air only that maketh an ill sea; but ill ways, ill markets, and, if you will consult with Momus,[3] ill neighbors. I speak not of many more: want of water, want of wood, shade, and shelter, want of fruitfulness, and mixture of grounds of several natures; want of prospect, want of level grounds, want of places at some near distance for sports of hunting, hawk-

---

[1] Site.   [2] Knoll.
[3] Momus was the god of ridicule and censure; he criticized Athena's house because it was not on wheels so that it could be moved away from undesirable neighbors.

ing, and races; too near the sea, too remote; having the commodity of navigable rivers, or the discommodity of their overflowing; too far off from great cities, which may hinder business; or too near them, which lurcheth [4] all provisions, and maketh every thing dear; where a man hath a great living laid together, and where he is scanted; all which, as it is impossible perhaps to find together, so it is good to know them, and think of them, that a man may take as many as he can; and if he have several dwellings, that he sort them so, that what he wanteth in the one he may find in the other. Lucullus answered Pompey well, who, when he saw his stately galleries and rooms so large and lightsome, in one of his houses, said, *Surely, an excellent place for summer, but how do you do in winter?* Lucullus answered, *Why, do you not think me as wise as some fowls are, that ever change their abode towards the winter?* [5]

To pass from the seat to the house itself, we will do as Cicero doth in the orator's art, who writes books *De Oratore*, and a book he entitles *Orator;* whereof the former delivers the precepts of the art, and the latter the perfection. We will therefore describe a princely palace, making a brief model thereof; for it is strange to see, now in Europe, such huge buildings as the Vatican and Escurial,[6]

[4] Eats up.
[5] Plutarch, *Lives*, III, 420.
[6] A palace and monastery twenty-seven miles from Madrid, built by Philip II.

and some others be, and yet scarce a very fair room in them.

First, therefore, I say, you cannot have a perfect palace, except you have two several sides; a side for the banquet, as is spoken of in the book of Hester,[7] and a side for the household; the one for feasts and triumphs,[8] and the other for dwelling. I understand both these sides to be not only returns, but parts of the front, and to be uniform without, though severally partitioned within; and to be on both sides of a great and stately tower in the midst of the front, that, as it were, joineth them together on either hand. I would have, on the side of the banquet in front, one only goodly room above stairs, of some forty foot high; and under it a room for a dressing or preparing place, at times of triumphs. On the other side, which is the household side, I wish it divided at the first into a hall and a chapel, (with a partition between), both of good state and bigness; and those not to go all the length, but to have at the further end a winter and a summer parlor, both fair; and under these rooms a fair and large cellar sunk under ground; and likewise some privy kitchens, with butteries, and pantries, and the like. As for the tower, I would have it two stories, of eighteen foot high apiece above the two wings; and a goodly leads upon the top, railed, with statues interposed; and the same tower to be divided into rooms, as shall be thought fit. The stairs likewise to the

[7] Esther, 1:5.   [8] Pageants.

Of Building

upper rooms, let them be upon a fair open newel, and finely railed in with images of wood cast into a brass color, and a very fair landing-place at the top. But this to be, if you do not point any of the lower rooms for a dining-place of servants; for, otherwise, you shall have the servants' dinner after your own; for the steam of it will come up as in a tunnel.[9] And so much for the front; only I understand the height of the first stairs to be sixteen foot, which is the height of the lower room.

Beyond this front is there to be a fair court, but three sides of it of a far lower building than the front; and in all the four corners of that court fair staircases, cast into turrets on the outside, and not within the row of buildings themselves; but those towers are not to be of the height of the front, but rather proportionable to the lower building. Let the court not be paved, for that striketh up a great heat in summer, and much cold in winter; but only some side alleys with a cross, and the quarters to graze, being kept shorn, but not too near shorn. The row of return on the banquet side, let it be all stately galleries; in which galleries let there be three or five fine cupolas in the length of it, placed at equal distance, and fine colored windows of several works; on the household side, chambers of presence [10] and ordinary entertainments, with some bedchambers; and let all three sides be a double house, without thorough lights on the sides, that you may have rooms

[9] The funnel of a chimney.   [10] State.

from the sun, both for forenoon and afternoon. Cast [11] it, also, that you may have rooms both for summer and winter; shady for summer, and warm for winter. You shall have sometimes fair houses so full of glass, that one cannot tell where to become [12] to be out of the sun or cold. For imbowed [13] windows, I hold them of good use; (in cities, indeed, upright [14] do better, in respect of the uniformity towards the street;) for they be pretty retiring places for conference; and, besides, they keep both the wind and sun off; for that which would strike almost through the room doth scarce pass the window: but let them be but few, four in the court, on the sides only.

Beyond this court, let there be an inward court of the same square and height, which is to be environed with the garden on all sides; and in the inside, cloistered on all sides upon decent and beautiful arches, as high as the first story; on the under story towards the garden, let it be turned to grotto, or place of shade, or estivation; and only have opening and windows towards the garden, and be level upon the floor, no whit sunk under ground to avoid all dampishness; and let there be a fountain, or some fair work of statues in the midst of this court, and to be paved as the other court was. These buildings to be for privy lodgings on both sides, and the end for privy galleries; whereof you must foresee that one of them be for an infirmary, if the prince or any special person should be sick,

[11] Plan.
[12] Where to go.
[13] Bay.
[14] Flush with the wall.

Of Building

with chambers, bedchamber, *anticamera*, and *recamera*,[15] joining to it; this upon the second story. Upon the ground story, a fair gallery, open, upon pillars; and upon the third story, likewise, an open gallery upon pillars, to take the prospect and freshness of the garden. At both corners of the further side, by way of return, let there be two delicate or rich cabinets, daintily paved, richly hanged, glazed with crystalline glass, and a rich cupola in the midst, and all other elegancy that can be thought upon. In the upper gallery, too, I wish that there may be, if the place will yield it, some fountains running in divers places from the wall, with some fine avoidances.[16] And thus much for the model of the palace, save that you must have, before you come to the front, three courts: a green court plain, with a wall about it; a second court of the same, but more garnished with little turrets, or rather embellishments, upon the wall; and a third court, to make a square with the front, but not to be built, nor yet inclosed with a naked wall, but inclosed with terraces leaded aloft, and fairly garnished on the three sides, and cloistered on the inside with pillars, and not with arches below. As for offices, let them stand at distance, with some low galleries to pass from them to the palace itself.

[15] Antechamber and withdrawing-room.
[16] Outlets.

46
Of Gardens

GOD Almighty first planted a garden; and, indeed, it is the purest of human pleasures; it is the greatest refreshment to the spirits of man; without which buildings and palaces are but gross handyworks; and a man shall ever see that, when ages grow to civility and elegancy, men come to build stately, sooner than to garden finely; as if gardening were the greater perfection. I do hold it, in the royal ordering of gardens, there ought to be gardens for all the months in the year, in which, severally, things of beauty may be then in season. For December and January and the latter part of November, you must take such things as are green all winter: holly, ivy, bays, juniper, cypress-trees, yew, pineapple trees;[1] fir trees, rosemary, lavender; periwinkle, the white, the purple, and the blue; germander, flags, orange trees, lemon trees, and myrtles, if they be stoved;[2] and sweet marjoram, warm set. There followeth, for the latter part of January and February, the mezereon tree, which then blossoms; crocus vernus,[3] both the yellow and the gray; primrose, anemones, the early tulip, the hyacinthus orientalis, chamaïris,[4] fritellaria. For March, there come violets, especially the single blue, which are the

[1] Pine trees.
[2] Kept warm in a greenhouse.
[3] The spring crocus.
[4] A variety of iris.

earliest; the yellow daffodil, the daisy, the almond tree in blossom, the peach tree in blossom, the cornelian tree in blossom, sweetbrier. In April, follow the double white violet, the wallflower, the stock-gillyflower, the cowslip, flower-de-luces, and lilies of all natures; rosemary flowers, the tulip, the double peony, the pale daffodil, the French honeysuckle, the cherry tree in blossom, the damascene [5] and plum trees in blossom, the white thorn in leaf, the lilac tree. In May and June come pinks of all sorts, especially the blush-pink; roses of all kinds, except the musk, which comes later; honeysuckles, strawberries, bugloss, columbine, the French marigold, flos Africanus,[6] cherry tree in fruit, ribes,[7] figs in fruit, rasps,[8] vine-flowers, lavender in flowers, the sweet satyrian, with the white flower; herba muscaria,[9] lilium convallium,[10] the apple tree in blossom. In July come gillyflowers of all varieties, musk-roses, the lime tree in blossom, early pears, and plums in fruit, genitings,[11] codlins. In August come plums of all sorts in fruit, pears, apricots, barberries, filberts, muskmelons, monkhoods, of all colors. In September come grapes, apples, poppies of all colors, peaches, melocotones,[12] nectarines, cornelians, wardens,[13] quinces. In October, and the be-

---

[5] The damson, or plum of Damascus.
[6] The African flower, another name for the French marigold.
[7] Currants, gooseberries and similar shrubs.
[8] Raspberries.
[9] The musked grape flower.
[10] Lilies-of-the-valley.
[11] A variety of early apples.
[12] A kind of quince.
[13] A species of pears.

ginning of November, come services,[14] medlars, bullaces,[15] roses cut or removed to come late, hollyoaks, and such like. These particulars are for the climate of London; but my meaning is perceived, that you may have *perpetual spring*,[16] as the place affords.

And because the breath of flowers is far sweeter in the air (where it comes and goes, like the warbling of music), than in the hand, therefore nothing is more fit for that delight than to know what be the flowers and plants that do best perfume the air. Roses, damask and red, are fast[17] flowers of their smell, so that you may walk by a whole row of them, and find nothing of their sweetness; yea, though it be in a morning's dew. Bays, likewise, yield no smell as they grow, rosemary little, nor sweet marjoram; that which, above all others, yields the sweetest smell in the air, is the violet, especially the white double violet, which comes twice a year, about the middle of April, and about Bartholomewtide.[18] Next to that is the musk-rose; then the strawberry leaves dying, with a most excellent cordial smell; then the flower of the vines, it is a little dust like the dust of a bent,[19] which grows upon the cluster in the first coming forth; then sweetbrier, then wallflowers, which are very delightful to be set under a parlor or lower chamber window; then pinks and gillyflowers, specially

---

[14] Shrubs allied to the shad bush. [15] A kind of plum tree.
[16] *Ver perpetuum.* Virgil, *Georgics*, II, 149.
[17] Stingy. [18] August 24.
[19] A species of grass found in pasture land, *e.g.*, the cat-tail.

Of Gardens

the matted pink and clove gillyflower; then the flowers of the lime tree; then the honeysuckles, so they be somewhat afar off. Of bean-flowers I speak not, because they are field flowers; but those which perfume the air most delightfully, not passed by as the rest, but being trodden upon and crushed, are three; that is, burnet, wild thyme, and water-mints; therefore you are to set whole alleys of them, to have the pleasure when you walk or tread.

For gardens (speaking of those which are indeed princelike, as we have done of buildings), the contents ought not well to be under thirty acres of ground, and to be divided into three parts; a green in the entrance, a heath, or desert, in the going forth, and the main garden in the midst, besides alleys on both sides; and I like well that four acres of ground be assigned to the green, six to the heath, four and four to either side, and twelve to the main garden. The green hath two pleasures: the one, because nothing is more pleasant to the eye than green grass kept finely shorn; the other, because it will give you a fair alley in the midst, by which you may go in front upon a stately hedge, which is to inclose the garden. But because the alley will be long, and in great heat of the year, or day, you ought not to buy the shade in the garden by going in the sun through the green; therefore you are, of either side the green, to plant a covert alley, upon carpenter's work, about twelve foot in height, by which you may go in shade into the garden. As for the making of knots or figures, with divers colored earths, that they may lie under the windows of the house on that side which the garden stands, they be but toys; you may see as good sights many times in tarts. The garden is best to be square, encompassed on all the four sides with a stately arched hedge: the arches to be upon pillars of carpenter's work, of some ten foot high, and six foot broad, and the spaces between of the same dimension with the breadth of the arch. Over the arches let there be an entire hedge of some four foot high, framed also upon carpenter's work; and upon the upper hedge, over every arch a little turret, with a belly enough to receive a cage of birds; and over every space between the arches some other little figure, with broad plates of round colored glass gilt, for the sun to play upon; but this hedge I intend to be raised upon a bank, not steep but gently slope, of some six foot, set all with flowers. Also I understand that this square of the garden should not be the whole breadth of the ground, but to leave on either side ground enough for diversity of side alleys, unto which the two covert alleys of the green may deliver you; but there must be no alleys with hedges at either end of this great inclosure; not at the hither end, for letting your prospect [20] upon this fair hedge from the green; nor at the further end for letting your prospect from the hedge through the arches upon the heath.

For the ordering of the ground within the great hedge, I leave it to variety of device; advising, nevertheless, that

[20] To shut off your view.

Of Gardens

whatsoever form you cast it into first, it be not too bushy, or full of work; wherein I, for my part, do not like images cut out in juniper or other garden stuff; they be for children. Little low hedges, round like welts [21] with some pretty pyramids, I like well; and in some places fair columns, upon frames of carpenter's work. I would also have the alleys spacious and fair. You may have closer alleys upon the side grounds, but none in the main garden. I wish, also, in the very middle, a fair mount, with three ascents and alleys, enough for four to walk abreast; which I would have to be perfect circles, without any bulwarks or embossments; and the whole mount to be thirty foot high, and some fine banqueting-house, with some chimneys neatly cast, and without too much glass.

For fountains, they are a great beauty and refreshment; but pools mar all, and make the garden unwholesome and full of flies and frogs. Fountains I intend to be of two natures, the one that sprinkleth or spouteth water; the other, a fair receipt [22] of water, of some thirty or forty foot square, but without fish, or slime, or mud. For the first, the ornaments of images, gilt or of marble, which are in use, do well; but the main matter is so to convey the water, as it never stay, either in the bowls or in the cistern; that the water be never by rest discolored, green, or red, or the like, or gather any mossiness or putrefaction; besides that, it is to be cleansed every day by the hand; also,

[21] Scalloped or arched.   [22] Pool.

some steps up to it and some fine pavement about it doth well. As for the other kind of fountain, which we may call a bathing-pool, it may admit much curiosity and beauty, wherewith we will not trouble ourselves: as, that the bottom be finely paved, and with images; the sides likewise; and withal, embellished with colored glass and such things of luster; encompassed, also, with fine rails of low statues. But the main point is the same that we mentioned in the former kind of fountain; which is, that the water be in perpetual motion, fed by a water higher than the pool, and delivered into it by fair spouts, and then discharged away under ground, by some equality of bores, that it stay little; and for fine devices, of arching water without spilling, and making it rise in several forms (of feathers, drinking glasses, canopies, and the like), they be pretty things to look on, but nothing to health and sweetness.

For the heath, which was the third part of our plot, I wish it to be framed as much as may be to a natural wildness. Trees I would have none in it, but some thickets made only of sweetbrier and honeysuckle, and some wild vine amongst; and the ground set with violets, strawberries, and primroses; for these are sweet, and prosper in the shade, and these to be in the heath here and there, not in any order. I like also little heaps, in the nature of molehills (such as are in wild heaths), to be set, some with wild thyme, some with pinks, some with germander, that gives a good flower to the eye; some with periwinkle, some with violets, some with strawberries, some with cowslips,

Of Gardens

some with daisies, some with red roses, some with lilium convallium, some with sweet williams red, some with bear's-foot, and the like low flowers, being withal sweet and sightly; part of which heaps to be with standards of little bushes pricked [23] upon their top, and part without; the standards to be roses, juniper, holly, barberries (but here and there, because of the smell of their blossom), red currants, gooseberries, rosemary, bays, sweetbrier, and such like; but these standards to be kept with cutting, that they grow not out of course.

For the side grounds, you are to fill them with variety of alleys, private, to give a full shade; some of them wheresoever the sun be. You are to frame some of them likewise for shelter, that when the wind blows sharp, you may walk as in a gallery: and those alleys must be likewise hedged at both ends, to keep out the wind; and these closer alleys must be ever finely gravelled, and no grass, because of going wet. In many of these alleys, likewise, you are to set fruit trees of all sorts, as well upon the walls as in ranges; [24] and this should be generally observed, that the borders wherein you plant your fruit trees be fair and large, and low, and not steep; and set with fine flowers, but thin and sparingly, lest they deceive [25] the trees. At the end of both the side grounds I would have a mount of some pretty height, leaving the wall of the inclosure breast high, to look abroad into the fields.

[23] Planted with little bushes that stand without support.
[24] In rows.   [25] Rob of nourishment.

For the main garden, I do not deny but there should be some fair alleys ranged on both sides with fruit trees, and some pretty tufts of fruit trees and arbors with seats, set in some decent order; but these to be by no means set too thick, but to leave the main garden so as it be not close, but the air open and free. For as for shade, I would have you rest upon the alleys of the side grounds, there to walk, if you be disposed, in the heat of the year or day; but to make account that the main garden is for the more temperate parts of the year, and in the heat of summer for the morning and the evening or overcast days.

For aviaries, I like them not, except they be of that largeness as they may be turfed, and have living plants and bushes set in them; that the birds may have more scope and natural nestling, and that no foulness appear in the floor of the aviary. So I have made a platform [26] of a princely garden, partly by precept, partly by drawing; not a model, but some general lines of it; and in this I have spared for no cost. But it is nothing for great princes, that for the most part taking advice with workmen, with no less cost set their things together, and sometimes add statues and such things for state and magnificence, but nothing to the true pleasure of a garden.

[26] Plan.

47
Of Negotiating

It is generally better to deal by speech than by letter; and by the mediation of a third than by a man's self. Letters are good, when a man would draw an answer by letter back again; or when it may serve for a man's justification afterwards to produce his own letter, or where it may be danger to be interrupted or heard by pieces. To deal in person is good, when a man's face breedeth regard, as commonly with inferiors; or in tender cases, where a man's eye upon the countenance of him with whom he speaketh may give him a direction how far to go; and, generally, where a man will reserve to himself liberty, either to disavow or to expound. In choice of instruments, it is better to choose men of a plainer sort that are like to do that that is committed to them, and to report back again faithfully the success, than those that are cunning to contrive out of other men's business somewhat to grace themselves, and will help the matter in report, for satisfaction sake. Use also such persons as affect [1] the business wherein they are employed, for that quickeneth much; and such as are fit for the matter, as bold men for expostulation, fairspoken men for persuasion, crafty men for inquiry and observation, froward and absurd [2] men for business that doth not

[1] Like.   [2] Stubborn and stupid.

well bear out itself. Use also such as have been lucky and prevailed before in things wherein you have employed them; for that breeds confidence, and they will strive to maintain their prescription. It is better to sound a person with whom one deals afar off than to fall upon the point at first, except you mean to surprise him by some short question. It is better dealing with men in appetite than with those that are where they would be. If a man deal with another upon conditions, the start of first performance is all; which a man cannot reasonably demand, except either the nature of the thing be such, which must go before; or else a man can persuade the other party that he shall still need him in some other thing; or else that he be counted the honester man. All practice is to discover or to work.[3] Men discover themselves in trust, in passion, at unawares; and, of necessity, when they would have somewhat done and cannot find an apt pretext. If you would work any man, you must either know his nature and fashions, and so lead him; or his ends, and so persuade him; or his weakness and disadvantages, and so awe him; or those that have interest in him, and so govern him. In dealing with cunning persons, we must ever consider their ends, to interpret their speeches; and it is good to say little to them, and that which they least look for. In all negotiations of difficulty, a man may not look to sow and reap at once; but must prepare business, and so ripen it by degrees.

[3] The whole knack is to find out about a person or to manipulate him.

48

Of Followers and Friends

COSTLY followers are not to be liked, lest, while a man maketh his train longer, he make his wings shorter. I reckon to be costly, not them alone which charge the purse, but which are wearisome and importune in suits. Ordinary followers ought to challenge no higher conditions than countenance, recommendation, and protection from wrongs. Factious followers are worse to be liked, which follow not upon affection to him with whom they range themselves, but upon discontentment conceived against some other; whereupon commonly ensueth that ill intelligence [1] that we many times see between great personages. Likewise glorious [2] followers, who make themselves as trumpets of the commendations of those they follow, are full of inconvenience, for they taint business through want of secrecy; and they export honor from a man, and make him a return in envy. There is a kind of followers, likewise, which are dangerous, being indeed espials; [3] which inquire the secrets of the house, and bear tales of them to others; yet such men many times are in great favor, for they are officious, and commonly exchange tales. The following, by certain estates [4] of men

[1] Misunderstanding.
[2] Boastful.
[3] Spies.
[4] Professions or classes.

answerable to that which a great person himself professeth (as of soldiers to him that hath been employed in the wars, and the like), hath ever been a thing civil and well taken even in monarchies, so it be without too much pomp or popularity. But the most honorable kind of following is to be followed as one that apprehendeth [5] to advance virtue and desert in all sorts of persons; and yet, where there is no eminent odds in sufficiency, it is better to take with the more passable than with the more able; and, besides, to speak truth in base times, active men are of more use than virtuous. It is true that, in government, it is good to use men of one rank equally; for to countenance some extraordinarily is to make them insolent, and the rest discontent, because they may claim a due: but, contrariwise, in favor, to use men with much difference and election is good: for it maketh the persons preferred more thankful, and the rest more officious, because all is of favor. It is good discretion not to make too much of any man at the first, because one cannot hold out that proportion. To be governed, as we call it, by one, is not safe, for it shows softness, and gives a freedom to scandal and disreputation; for those that would not censure, or speak ill of a man immediately, will talk more boldly of those that are so great with them, and thereby wound their honor; yet to be distracted with many is worse, for it makes men to be of the last impression, and full of change. To take advice

[5] Understands as his purpose.

of some few friends is ever honorable; for lookers-on many times see more than gamesters, and the vale best discovereth the hill. There is little friendship in the world, and least of all between equals, which was wont to be magnified. That that is, is between superior and inferior, whose fortunes may comprehend [6] the one the other.

[6] Include.

49
Of Suitors

MANY ill matters and projects are undertaken;[1] and private suits do putrefy the public good. Many good matters are undertaken with bad minds; I mean not only corrupt minds, but crafty minds, that intend not performance. Some embrace suits, which never mean to deal effectually in them; but if they see there may be life in the matter, by some other mean they will be content to win a thank, or take a second[2] reward, or, at least, to make use in the meantime of the suitor's hopes. Some take hold of suits only for an occasion to cross some other, or to make an information, whereof they could not otherwise have apt pretext, without care what become of the suit when that turn is served; or, generally, to make other men's business a kind of entertainment[3] to bring in their own: nay, some undertake suits with a full purpose to let them fall, to the end to gratify the adverse party, or competitor. Surely, there is in some sort a right in every suit; either a right of equity, if it be a suit of controversy, or a right of desert, if it be a suit of petition. If affection lead a man to favor the wrong side in justice, let him rather use his coun-

---

[1] Taken up by the "undertaker" or go-between who tries to advance the suitor's interest at court or even with the king himself.
[2] Inferior.   [3] Introduction.

Of Suitors

tenance to compound the matter than to carry it. If affection lead a man to favor the less worthy in desert, let him do it without depraving [4] or disabling the better deserver. In suits which a man doth not well understand, it is good to refer them to some friend of trust and judgment, that may report whether he may deal in them with honor; but let him choose well his referendaries,[5] for else he may be led by the nose. Suitors are so distasted with delays and abuses that plain dealing in denying to deal in suits at first, and reporting the success barely,[6] and in challenging no more thanks than one hath deserved, is grown not only honorable, but also gracious. In suits of favor, the first coming ought to take little place;[7] so far forth[8] consideration may be had of his trust, that if intelligence of the matter could not otherwise have been had but by him, advantage be not taken of the note,[9] but the party left to his other means, and in some sort recompensed for his discovery. To be ignorant of the value of a suit is simplicity; as well as to be ignorant of the right thereof is want of conscience. Secrecy in suits is a great mean of obtaining; for voicing them to be in forwardness may discourage some kind of suitors, but doth quicken and awake others. But timing of the suit is the principal; timing, I say, not only in respect of the person that should grant it, but in

---

[4] Lowering, or humiliating.   [5] Referees.
[6] Forthrightly; without elaboration.
[7] To have little effect.
[8] To this extent.   [9] Of the information.

respect of those which are like to cross it. Let a man, in the choice of his mean, rather choose the fittest mean, than the greatest mean; and rather them that deal in certain things, than those that are general. The reparation of a denial is sometimes equal to the first grant, if a man show himself neither dejected nor discontented. *Ask more than is fair in order to get what is just*,[10] is a good rule, where a man hath strength of favor; but otherwise a man were better rise in his suit; for he that would have ventured at first to have lost the suitor, will not, in the conclusion, lose both the suitor and his own former favor. Nothing is thought so easy a request to a great person as his letter: and yet if it be not in a good cause, it is so much out of his reputation. There are no worse instruments than these general contrivers of suits; for they are but a kind of poison and infection to public proceedings.

[10] *Iniquum petas, ut aequum feras.* Quintilian, *On the Institutes of Oratory,* IV, v, 16.

50
Of Studies

STUDIES serve for delight, for ornament, and for ability. Their chief use for delight is in privateness and retiring; for ornament, is in discourse; and for ability, is in the judgment and disposition of business; for expert men can execute and perhaps judge of particulars one by one; but the general counsels, and the plots and marshalling of affairs, come best from those that are learned. To spend too much time in studies is sloth; to use them too much for ornament is affectation; to make judgment wholly by their rules is the humor of a scholar. They perfect nature, and are perfected by experience; for natural abilities are like natural plants, that need proyning [1] by study; and studies themselves do give forth directions too much at large, except they be bounded in by experience. Crafty men contemn studies, simple men admire them, and wise men use them; for they teach not their own use; but that is a wisdom without them and above them, won by observation. Read not to contradict and confute, nor to believe and take for granted, nor to find talk and discourse, but to weigh and consider. Some books are to be tasted, others to be swal-

[1] Pruning.

lowed, and some few to be chewed and digested; that is, some books are to be read only in parts; others to be read, but not curiously;[2] and some few to be read wholly, and with diligence and attention. Some books also may be read by deputy, and extracts made of them by others; but that would be only in the less important arguments and the meaner sort of books; else distilled books are, like common distilled waters, flashy[3] things. Reading maketh a full man; conference a ready man; and writing an exact man; and, therefore, if a man write little, he had need have a great memory; if he confer little, he had need have a present wit; and if he read little, he had need have much cunning, to seem to know that he doth not. Histories make men wise; poets, witty; the mathematics, subtile; natural philosophy, deep; moral, grave; logic and rhetoric, able to contend: *Studies go to form character;*[4] nay, there is no stand or impediment in the wit, but may be wrought out by fit studies. Like as diseases of the body may have appropriate exercises, bowling is good for the stone and reins,[5] shooting for the lungs and breast, gentle walking for the stomach, riding for the head and the like; so, if a man's wit be wandering, let him study the mathematics; for in demonstrations, if his wit be called away never so little, he must begin again; if his wit be not apt to distinguish or find difference, let him study the schoolmen, for they are

---

[2] With great care.   [3] Tasteless or showy.
[4] *Abeunt studia in mores.* Ovid, *Heroides*, XV, 83.
[5] Kidneys.

Of Studies

hair-splitters.[6] If he be not apt to beat over matters, and to call up one thing to prove and illustrate another, let him study the lawyers' cases; so every defect of the mind may have a special receipt.

[6] *Cymini sectores.* Literally, "cutters of cumin seed."

51
Of Faction

MANY have an opinion not wise, that for a prince to govern his estate or for a great person to govern his proceedings, according to the respect of factions, is a principal part of policy; whereas, contrariwise, the chiefest wisdom is, either in ordering those things which are general, and wherein men of several factions do nevertheless agree, or in dealing with correspondence to particular persons, one by one; but I say not that the consideration of factions is to be neglected. Mean men in their rising must adhere; but great men, that have strength in themselves, were better to maintain themselves indifferent and neutral; yet, even in beginners, to adhere so moderately, as he be a man of the one faction, which is most passable with the other, commonly giveth best way. The lower and weaker faction is the firmer in conjunction; and it is often seen that a few that are stiff do tire out a great number that are more moderate. When one of the factions is extinguished, the remaining subdivideth; as the faction between Lucullus and the rest of the nobles of the senate (which they called *optimates*), held out a while against the faction of Pompey and Caesar; but when the senate's authority was pulled down, Caesar and Pompey soon after brake. The faction or party of Antonius and Octavianus Caesar, against Bru-

Of Faction

tus and Cassius, held out likewise for a time; but when Brutus and Cassius were overthrown, then soon after Antonius and Octavianus brake and subdivided. These examples are of wars, but the same holdeth in private factions; and, therefore, those that are seconds in factions do many times, when the faction subdivideth, prove principals; but many times also they prove ciphers, and cashiered, for many a man's strength is in opposition; and when that faileth, he groweth out of use. It is commonly seen, that men once placed, take in with the contrary faction to that by which they enter; thinking, belike, that they have the first sure, and now are ready for a new purchase. The traitor in faction lightly goeth away with it; for when matters have stuck long in balancing, the winning of some one man casteth them,[1] and he getteth all the thanks. The even carriage between two factions proceedeth not always of moderation, but of a trueness to a man's self, with end to make use of both. Certainly, in Italy, they hold it a little suspect in popes, when they have often in their mouth, *Common Father*,[2] and take it to be a sign of one that meaneth to refer all to the greatness of his own house. Kings had need beware how they side themselves, and make themselves as of a faction or party; for leagues within the state are ever pernicious to monarchies; for they raise an obligation paramount to obligation of sovereignty, and make the king *like one of us*,[3] as was to be seen in the

---

[1] Causes one side to preponderate.
[2] *Padre commune.*
[3] *Tanquam unus ex nobis.*

League of France. When factions are carried too high and too violently, it is a sign of weakness in princes, and much to the prejudice both of their authority and business. The motions of factions under kings ought to be like the motions (as the astronomers speak) of the inferior orbs, which may have their proper motions, but yet still are quietly carried by the higher motion of *primum mobile*.

52
Of Ceremonies and Respects

HE THAT is only real had need have exceeding great parts of virtue; as the stone had need to be rich that is set without foil; but if a man mark it well, it is in praise and commendation of men, as it is in gettings and gains; for the proverb is true, that *Light gains make heavy purses;* for light gains come thick, whereas great come but now and then. So it is true, that small matters win great commendation, because they are continually in use and in note; whereas the occasion of any great virtue cometh but on festivals; therefore it doth much add to a man's reputation, and is (as Queen Isabella [1] said) like perpetual letters commendatory, to have good forms. To attain them, it almost sufficeth not to despise them; for so shall a man observe them in others; and let him trust himself with the rest; for if he labor too much to express them, he shall lose their grace, which is to be natural and unaffected. Some men's behavior is like a verse wherein every syllable is measured; how can a man comprehend great matters, that breaketh his mind too much to small observations? Not to use ceremonies at all is to teach others not to use them again, and so diminisheth respect to himself; especially they be not to

[1] Of Castile, the patroness of Columbus.

be omitted to strangers and formal natures; but the dwelling upon them, and exalting them above the moon, is not only tedious, but doth diminish the faith and credit of him that speaks; and, certainly, there is a kind of conveying of effectual and imprinting[2] passages amongst compliments, which is of singular use, if a man can hit upon it. Amongst a man's peers, a man shall be sure of familiarity, and, therefore, it is good a little to keep state. Amongst a man's inferiors, one shall be sure of reverence, and therefore it is good a little to be familiar. He that is too much in any thing, so that he giveth another occasion of satiety, maketh himself cheap. To apply one's self to others is good, so it be with demonstration that a man doth it upon regard, and not upon facility. It is a good precept generally in seconding another, yet to add somewhat of one's own; as, if you will grant his opinion, let it be with some distinction; if you will follow his motion, let it be with condition; if you allow his counsel, let it be with alleging further reason. Men had need beware how they be too perfect in compliments; for be they never so sufficient otherwise, their enviers will be sure to give them that attribute to the disadvantage of their greater virtues. It is loss, also, in business, to be too full of respects, or to be too curious[3] in observing times and opportunities. Solomon saith, *He that considereth the wind shall not sow, and he that looketh to the clouds shall not reap.*[4] A wise man will

---

[2] Impressive.
[3] Careful.   [4] Ecclesiastes, 11:4.

Of Ceremonies and Respects

make more opportunities than he finds. Men's behavior should be like their apparel, not too strait or point device,[5] but free for exercise or motion.

[5] Strait-laced or precise.

53
Of Praise

PRAISE is the reflection of virtue; but it is glass, or body, which giveth the reflection. If it be from the common people, it is commonly false and naught, and rather followeth vain persons than virtuous; for the common people understand not many excellent virtues. The lowest virtues draw praise from them, the middle virtues work in them astonishment or admiration, but of the highest virtues they have no sense or perceiving at all; but shows and *appearances resembling virtues*[1] serve best with them. Certainly fame is like a river that beareth up things light and swollen and drowns things weighty and solid; but if persons of quality and judgment concur, then it is (as the Scripture saith), *A good name is like sweet-smelling ointment*,[2] it filleth all round about, and will not easily away; for the odors of ointments are more durable than those of flowers. There be so many false points of praise, that a man may justly hold it a suspect. Some praises proceed merely of flattery; and if he be an ordinary flatterer, he will have certain common attributes,[3] which may serve every man; if he be a cunning flatterer, he

---

[1] *Species virtutibus similes.* Tacitus, *Annals*, XV, 48.
[2] *Nomen bonum instar unguenti fragrantis.* Ecclesiastes, 7:1.
[3] To ascribe to the man he is flattering.

Of Praise

will follow the arch-flatterer, which is a man's self, and wherein a man thinketh best of himself, therein the flatterer will uphold him most. But if he be an impudent flatterer, look wherein a man is conscious to himself that he is most defective, and is most out of countenance in himself, that will the flatterer entitle him to, perforce, *despising his conscience*.[4] Some praises come of good wishes and respects, which is a form due in civility to kings and great persons, *to instruct through praise*,[5] when, by telling men what they are, they represent to them what they should be; some men are praised maliciously to their hurt, thereby to stir envy and jealousy towards them: *The worst kind of enemies are flatterers;*[6] insomuch as it was a proverb amongst the Grecians that *he that was praised to his hurt, should have a push*[7] *rise upon his nose;* as we say that a blister will rise upon one's tongue that tells a lie; certainly moderate praise, used with opportunity, and not vulgar, is that which doth the good. Solomon saith: *He that praiseth his friend aloud, rising early, it shall be to him no better than a curse.*[8] Too much magnifying of man or matter doth irritate contradiction, and procure envy and scorn. To praise a man's self cannot be decent, except it be in rare cases; but to praise a man's office or profession, he may do it with good grace, and with a kind of magnanimity. The cardinals of

---

[4] *Spretâ conscientiâ.* [5] *Laudando praecipere.*
[6] *Pessimum genus inimicorum laudantium.*
[7] Pimple. [8] Proverbs, 27:14.

Rome, which are theologues,[9] and friars, and schoolmen, have a phrase of notable contempt and scorn towards civil business; for they call all temporal business of wars, embassages, judicature, and other employments, *shirrerie*, which is *under-sheriffries*, as if they were but matters for under-sheriffs and catchpoles; though many times those under-sheriffries do more good than their high speculations. St. Paul, when he boasts of himself, he doth oft interlace, *I speak like a fool:* [10] but speaking of his calling, he saith, *I will magnify mine office.*[11]

[9] Theologians.
[10] II Corinthians, 11:23.
[11] Romans, 11:13.

54
Of Vainglory

It was prettily devised of Aesop, the fly sat upon the axle-tree of the chariot-wheel, and said, *What a dust do I raise!* So are there some vain persons, that, whatsoever goeth alone, or moveth upon greater means, if they have never so little hand in it, they think it is they that carry it. They that are glorious must needs be factious; for all bravery[1] stands upon comparisons. They must needs be violent to make good their own vaunts; neither can they be secret, and therefore not effectual; but, according to the French proverb, *Beaucoup de bruit, peu de fruit;—much bruit,*[2] *little fruit.* Yet certainly there is use of this quality in civil affairs: where there is an opinion and fame to be created, either of virtue or greatness, these men are good trumpeters. Again, as Titus Livius noteth, in the case of Antiochus and the Aetolians, there are sometimes great effects of cross lies; as if a man that negotiates between two princes, to draw them to join in a war against the third, doth extol the forces of either of them above measure, the one to the other; and sometimes he that deals between man and man raiseth his own credit with both, by pretending greater interest than he hath in either; and in these, and the like kinds, it often falls out,

[1] Vaunting, or boasting.   [2] Noise.

that somewhat is produced of nothing; for lies are sufficient to breed opinion, and opinion brings on substance. In military commanders and soldiers, vainglory is an essential point; for as iron sharpens iron, so by glory one courage sharpeneth another. In cases of great enterprise upon charge and adventure,[3] a composition of glorious natures doth put life into business; and those that are of solid and sober natures have more of the ballast than of the sail. In fame of learning, the flight will be slow without some feathers of ostentation: *Those who write books on the worthlessness of glory take care to put their names on the title page.*[4] Socrates, Aristotle, Galen, were men full of ostentation. Certainly vainglory helpeth to perpetuate a man's memory; and virtue was never so beholden to human nature, as it received its due at the second hand. Neither had the fame of Cicero, Seneca, Plinius Secundus, borne her age so well if it had not been joined with some vanity in themselves; like unto varnish, that makes ceilings not only shine but last. But all this while, when I speak of vainglory, I mean not of that property that Tacitus doth attribute to Mucianus, *A man who by a kind of art set forth to advantage all that he had said and done;*[5] for that proceeds not of vanity,

---

[3] Expense and risk.
[4] *Qui de contemnendâ gloriâ libros scribunt, nomen suum inscribunt.* Bacon here quotes incorrectly from Cicero's *Tusculanae Disputationes*, I, 15.
[5] *Omnium, quae dixerat feceratque, arte quâdam ostentator. History,* II, 80.

Of Vainglory

but of natural magnanimity and discretion; and in some persons is not only comely but gracious; for excusations,[6] cessions,[7] modesty itself, well governed, are but arts of ostentation; and amongst those arts there is none better than that which Plinius Secundus speaketh of, which is to be liberal of praise and commendation to others, in that wherein a man's self hath any perfection. For, saith Pliny, very wittily, *In commending another, you do yourself right; for he that you commend is either superior to you in that you commend, or inferior: if he be inferior, if he be to be commended, you much more; if he be superior, if he be not to be commended, you much less.*[8] Glorious[9] men are the scorn of wise men, the admiration of fools, the idols of parasites, and the slaves of their own vaunts.

[6] Apologies.
[7] Concessions.
[8] *Epistles*, VI, 17.
[9] Boastful.

55
Of Honor and Reputation

THE winning of honor is but the revealing of a man's virtue and worth without disadvantage; for some in their actions do woo and affect honor and reputation; which sort of men are commonly much talked of, but inwardly little admired; and some, contrariwise, darken their virtue in the show of it, so as they be undervalued in opinion. If a man perform that which hath not been attempted before, or attempted and given over, or hath been achieved, but not with so good circumstance, he shall purchase more honor than by affecting a matter of greater difficulty or virtue, wherein he is but a follower. If a man so temper his actions, as in some one of them he doth content every faction or combination of people, the music will be the fuller. A man is an ill husband of his honor that entereth into any action, the failing wherein may disgrace him more than the carrying of it through can honor him. Honor that is gained and broken upon another hath the quickest reflection, like diamonds cut with facets; and therefore let a man contend to excel any competitors of his in honor, in outshooting them, if he can, in their own bow. Discreet followers and servants help much to repu-

Of Honor and Reputation

tation: *All fame emanates from servants.*[1] Envy, which is the canker of honor, is best extinguished by declaring a man's self in his ends, rather to seek merit than fame; and by attributing a man's successes rather to Divine providence and felicity than to his own virtue or policy. The true marshalling of the degrees of sovereign honor are these. In the first place are *conditores imperiorum*, founders of states and commonwealths; such as were Romulus, Cyrus, Caesar, Ottoman, Ismael. In the second place are *legislatores*, lawgivers, which are also called second founders, or *perpetui principes*, because they govern by their ordinances after they are gone; such were Lycurgus, Solon, Justinian, Edgar,[2] Alphonsus of Castile, the Wise, that made the *Siete Partidas*.[3] In the third place are *deliverers* or *preservers*,[4] such as compound the long miseries of civil wars, or deliver their countries from servitude of strangers or tyrants, as Augustus Caesar, Vespasianus, Aurelianus, Theodoricus, King Henry the Seventh of England, King Henry the Fourth of France. In the fourth place are *extenders* or *defenders of the empire*,[5] such as in honorable wars enlarge their territories, or make noble defense against invaders. And, in the last

---

[1] *Omnis fama a domesticis emanat.* Cicero, *On the Petition of the Consulate*, V.
[2] Surnamed the Peaceful, who ascended the throne of England in 959.
[3] The Seven Laws, a collection of Spanish law made by Alphonso X in the thirteenth century.
[4] *Liberatores* or *salvatores*.
[5] *Propagatores* or *propugnatores imperii*.

place are *fathers of their country*,[6] which reign justly, and make the times good wherein they live; both which last kinds need no examples, they are in such number. Degrees of honor in subjects are, first, *sharers of cares*,[7] those upon whom princes do discharge the greatest weight of their affairs, their right hands, as we call them; the next are *leaders in war*,[8] great leaders, such as are princes' lieutenants, and do them notable services in the wars; the third are *gratiosi*, favorites, such as exceed not this scantling,[9] to be solace to the sovereign, and harmless to the people; and the fourth *equals in affairs*,[10] such as have great places under princes, and execute their places with sufficiency. There is an honor, likewise, which may be ranked amongst the greatest, which happeneth rarely; that is, of such as sacrifice themselves to death or danger for the good of their country as was M. Regulus and the two Decii.[11]

---

[6] *Patres patriae.*
[7] *Participes curarum.*
[8] *Duces belli.*
[9] Dimension.
[10] *Negotiis pares.*
[11] Regulus, a Roman general captured in the Punic War, when sent to Rome to arrange a transfer of prisoners, urged the Senate not to permit it. He returned to Carthage and was put to death. Decius and his son met their death rushing headlong into the ranks of the enemy.

56
Of Judicature

JUDGES ought to remember that their office is *jus dicere*, and not *jus dare*; to interpret law, and not to make law, or give law; else will it be like the authority claimed by the Church of Rome, which, under pretext of exposition of Scripture, doth not stick to add and alter, and to pronounce that which they do not find, and, by show of antiquity, to introduce novelty. Judges ought to be more learned than witty, more reverend than plausible,[1] and more advised[2] than confident. Above all things, integrity is their portion and proper virtue. *Cursed* (saith the law)[3] *is he that removeth the landmark.* The mislayer of a *mere-stone*[4] is to blame; but it is the unjust judge that is the capital remover of landmarks, when he defineth amiss of lands and property. One foul sentence doth more hurt than many foul examples; for these do but corrupt the stream, the other corrupteth the fountain: so saith Solomon, *A righteous man falling down before the wicked is as a troubled fountain and a corrupt spring.*[5] The office of judges may have reference unto the parties that sue, unto

[1] Applauded.   [2] Reserved.
[3] Deuteronomy, 27:17.   [4] Boundary mark.
[5] *Fons turbatus et vena corrupta est justus cadens in causâ suâ coram adversario.* Proverbs, 25:26.

the advocates that plead, unto the clerks and ministers of justice underneath them, and to the sovereign or state above them.

First, for the causes or parties that sue. *There be* (saith the Scripture) *that turn judgment into wormwood;*[6] and surely there be, also, that turn it into vinegar; for injustice maketh it bitter, and delays make it sour. The principal duty of a judge is to suppress force and fraud; whereof force is the more pernicious when it is open, and fraud when it is close and disguised. Add thereto contentious suits, which ought to be spewed out, as the surfeit of courts. A judge ought to prepare his way to a just sentence, as God useth to prepare his way, by raising valleys and taking down hills; so when there appeareth on either side a high hand, violent prosecution, cunning advantages taken, combination, power, great counsel, then is the virtue of a judge seen to make inequality equal, that he may plant his judgment as upon an even ground. *He who wrings the nose hard brings blood;*[7] and where the wine-press is hard wrought, it yields a harsh wine that tastes of the grape-stone. Judges must beware of hard constructions and strained inferences, for there is no worse torture than the torture of laws. Especially in case of laws penal, they ought to have care that that which was meant for terror be not turned into rigor; and that

---

[6] Amos, 5:7.
[7] *Qui fortiter emungit, elicit sanguinem.* See Proverbs, 30:33.

Of Judicature

they bring not upon the people that shower whereof the Scripture speaketh, *He shall rain snares upon them;*[8] for penal laws pressed, are a shower of snares upon the people. Therefore let penal laws, if they have been sleepers of long, or if they be grown unfit for the present time, be by wise judges confined in the execution; *It is the duty of a judge to consider not only the facts, but the circumstances of the case,*[9] etc. In causes of life and death, judges ought (as far as law permitteth) in justice to remember mercy; and to cast a severe eye upon the example, but a merciful eye upon the person.

Secondly, for the advocates and counsel that plead. Patience and gravity of hearing is an essential part of justice, and an overspeaking judge is no well-tuned cymbal. It is no grace to a judge first to find that which he might have heard in due time from the bar; or to show quickness of conceit[10] in cutting off evidence or counsel too short, or to prevent[11] information by questions, though pertinent. The parts of a judge in hearing are four: to direct the evidence; to moderate length, repetition, or impertinency of speech; to recapitulate, select, and collate the material points of that which hath been said; and to give the rule or sentence. Whatsoever is above these is too much, and proceedeth either of glory, and willingness to speak, or of impatience to hear, or of short-

---

[8] *Pluet super eos laqueos.* See Psalm 11:6.
[9] *Judicis officium est, ut res, ita tempora rerum.* Ovid, *Sorrows*, I, i, 37.
[10] Understanding.   [11] Anticipate.

ness of memory, or of want of a staid and equal attention. It is a strange thing to see that the boldness of advocates should prevail with judges; whereas they should imitate God in whose seat they sit, who *represseth the presumptuous, and giveth grace to the modest;*[12] but it is more strange that judges should have noted favorites, which cannot but cause multiplication of fees, and suspicion of by-ways. There is due from the judge to the advocate some commendation and gracing, where causes are well handled and fair pleaded, especially towards the side which obtaineth not;[13] for that upholds in the client the reputation of his counsel, and beats down in him the conceit[14] of his cause. There is likewise due to the public a civil reprehension of advocates, where there appeareth cunning counsel, gross neglect, slight information, indiscreet pressing, or an over-bold defense; and let not the counsel at the bar chop[15] with the judge, nor wind himself into the handling of the cause anew after the judge hath declared his sentence; but, on the other side, let not the judge meet the cause half way, nor give occasion to the party to say his counsel or proofs were not heard.

Thirdly, for that that concerns clerks and ministers. The place of justice is a hallowed place; and therefore not only the bench, but the foot-pace and precincts, and

---

[12] Proverbs, 3:34.
[13] Is not successful.
[14] Makes him feel less confidence in his cause.
[15] Argue.

Of Judicature

purprise thereof, ought to be preserved without scandal and corruption; for certainly *Grapes* (as the Scripture saith) *will not be gathered of thorns or thistles;* [16] neither can justice yield her fruit with sweetness amongst the briers and brambles of catching and polling [17] clerks and ministers. The attendance of courts is subject to four bad instruments: first, certain persons that are sowers of suits, which make the court swell and the country pine; the second sort is of those that engage courts in quarrels of jurisdiction, and are not truly *friends of the court*, but *parasites of the court*,[18] in puffing a court up beyond her bounds for their own scraps and advantage; the third sort is of those that may be accounted the left hands of courts; persons that are full of nimble and sinister tricks and shifts, whereby they pervert the plain and direct courses of courts, and bring justice into oblique lines and labyrinths; and the fourth is the poller [19] and exacter of fees; which justifies the common resemblance of the courts of justice to the bush, whereunto while the sheep flies for defense in weather, he is sure to lose part of his fleece. On the other side, an ancient clerk, skillful in precedents, wary in proceeding, and understanding in the business of the court, is an excellent finger of a court, and doth many times point the way to the judge himself.

Fourthly, for that which may concern the sovereign

---

[16] See Matthew, 7:16.
[17] Plundering.
[18] *Amici curiae; parasiti curiae.*
[19] Grafter.

and estate. Judges ought, above all, to remember the conclusion of the Roman Twelve Tables, *The welfare of the people is the supreme law;* [20] and to know that laws, except they be in order to that end, are but things captious, and oracles not well inspired; therefore it is a happy thing in a state, when kings and states do often consult with judges; and again, when judges do often consult with the king and state: the one, when there is matter of law intervenient in business of state; the other, when there is some consideration of state intervenient in matter of law; for many times the things deduced to judgment may be *meum* and *tuum*,[21] when the reason and consequence thereof may trench to point of estate. I call matter of estate, not only the parts of sovereignty, but whatsoever introduceth any great alteration, or dangerous precedent, or concerneth manifestly any great portion of people; and let no man weakly conceive that just laws and true policy have any antipathy, for they are like the spirits and sinews, that one moves with the other. Let judges also remember that Solomon's throne was supported by lions [22] on both sides; let them be lions, but yet lions under the throne, being circumspect that they do not check or oppose any points of sovereignty. Let not judges also be so ignorant of their own right, as to think there is not left to them, as a principal part of their office, a wise

---

[20] *Salus populi suprema lex.*
[21] Mine and thine.   [22] See I Kings, 10:18-20.

use and application of laws; for they may remember what the apostle saith of a greater law than theirs: *We know that the law is good if a man use it lawfully.*[23]

[23] *Nos scimus quia lex bona est, modo quis eâ utatur legitime.* I Timothy 1:8.

57
Of Anger

To SEEK to extinguish anger utterly is but a bravery[1] of the Stoics. We have better oracles. *Be angry, but sin not; let not the sun go down upon your anger.*[2] Anger must be limited and confined, both in race and in time. We will first speak how the natural inclination and habit to be angry may be attempered and calmed; secondly, how the particular motions of anger may be repressed, or at least refrained from doing mischief; thirdly, how to raise anger, or appease anger in another.

For the first, there is no other way but to meditate and ruminate well upon the effects of anger, how it troubles man's life; and the best time to do this is to look back upon anger when the fit is thoroughly over. Seneca saith well, *that anger is like ruin, which breaks itself upon that it falls.*[3] The Scripture exhorteth us *to possess our souls in patience;*[4] whosoever is out of patience, is out of possession of his soul. Men must not turn bees, *and put their very lives into the sting.*[5] Anger is certainly a kind of baseness; as it appears well in the weakness of those subjects in whom it reigns, children, women, old folks, sick folks.

[1] Boast.
[2] Ephesians, 4:26.
[3] *On Anger*, I, 1.
[4] Luke, 21:19.
[5] *Animasque in vulnere ponunt.* Virgil, *Georgics*, IV, 238.

Only men must beware that they carry their anger rather with scorn than with fear; so that they may seem rather to be above the injury than below it; which is a thing easily done, if a man will give law to himself in it.

For the second point, the causes and motives of anger are chiefly three. First, to be too sensible of hurt, for no man is angry that feels not himself hurt and therefore tender and delicate persons must need be oft angry, they have so many things to trouble them, which more robust natures have little sense of: the next is, the apprehension and construction of the injury offered, to be, in the circumstances thereof, full of contempt; for contempt is that which putteth an edge upon anger, as much, or more, than the hurt itself; and therefore, when men are ingenious in picking out circumstances of contempt, they do kindle their anger much: lastly, opinion of the touch of a man's reputation doth multiply and sharpen anger; wherein the remedy is that a man should have, as Gonsalvo [6] was wont to say, *A thicker covering for his honor.*[7] But in all refrainings of anger, it is the best remedy to win time, and to make a man's self believe that the opportunity of his revenge is not yet come; but that he foresees a time for it, and so to still himself in the meantime, and reserve it.

To contain anger from mischief, though it take hold of a man, there be two things whereof you must have

---

[6] Gonsalvo Hernandez de Cordova, a Spanish general known as The Great Captain.   [7] *Telam honoris crassiorem.*

special caution: the one, of extreme bitterness of words, especially if they be aculeate and proper,[8] for *general revilings*[9] are nothing so much; and again, that in anger a man reveal no secrets, for that makes him not fit for society: the other, that you do not peremptorily break off in any business in a fit of anger; but, howsoever you show bitterness, do not act any thing that is not revocable.

For raising and appeasing anger in another, it is done chiefly by choosing of times when men are frowardest and worst disposed to incense them; again, by gathering (as was touched before) all that you can find out to aggravate the contempt: and the two remedies are by the contraries; the former to take good times, when first to relate to a man an angry business, for the first impression is much; and the other is to sever, as much as may be, the construction of the injury from the point of contempt; imputing it to misunderstanding, fear, passion, or what you will.

[8] Pointed and peculiarly appropriate to the party attacked.
[9] *Communia maledicta.*

58
Of Vicissitude of Things

SOLOMON saith, *There is no new thing upon the earth;*[1] so that as Plato[2] had an imagination that all knowledge was but remembrance, so Solomon giveth his sentence, *That all novelty is but oblivion;*[3] whereby you may see, that the river of Lethe[4] runneth as well above ground as below. There is an abstruse astrologer that saith, if it were not for two things that are constant (the one is that the fixed stars ever stand at like distance one from another and never come nearer together, nor go further asunder; the other, that the diurnal motion perpetually keepeth time), no individual would last one moment; certain it is that the matter is in a perpetual flux, and never at a stay. The great winding-sheets that bury all things in oblivion are two—deluges and earthquakes. As for conflagrations and great droughts, they do not merely dispeople, but destroy. Phaeton's car went but a day; and the three years' drought in the time of Elias,[5] was but particular,[6] and left people alive. As for the great burnings by lightnings, which are often in the West Indies,[7] they are but narrow;

[1] Ecclesiastes, 1:9.
[2] *Phaedo.*
[3] See Ecclesiastes, 1:11.
[4] River of oblivion.
[5] Elijah. See I Kings, 17:1; 18:1.
[6] Confined to a limited space.
[7] The whole of the American continent then discovered is included under this name.

but in the other two destructions, by deluge and earthquake, it is further to be noted that the remnant of people which happen to be reserved are commonly ignorant and mountainous people that can give no account of the time past; so that the oblivion is all one, as if none had been left. If you consider well of the people of the West Indies, it is very probable that they are a newer or a younger people than the people of the old world; and it is much more likely that the destruction that hath heretofore been there, was not by earthquakes, (as the Egyptian priest told Solon, concerning the Island of Atlantis,[8] that it was swallowed by an earthquake), but rather that it was desolated by a particular deluge, for earthquakes are seldom in those parts; but, on the other side, they have such pouring rivers, as the rivers of Asia and Africa and Europe are but brooks to them. Their Andes, likewise, or mountains, are far higher than those with us; whereby it seems that the remnants of generations of men were in such a particular deluge saved. As for the observation that Machiavel hath, that the jealousy of sects doth much extinguish the memory of things,[9] traducing Gregory the Great, that he did what in him lay to extinguish all heathen antiquities, I do not find that those zeals do any great effects, nor last long; as it appeared in the succession of Sabinian,[10] who did revive the former antiquities.

---

[8] Plato, *Timæus* III, 24, seq.   [9] *Discourses*, II, 5.
[10] Sabinian succeeded Gregory the Great as pope in 604. Under him there was a revival of the earlier attachment to the ancient gods.

Of Vicissitude of Things

The vicissitude or mutations in the superior globe are no fit matter for this present argument. It may be, Plato's great year,[11] if the world should last so long, would have some effect, not in renewing the state of like individuals (for that is the fume [12] of those that conceive the celestial bodies have more accurate influences upon these things below, than indeed they have), but in gross. Comets, out of question, have likewise power and effect over the gross and mass of things; but they are rather gazed, and waited upon in their journey, than wisely observed in their effects, especially in their respective effects; that is, what kind of comet for magnitude, color, version of the beams, placing in the region of heaven, or lasting, produceth what kind of effects.

There is a toy,[13] which I have heard and I would not have it given over, but waited upon a little. They say it is observed in the Low Countries (I know not in what part) that every five and thirty years the same kind and suit of years and weather comes about again; as great frosts, great wet, great droughts, warm winters, summers with little heat, and the like; and they call it the prime. It is a thing I do the rather mention, because, computing backwards, I have found some concurrence.

But to leave these points of nature, and to come to

---

[11] The time required for all the heavenly bodies, having completed their revolutions, to return to the places they had at the beginning of the world. See Plato, *Timaeus*, III, 38.
[12] Imagining.   [13] A curious fancy.

men. The greatest vicissitude of things amongst men is the vicissitude of sects and religions; for those orbs rule in men's minds most. The true religion is built upon the rock; the rest are tossed upon the waves of time. To speak, therefore, of the causes of new sects, and to give some counsel concerning them, as far as the weakness of human judgment can give stay to so great revolutions.

When the religion formerly received is rent by discords, and when the holiness of the professors of religion is decayed and full of scandal, and, withal, the times be stupid, ignorant, and barbarous, you may doubt the springing up of a new sect; if then, also, there should arise any extravagant and strange spirit to make himself author thereof; all which points held when Mahomet published his law. If a new sect have not two properties, fear it not, for it will not spread. The one is the supplanting or the opposing of authority established, for nothing is more popular than that; the other is, the giving license to pleasures and a voluptuous life; for as for speculative heresies (such as were in ancient times the Arians,[14] and now the Arminians),[15] though they work mightily upon men's wits, yet they do not produce any great alterations in states, except it be by the help of civil occasions. There be three manner of plantations of new sects: by the power

[14] The followers of Arius (256-336) whose doctrines tended to deny the divinity of Christ.
[15] The followers of Arminius, or Jacob Harmensen (1560-1609), who protested against the Calvinistic doctrine of total predestination.

Of Vicissitude of Things

of signs and miracles; by the eloquence and wisdom of speech and persuasion; and by the sword. For martyrdoms, I reckon them amongst miracles, because they seem to exceed the strength of human nature; and I may do the like of superlative and admirable holiness of life. Surely there is no better way to stop the rising of new sects and schisms than to reform abuses; to compound the smaller differences; to proceed mildly, and not with sanguinary persecutions; and rather to take off the principal authors, by winning and advancing them, than to enrage them by violence and bitterness.

The changes and vicissitude in wars are many, but chiefly in three things: in the seats or stages of the war, in the weapons, and in the manner of the conduct. Wars, in ancient time, seemed more to move from east to west; for the Persians, Assyrians, Arabians, Tartars (which were the invaders), were all eastern people. It is true the Gauls were western; but we read but of two incursions of theirs, the one to Gallo-Graecia,[16] the other to Rome: but east and west have no certain points of heaven; and no more have the wars, either from the east or west, any certainty of observation; but north and south are fixed; and it hath seldom or never been seen that the far southern people have invaded the northern, but contrariwise: whereby it is manifest that the northern tract of the world is in nature the more martial region, be it in respect of

[16] Galatia.

the stars of that hemisphere, or of the great continents that are upon the north; whereas the south part, for aught that is known, is almost all sea; or (which is most apparent) of the cold of the northern parts, which is that which, without aid of discipline, doth make the bodies hardest, and the courage warmest.

Upon the breaking and shivering of a great state and empire, you may be sure to have wars; for great empires, while they stand, do enervate and destroy the forces of the natives which they have subdued, resting upon their own protecting forces; and then, when they fail also, all goes to ruin, and they become a prey. So was it in the decay of the Roman empire, and likewise in the empire of Almaigne,[17] after Charles the Great, every bird taking a feather, and were not unlike to befall to Spain, if it should break. The great accessions and unions of kingdoms do likewise stir up wars; for when a state grows to an overpower, it is like a great flood that will be sure to overflow, as it hath been seen in the states of Rome, Turkey, Spain, and others. Look when the world hath fewest barbarous people, but such as commonly will not marry or generate, except they know means to live (as it is almost everywhere at this day, except Tartary), there is no danger of inundations of people; but when there be great shoals of people, which go on to populate, without foreseeing means of life and sustenation,[18] it is of necessity

[17] Germany. [18] Support.

Of Vicissitude of Things

that once in an age or two they discharge a portion of their people upon other nations, which the ancient northern people were wont to do by lot; casting lots what part should stay at home, and what should seek their fortunes. When a warlike state grows soft and effeminate, they may be sure of a war, for commonly such states are grown rich in the time of their degenerating; and so the prey inviteth, and their decay in valor encourageth a war.

As for the weapons, it hardly falleth under rule and observation, yet we see even they have returns and vicissitudes; for certain it is that ordnance [19] was known in the city of the Oxidraces, in India, and was that which the Macedonians called thunder and lightning, and magic; and it is well known that the use of ordnance hath been in China above two thousand years. The conditions of weapons, and their improvements are, first, the fetching [20] afar off, for that outruns the danger, as it is seen in ordnance and muskets; secondly, the strength of the percussion, wherein, likewise, ordnance do exceed all arietations,[21] and ancient inventions; the third is, the commodious use of them, as that they may serve in all weathers, that the carriage may be light and manageable, and the like.

For the conduct of the war: at the first, men rested extremely upon number; they did put the wars likewise upon main force and valor, pointing days for pitched

---

[19] Gunpowder.   [20] Striking.   [21] Battering-rams.

fields,[22] and so trying it out upon an even match; and they were more ignorant in ranging and arraying their battles. After they grew to rest upon number, rather competent than vast, they grew to advantages of place, cunning diversions, and the like, and they grew more skillful in the ordering of their battles.

In the youth of a state, arms do flourish; in the middle age of a state, learning; and then both of them together for a time; in the declining age of a state, mechanical arts and merchandise. Learning hath his infancy when it is but beginning, and almost childish; then his youth, when it is luxuriant and juvenile; then his strength of years, when it is solid and reduced;[23] and, lastly, his old age, when it waxeth dry and exhaust. But it is not good to look too long upon these turning wheels of vicissitude, lest we become giddy; as for the philology[24] of them, that is but a circle of tales, and therefore not fit for this writing.

[22] Appointing days for pitched battles.
[23] Concentrated.   [24] History.

New Atlantis

New Atlantis

WE SAILED from Peru (where we had continued by the space of one whole year) for China and Japan, by the South Sea, taking with us victuals for twelve months; and had good winds from the east, though soft and weak, for five months' space and more. But then the wind came about, and settled in the west for many days, so as we could make little or no way, and were sometimes in purpose to turn back. But then again there arose strong and great winds from the south, with a point east; which carried us up, for all that we could do, towards the north; by which time our victuals failed us, though we had made good spare of them. So that finding ourselves in the midst of the greatest wilderness of waters in the world without victual, we gave ourselves for lost men, and prepared for death. Yet we did lift up our hearts and voices to God above, who "showeth his wonders in the deep," beseeching him of his mercy, that as in the beginning he discovered the face of the deep, and brought forth dry land, so he would now discover land to us that we mought not perish.

And it came to pass that the next day about evening we saw within a kenning [1] before us, towards the north,

[1] Perceptible distance.

as it were thick clouds, which did put us in some hope of land; knowing how that part of the South Sea was utterly unknown; and might have islands or continents that hitherto were not come to light. Wherefore we bent our course thither, where we saw the appearance of land, all that night; and in the dawning of the next day, we might plainly discern that it was a land, flat to our sight, and full of boscage,[2] which made it show the more dark. And after an hour and a half's sailing, we entered into a good haven, being the port of a fair city: not great indeed, but well built, and that gave a pleasant view from the sea. And we thinking every minute long till we were on land came close to the shore and offered to land. But straightways we saw divers of the people, with bastons[3] in their hands, as it were, forbidding us to land: yet without any cries or fierceness, but only as warning us off by signs that they made. Whereupon being not a little discomforted, we were advising with ourselves what we should do.

During which time there made forth to us a small boat with about eight persons in it, whereof one of them had in his hand a tipstaff[4] of a yellow cane, tipped at both ends with blue, who came aboard our ship, without any show of distrust at all. And when he saw one of our number present himself somewhat afore the rest, he drew forth a little scroll of parchment (somewhat yellower than our parchment and shining like the leaves of writing

[2] Woods.   [3] Staves.
[4] A staff carried as symbol of authority.

tables, but otherwise soft and flexible), and delivered it to our foremost man. In which scroll were written in ancient Hebrew, and in ancient Greek, and in good Latin of the School,[5] and in Spanish, these words: "Land ye not, none of you, and provide to be gone from this coast within sixteen days, except you have further time given you. Meanwhile, if you want fresh water, or victual, or help for your sick, or that your ship needeth repair, write down your wants, and you shall have that which belongeth to mercy." This scroll was signed with a stamp of cherubin's wings, not spread, but hanging downwards; and by them a cross. This being delivered, the officer returned, and left only a servant with us to receive our answer.

Consulting hereupon amongst ourselves, we were much perplexed. The denial of landing, and hasty warning us away, troubled us much: on the other side, to find that the people had[6] languages, and were so full of humanity, did comfort us not a little. And above all, the sign of the cross to that instrument was to us a great rejoicing, and as it were a certain presage of good. Our answer was in the Spanish tongue, "That for our ship, it was well; for we had rather met with calms and contrary winds, than any tempests. For our sick, they were many, and in very ill case; so that if they were not permitted to land, they ran in danger of their lives." Our other wants we set down in particular, adding, "That we had some little store of mer-

[5] Classical Latin. [6] Knew.

chandise, which if it pleased them to deal for, it might supply our wants, without being chargeable unto them." We offered some reward in pistolets [7] unto the servant, and a piece of crimson velvet to be presented to the officer: but the servant took them not, nor would scarce look upon them; and so left us, and went back in another little boat which was sent for him.

About three hours after we had dispatched our answer there came towards us a person (as it seemed) of place.[8] He had on him a gown with wide sleeves, of a kind of water chamolet,[9] of an excellent azure color, far more glossy than ours; his under apparel was green, and so was his hat, being in the form of a turban, daintily made, and not so huge as the Turkish turbans; and the locks of his hair came down below the brims of it. A reverend man was he to behold. He came in a boat, gilt in some parts of it, with four persons more only in that boat; and was followed by another boat, wherein were some twenty. When he was come within a flight-shot [10] of our ship, signs were made to us that we should send forth some to meet him upon the water, which we presently did in our ship-boat, sending the principal man amongst us save one, and four of our number with him.

When we were come within six yards of their boat, they called to us to stay, and not to approach farther, which we did. And thereupon the man whom I before described

[7] Spanish coins.
[8] Man of authority.
[9] A fabric made of goat's hair.
[10] Distance an arrow can be shot.

New Atlantis

stood up, and with a loud voice, in Spanish, asked, "Are ye Christians?" We answered, we were; fearing the less, because of the cross we had seen in the subscription. At which answer the said person lift up his right hand towards heaven, and drew it softly to his mouth (which is the gesture they use when they thank God), and then said: "If ye will swear, all of you, by the merits of the Saviour, that ye are no pirates, nor have shed blood, lawfully nor unlawfully, within forty days past, you may have license to come on land." We said we were all ready to take that oath. Whereupon one of those that were with him, being (as it seemed) a notary, made an entry of this act. Which done, another of the attendants of the great person, which was with him in the same boat, after his lord had spoken a little to him, said aloud: "My lord would have you know that it is not of pride, or greatness, that he cometh not aboard your ship: but for that, in your answer, you declare that you have many sick amongst you, he was warned by the Conservator of Health of the city that he should keep a distance." We bowed ourselves towards him, and answered we were his humble servants; and accounted for great honor and singular humanity towards us, that which was already done; but hoped well that the nature of the sickness of our men was not infectious. So he returned; and a while after came the notary to us aboard our ship, holding in his hand a fruit of that country, like an orange, but of color between orange-tawny and scarlet, which cast a most excellent odor. He used it (as it seemed) for a preservative against infection. He gave us our oath, "By the name of Jesus, and his merits"; and after told us that the next day, by six of the clock in the morning, we should be sent to, and brought to the Strangers' House (so he called it), where we should be accommodated of things, both for our whole and for our sick. So he left us; and when we offered him some pistolets, he smiling said he must not be twice paid for one labor: meaning (as I take it) that he had salary sufficient of the state for his service. For (as I after learned) they call an officer that taketh rewards twice-paid.

The next morning early there came to us the same officer that came to us at first with his cane, and told us: "He came to conduct us to the Strangers' House; and that he had prevented [11] the hour, because we might have the whole day before us for our business. For (said he) if you will follow my advice, there shall first go with me some few of you, and see the place, and how it may be made convenient for you; and then you may send for your sick, and the rest of your number, which ye will bring on land." We thanked him, and said that this care which he took of desolate strangers, God would reward. And so six of us went on land with him; and when we were on land, he went before us, and turned to us, and said he was but our servant, and our guide. He led us through three fair streets; and all the way we went there were gathered some people

[11] Anticipated.

on both sides, standing in a row; but in so civil a fashion, as if it had been not to wonder at us but to welcome us! and divers of them, as we passed by them, put their arms a little abroad, which is their gesture when they bid any welcome.

The Strangers' House is a fair and spacious house built of brick, of somewhat a bluer color than our brick; and with handsome windows, some of glass, some of a kind of cambric oiled. He brought us first into a fair parlor above stairs, and then asked us what number of persons we were? and how many sick? We answered we were in all (sick and whole) one and fifty persons, whereof our sick were seventeen. He desired us to have patience a little, and to stay till he came back to us, which was about an hour after; and then he led us to see the chambers which were provided for us, being in number nineteen. They having cast [12] it (as it seemeth) that four of those chambers, which were better than the rest, might receive four of the principal men of our company; and lodge them alone by themselves; and the other fifteen chambers were to lodge us, two and two together. The chambers were handsome and cheerful chambers, and furnished civilly. Then he led us to a long gallery, like a dorture,[13] where he showed us all along the one side (for the other side was but wall and window) seventeen cells, very neat ones, having partitions of cedar wood. Which gallery and cells,

[12] Arranged.   [13] Dormitory.

being in all forty (many more than we needed), were instituted as an infirmary for sick persons. And he told us withal that as any of our sick waxed well, he might be removed from his cell to a chamber: for which purpose there were set forth ten spare chambers, besides the number we spake of before. This done, he brought us back to the parlor, and lifting up his cane a little (as they do when they give any charge or command), said to us, "Ye are to know that the custom of the land requireth that after this day and tomorrow (which we give you for removing your people from your ship), you are to keep within doors for three days. But let it not trouble you, nor do not think yourselves restrained, but rather left to your ease and rest. You shall want nothing, and there are six of our people appointed to attend you for any business you may have abroad." We gave him thanks with all affection and respect, and said, "God surely is manifested in this land." We offered him also twenty pistolets; but he smiled, and only said:

"What? twice paid!" And so he left us.

Soon after our dinner was served in; which was right good viands, both for bread and meat: better than any collegiate diet [14] that I have known in Europe. We had also drink of three sorts, all wholesome and good; wine of the grape; a drink of grain, such as is with us our ale, but more clear; and a kind of cider made of a fruit of that country;

[14] Meals in a college hall.

a wonderful pleasing and refreshing drink. Besides, there were brought in to us great store of those scarlet oranges for our sick; which (they said) were an assured remedy for sickness taken at sea. There was given us also a box of small gray or whitish pills, which they wished our sick should take, one of the pills every night before sleep; which (they said) would hasten their recovery.

The next day, after that our trouble of carriage and removing of our men and goods out of our ship was somewhat settled and quiet, I thought good to call our company together, and when they were assembled, said unto them, "My dear friends, let us know ourselves, and how it standeth with us. We are men cast on land, as Jonas was out of the whale's belly, when we were as buried in the deep; and now we are on land, we are but between death and life, for we are beyond both the Old World and the New; and whether ever we shall see Europe, God only knoweth. It is a kind of miracle hath brought us hither, and it must be little less than shall bring us hence. Therefore in regard of our deliverance past, and our danger present and to come, let us look up to God, and every man reform his own ways. Besides we are come here amongst a Christian people, full of piety and humanity: let us not bring that confusion of face upon ourselves, as to show our vices or unworthiness before them. Yet there is more, for they have by commandment (though in form of courtesy) cloistered us within these walls for three days:

who knoweth whether it be not to take some taste of our manners and conditions? And if they find them bad, to banish us straightways; if good, to give us further time. For these men that they have given us for attendance may withal have an eye upon us. Therefore, for God's love, and as we love the weal of our souls and bodies, let us so behave ourselves, as we may be at peace with God, and may find grace in the eyes of this people." Our company with one voice thanked me for my good admonition, and promised me to live soberly and civilly, and without giving any the least occasion of offense. So we spent our three days joyfully, and without care, in expectation what would be done with us when they were expired. During which time, we had every hour joy of the amendment of our sick, who thought themselves cast into some divine pool of healing, they mended so kindly [15] and so fast.

The morrow after our three days were past, there came to us a new man, that we had not seen before, clothed in blue as the former was, save that his turban was white with a small red cross on the top. He had also a tippet [16] of fine linen. At his coming in he did bend to us a little, and put his arms abroad. We of our parts saluted him in a very lowly and submissive manner; as looking that from him we should receive sentence of life or death. He desired to speak with some few of us. Whereupon six of us only stayed, and the rest avoided [17] the room. He said, "I am

---

[15] Naturally.
[16] Scarf worn about the neck.   [17] Left.

by office Governor of this House of Strangers, and by vocation I am a Christian priest; and therefore am come to you to offer you my service, both as strangers, and chiefly as Christians. Some things I may tell you, which I think you will not be unwilling to hear. The state hath given you license to stay on land for the space of six weeks: and let it not trouble you, if your occasions [18] ask further time, for the law in this point is not precise; and I do not doubt but myself shall be able to obtain for you such further time as shall be convenient. Ye shall also understand that the Strangers' House is at this time rich, and much aforehand; for it hath laid up revenue these thirty-seven years, for so long it is since any stranger arrived in this part; and therefore take ye no care; the state will defray you all the time you stay. Neither shall you stay one day the less for that. As for any merchandise ye have brought, ye shall be well used, and have your return, either in merchandise or in gold and silver: for to us it is all one. And if you have any other request to make, hide it not; for ye shall find we will not make your countenance to fall by the answer ye shall receive. Only this I must tell you, that none of you must go above a karan (that is with them a mile and a half) from the walls of the city, without especial leave."

We answered, after we had looked awhile one upon another, admiring this gracious and parent-like usage, that

[18] Needs.

we could not tell what to say, for we wanted words to express our thanks; and his noble free offers left us nothing to ask. It seemed to us that we had before us a picture of our salvation in heaven; for we that were awhile since in the jaws of death, were now brought into a place where we found nothing but consolations. For the commandment laid upon us, we would not fail to obey it, though it was impossible but our hearts should be inflamed to tread further upon this happy and holy ground. We added that our tongues should first cleave to the roofs of our mouths ere we should forget, either his reverend person or this whole nation, in our prayers. We also most humbly besought him to accept of us as his true servants, by as just a right as ever men on earth were bounden; laying and presenting both our persons and all we had at his feet. He said he was a priest, and looked for a priest's reward; which was our brotherly love, and the good of our souls and bodies. So he went from us, not without tears of tenderness in his eyes, and left us also confused with joy and kindness, saying amongst ourselves that we were come into a land of angels, which did appear to us daily, and prevent [19] us with comforts which we thought not of, much less expected.

The next day, about ten of the clock, the Governor came to us again, and after salutations, said familiarly that he was come to visit us; and called for a chair, and sat him

[19] Anticipate.

New Atlantis

down; and we, being some ten of us (the rest were of the meaner sort, or else gone abroad),[20] sat down with him; and when we were set, he began thus: "We of this island of Bensalem (for so they called it in their language) have this: that by means of our solitary situation, and of the laws of secrecy, which we have for our travellers, and our rare admission of strangers, we know well most part of the habitable world, and are ourselves unknown. Therefore because he that knoweth least is fitted to ask questions, it is more reason, for the entertainment of the time, that ye ask me questions than that I ask you."

We answered that we humbly thanked him that he would give us leave so to do: and that we conceived, by the taste we had already, that there was no worldly thing on earth more worthy to be known than the state of that happy land. But above all (we said) since that we were met from the several ends of the world, and hoped assuredly that we should meet one day in the kingdom of heaven (for that we were both part Christians), we desired to know (in respect that land was so remote, and so divided by vast and unknown seas from the land where our Saviour walked on earth) who was the apostle of that nation, and how it was converted to the faith? It appeared in his face that he took great contentment in this our question; he said, "Ye knit my heart to you by asking this question in the first place: for it showeth that you first

[20] Of inferior rank or else gone out.

seek the kingdom of heaven: and I shall gladly, and briefly, satisfy your demand.

"About twenty years after the ascension of our Saviour it came to pass that there was seen by the people of Renfusa (a city upon the eastern coast of our island), within sight (the night was cloudy and calm), as it might be some mile in the sea, a great pillar of light; not sharp, but in form of a column or cylinder, rising from the sea a great way up towards heaven; and on the top of it was seen a large cross of light, more bright and resplendent than the body of the pillar. Upon which so strange a spectacle the people of the city gathered apace together upon the sands, to wonder; and so after put themselves into a number of small boats to go nearer to this marvellous sight. But when the boats were come within about sixty yards of the pillar they found themselves all bound, and could go no further, yet so as they might move to go about, but might not approach nearer: so as the boats stood all as in a theatre, beholding this light, as an heavenly sign. It so fell out that there was in one of the boats one of our wise men, of the Society of Solomon's House; which house or college, my good brethren, is the very eye of this kingdom, who having awhile attentively and devoutly viewed and contemplated this pillar and cross, fell down upon his face; and then raised himself upon his knees, and lifting up his hands to heaven, made his prayers in this manner:

" 'Lord God of heaven and earth, thou hast vouchsafed

New Atlantis

of thy grace, to those of our order, to know thy works of creation, and the secrets of them; and to discern (as far as appertaineth to the generations of men) between divine miracles, works of nature, works of art, and impostures and illusions of all sorts. I do here acknowledge and testify before this people, that the thing which we now see before our eyes is thy finger, and a true miracle. And forasmuch as we learn in our books that thou workest miracles but to a divine and excellent end (for the laws of nature are thine own laws, and thou exceedest them not but upon great cause), we most humbly beseech thee to prosper this great sign, and to give us the interpretation and use of it in mercy; which thou dost in some part secretly promise, by sending it unto us.'

"When he had made his prayer, he presently found the boat he was in movable and unbound; whereas all the rest remained still fast; and taking that for an assurance of leave to approach, he caused the boat to be softly and with silence rowed towards the pillar. But ere he came near it, the pillar and cross of light broke up, and cast itself abroad, as it were, into a firmament of many stars, which also vanished soon after, and there was nothing left to be seen but a small ark or chest of cedar, dry, and not wet at all with water, though it swam. And in the fore-end of it, which was towards him, grew a small green branch of palm; and when the wise man had taken it with all reverence into his boat, it opened of itself, and there were found in it a book and a letter, both written in fine parchment, and wrapped in sindons [21] of linen. The book contained all the canonical books of the Old and New Testament, according as you have them (for we know well that the Churches with you receive), and the Apocalypse itself; and some other books of the New Testament, which were not at that time written, were nevertheless in the book. And for the letter, it was in these words:

"'I Bartholomew, a servant of the Highest, and apostle of Jesus Christ, was warned by an angel that appeared to me in a vision of glory that I should commit this ark to the floods of the sea. Therefore I do testify and declare unto that people where God shall ordain this ark to come to land, that in the same day is come unto them salvation and peace and goodwill from the Father, and from the Lord Jesus.'

"There was also in both these writings, as well the book as the letter, wrought a great miracle, conform [22] to that of the apostles, in the original gift of tongues. For there being at that time, in this land, Hebrews, Persians, and Indians, besides the natives, every one read upon the book and letter, as if they had been written in his own language. And thus was this land saved from infidelity (as the remain of the Old World was from water) by an ark, through the apostolical and miraculous evangelism of St. Bartholomew." And here he paused, and a messenger

[21] Pieces. [22] Similar.

New Atlantis

came, and called him forth from us. So this was all that passed in that conference.

The next day the same Governor came again to us, immediately after dinner, and excused himself, saying that the day before he was called from us somewhat abruptly, but now he would make us amends, and spend time with is, if we held his company and conference agreeable. We answered that we held it so agreeable and pleasing to us, as we forgot both dangers past and fears to come, for the time we heard him speak; and that we thought an hour spent with him was worth years of our former life. He bowed himself a little to us, and after we were set again, he said, "Well, the questions are on your part."

One of our number said, after a little pause, that there was a matter we were no less desirous to know than fearful to ask, lest we might presume too far. But encouraged by his rare humanity towards us (that could scarce think ourselves strangers, being his vowed and professed servants), we would take the hardiness to propound it; humbly beseeching him, if he thought it not fit to be answered, that he would pardon it, though he rejected it. We said we well observed those his words, which he formerly spake, that this happy island where we now stood was known to few, and yet knew most of the nations of the world, which we found to be true, considering they had the languages of Europe, and knew much of our state and business; and yet we in Europe (notwithstanding all the remote discoveries and navigations of this last age) never heard any of the least inkling or glimpse of this island. This we found wonderful strange; for that all nations have interknowledge one of another, either by voyage into foreign parts, or by strangers that come to them; and though the traveller into a foreign country doth commonly know more by the eye than he that stayeth at home can by relation of the traveller; yet both ways suffice to make a mutual knowledge, in some degree, on both parts. But for this island, we never heard tell of any ship of theirs that had been seen to arrive upon any shore of Europe; no, nor of either the East or West Indies, nor yet of any ship of any other part of the world that had made return from them. And yet the marvel rested not in this; for the situation of it (as his lordship said) in the secret conclave of such a vast sea mought cause it. But then, that they should have knowledge of the languages, books, affairs, of those that lie such a distance from them, it was a thing we could not tell what to make of; for that it seemed to us a condition and propriety [23] of divine powers, and beings to be hidden and unseen to others, and yet to have others open, and as in a light to them.

At this speech the Governor gave a gracious smile and said that we did well to ask pardon for this question we now asked, for that it imported, as if we thought this land a land of magicians, that sent forth spirits of the air into all parts, to bring them news and intelligence of other

[23] Property.

countries. It was answered by us all, in all possible humbleness, but yet with a countenance taking knowledge,[24] that we knew he spake it but merrily; that we were apt enough to think there was somewhat supernatural in this island, but yet rather as angelical than magical. But to let his lordship know truly what it was that made us tender and doubtful to ask this question, it was not any such conceit, but because we remembered he had given a touch [25] in his former speech that this land had laws of secrecy touching strangers. To this he said, "You remember it aright; and therefore in that I shall say to you, I must reserve some particulars, which it is not lawful for me to reveal, but there will be enough left to give you satisfaction.

"You shall understand (that which perhaps you will scarce think credible) that about three thousand years ago, or somewhat more, the navigation of the world (especially for remote voyages) was greater than at this day. Do not think with yourselves that I know not how much it is increased with you, within these six-score years; I know it well, and yet I say, greater then than now; whether it was that the example of the Ark, that saved the remnant of men from the universal Deluge, gave men confidence to adventure upon the waters, or what it was; but such is the truth. The Phoenicians, and specially the Tyrians, had great fleets; so had the Carthaginians their colony, which

[24] Acknowledging.   [25] Hinted.

is yet further west. Towards the east the shipping of Egypt, and of Palestine, was likewise great. China also, and the Great Atlantis (that you call America), which have now but junks and canoes, abounded then in tall ships. This island (as appeareth by faithful registers of those times) had then fifteen hundred strong ships, of great content. Of all this there is with you sparing [26] memory, or none; but we have large knowledge thereof.

"At that time this land was known and frequented by the ships and vessels of all the nations before named. And (as it cometh to pass) they had many times men of other countries that were no sailors that came with them; as Persians, Chaldeans, Arabians, so as almost all nations of might and fame resorted hither; of whom we have some stirps [27] and little tribes with us at this day. And for our own ships, they went sundry voyages, as well to your straits,[28] which you call the Pillars of Hercules, as to other parts in the Atlantic and Mediterranean Seas; as to Paguin [29] (which is the same with Cambaline) and Quinzy, upon the Oriental Seas, as far as to the borders of the East Tartary.

"At the same time, and an age after or more, the inhabitants of the Great Atlantis did flourish. For though the narration and description which is made by a great man [30] with you, that the descendants of Neptune planted there,

[26] Slight.
[27] Families.
[28] Of Gibraltar.
[29] Peking.
[30] Plato describes Atlantis in the *Critias*.

New Atlantis

and of the magnificent temple, palace, city, and hill; and the manifold streams of goodly navigable rivers (which as so many chains environed the same site and temple); and the several degrees of ascent, whereby men did climb up to the same, as if it had been a *scala coeli*,[31] be all poetical and fabulous; yet so much is true, that the said country of Atlantis, as well that of Peru, then called Coya, as that of Mexico, then named Tyrambel, were mighty and proud kingdoms, in arms, shipping, and riches: so mighty as at one time (or at least within the space of ten years), they both made two great expeditions; they of Tyrambel through the Atlantic to the Mediterranean Sea; and they of Coya, through the South Sea upon this our island; and for the former of these, which was into Europe, the same author amongst you (as it seemeth) had some relation [32] from the Egyptian priest, whom he citeth. For assuredly such a thing there was. But whether it were the ancient Athenians that had the glory of the repulse and resistance of those forces, I can say nothing; but certain it is there never came back either ship or man from that voyage. Neither had the other voyage of those of Coya upon us had better fortune, if they had not met with enemies of greater clemency. For the king of this island, by name Altabin, a wise man and a great warrior, knowing well both his own strength and that of his enemies, handled the matter so, as he cut off their land forces from their ships,

[31] A ladder to Heaven. See Genesis, 28:12.
[32] Report.

and entoiled[33] both their navy and their camp with a greater power than theirs, both by sea and land, and compelled them to render themselves without striking stroke; and after they were at his mercy, contenting himself only with their oath that they should no more bear arms against him, dismissed them all in safety.

"But the divine revenge overtook not long after those proud enterprises. For within less than the space of one hundred years the Great Atlantis was utterly lost and destroyed; not by a great earthquake, as your man saith (for that whole tract is little subject to earthquakes), but by a particular deluge or inundation, those countries having at this day far greater rivers and far higher mountains to pour down waters than any part of the Old World. But it is true that the same inundation was not deep, not past forty foot in most places from the ground, so that although it destroyed man and beast generally, yet some few wild inhabitants of the wood escaped. Birds also were saved by flying to the high trees and woods. For as for men, although they had buildings in many places higher than the depth of the water, yet that inundation, though it were shallow, had a long continuance, whereby they of the vale that were not drowned perished for want of food, and other things necessary.

"So as marvel you not at the thin population of America, nor at the rudeness and ignorance of the people; for you must account your inhabitants of America as a young

[33] Trapped.

people, younger a thousand years at the least than the rest of the world, for that there was so much time between the universal Flood and their particular inundation. For the poor remnant of human seed which remained in their mountains peopled the country again slowly, by little and little, and being simple and savage people (not like Noah and his sons, which was the chief family of the earth) they were not able to leave letters, arts, and civility to their posterity; and having likewise in their mountainous habitations been used (in respect of the extreme cold of those regions) to clothe themselves with the skins of tigers, bears, and great hairy goats, that they have in those parts; when after they came down into the valley, and found the intolerable heats which are there, and knew no means of lighter apparel, they were forced to begin the custom of going naked, which continueth at this day. Only they take great pride and delight in the feathers of birds, and this also they took from those their ancestors of the mountains, who were invited unto it, by the infinite flight of birds that came up to the high grounds, while the waters stood below. So you see, by this main accident of time, we lost our traffic with the Americans, with whom of all others, in regard they lay nearest to us, we had most commerce.

"As for the other parts of the world, it is most manifest that in the ages following (whether it were in respect of wars, or by a natural revolution of time) navigation did everywhere greatly decay, and specially far voyages (the rather by the use of galleys and such vessels as could hardly brook the ocean) were altogether left and omitted. So then, that part of intercourse which could be from other nations, to sail to us, you see how it hath long since ceased; except it were by some rare accident, as this of yours. But now of the cessation of that other part of intercourse, which mought be by our sailing to other nations, I must yield you some other cause. For I cannot say, if I shall say truly, but our shipping, for number, strength, mariners, pilots, and all things that appertain to navigation, is as great as ever; and therefore why we should sit at home, I shall now give you an account by itself; and it will draw nearer, to give you satisfaction, to your principal question.

"There reigned in this island about 1,900 years ago a king, whose memory of all others we most adore; not superstitiously, but as a divine instrument, though a mortal man: his name was Solamona; and we esteem him as the lawgiver of our nation. This king had a large heart, inscrutable for good,[34] and was wholly bent to make his kingdom and people happy. He therefore taking into consideration how sufficient and substantive [35] this land was to maintain itself without any aid at all of the foreigner, being 5,600 miles in circuit, and of rare fertility of soil in the greatest part thereof; and finding also the shipping of this country mought be plentifully set on work, both by fishing and by transportations from port to port, and likewise by sailing unto some small islands that are not far

[34] Unfathomable, inexhaustible.   [35] Self-sustaining.

from us, and are under the crown and laws of this state; and recalling into his memory the happy and flourishing estate wherein this land then was, so as it mought be a thousand ways altered to the worse, but scarce any one way to the better; though nothing wanted to his noble and heroical intentions, but only (as far as human foresight mought reach) to give perpetuity to that which was in his time so happily established. Therefore amongst his other fundamental laws of this kingdom he did ordain the interdicts and prohibitions which we have touching entrance of strangers; which at that time (though it was after the calamity of America) was frequent; doubting [36] novelties and commixture of manners. It is true, the like law against the admission of strangers without license is an ancient law in the kingdom of China, and yet continued in use. But there it is a poor thing; and hath made them a curious, ignorant, fearful, foolish nation. But our lawgiver made his law of another temper. For first, he hath preserved all points of humanity, in taking order and making provision for the relief of strangers distressed; whereof you have tasted."

At which speech (as reason was) we all rose up, and bowed ourselves. He went on:

"That king also still desiring to join humanity and policy together; and thinking it against humanity to detain strangers here against their wills; and against policy

[36] Fearing.

that they should return and discover [37] their knowledge of this estate, he took this course: he did ordain that of the strangers that should be permitted to land, as many (at all times) mought depart as would; but as many as would stay should have very good conditions, and means to live from the state. Wherein he saw so far, that now in so many ages since the prohibition, we have memory not of one ship that ever returned, and but of thirteen persons only, at several times, that chose to return in our bottoms. What those few that returned may have reported abroad I know not. But you must think whatsoever they have said could be taken where they came but for a dream. Now for our travelling from hence into parts abroad, our lawgiver thought fit altogether to restrain it. So is it not in China. For the Chinese sail where they will or can; which showeth that their law of keeping out strangers is a law of pusillanimity and fear. But this restraint of ours hath one only exception, which is admirable; preserving the good which cometh by communicating with strangers, and avoiding the hurt: and I will now open it to you. And here I shall seem a little to digress, but you will by and by find it pertinent.

"Ye shall understand, my dear friends, that amongst the excellent acts of that king, one above all hath the pre-eminence. It was the erection and institution of an order, or society, which we call Solomon's House; the

[37] Reveal.

taken for their relief, and competent means to live. There, if any be subject to vice or take ill courses, they are reproved and censured. So likewise direction is given touching marriages, and the courses of life which any of them should take, with divers other the like orders and advices. The Governor assisteth,[49] to the end to put in execution by his public authority the decrees and orders of the Tirsan, if they should be disobeyed; though that seldom needeth, such reverence and obedience they give to the order of nature. The Tirsan doth also then ever choose one man from amongst his sons to live in house with him; who is called ever after the Son of the Vine. The reason will hereafter appear.

On the feast day, the father or Tirsan cometh forth after divine service into a large room where the feast is celebrated; which room hath an half-pace[50] at the upper end. Against the wall, in the middle of the half-pace, is a chair placed for him, with a table and carpet before it. Over the chair is a state[51] made round or oval, and it is of ivy; an ivy somewhat whiter than ours, like the leaf of a silver asp, but more shining; for it is green all winter. And the state is curiously wrought with silver and silk of divers colors, broiding or binding in the ivy; and is ever of the work of some of the daughters of the family, and veiled over at the top, with a fine net of silk and silver. But the substance of it is true ivy; whereof, after it is taken

[49] Attends.   [50] Platform.   [51] Canopy.

down, the friends of the family are desirous to have some leaf or sprig to keep.

The Tirsan cometh forth with all his generation or lineage, the males before him, and the females following him; and if there be a mother from whose body the whole lineage is descended, there is a traverse [52] placed in a loft above, on the right hand of the chair, with a privy door, and a carved window of glass, leaded with gold and blue, where she sitteth, but is not seen. When the Tirsan is come forth, he sitteth down in the chair; and all the lineage place themselves against the wall, both at his back, and upon the return [53] of the half-pace, in order of their years, without difference of sex, and stand upon their feet. When he is set, the room being always full of company, but well kept and without disorder, after some pause there cometh in from the lower end of the room a Taratan (which is as much as an herald), and on either side of him two young lads, whereof one carrieth a scroll of their shining yellow parchment and the other a cluster of grapes of gold, with a long foot or stalk. The herald and children are clothed with mantles of sea-water green satin; but the herald's mantle is streamed with gold and hath a train.

Then the herald with three curtsies, or rather inclinations,[54] cometh up as far as the half-pace, and there first taketh into his hand the scroll. This scroll is the king's

---

[52] Screened compartment.
[53] Sides.
[54] Bows.

charter, containing gift of revenue, and many privileges, exemptions, and points of honor, granted to the father of the family; and it is ever styled and directed. "To such an one, our well-beloved friend and creditor," which is a title proper only to this case. For they say, the king is debtor to no man, but for propagation of his subjects. The seal set to the king's charter is the king's image, embossed or molded in gold; and though such charters be expedited [55] of course, and as of right, yet they are varied by discretion, according to the number and dignity of the family. This charter the herald readeth aloud; and while it is read, the father or Tirsan standeth up, supported by two of his sons, such as he chooseth. Then the herald mounteth the half-pace, and delivereth the charter into his hand; and with that there is an acclamation, by all that are present, in their language, which is thus much, "Happy are the people of Bensalem."

Then the herald taketh into his hand from the other child the cluster of grapes, which is of gold; both the stalk and the grapes. But the grapes are daintily enamelled; and if the males of the family be the greater number, the grapes are enamelled purple, with a little sun set on the top; if the females, then they are enamelled into a greenish yellow, with a crescent on the top. The grapes are in number as many as there are descendants of the family. This golden cluster the herald delivereth also to the Tirsan, who

[55] Granted.

presently delivereth it over to that son that he had formerly chosen to be in house with him; who beareth it before his father, as an ensign of honor, when he goeth in public ever after; and is thereupon called the Son of the Vine.

After this ceremony ended the father or Tirsan retireth; and after some time cometh forth again to dinner, where he sitteth alone under the state as before; and none of his descendants sit with him, of what degree or dignity soever, except he hap to be of Solomon's House. He is served only by his own children, such as are male; who perform unto him all service of the table upon the knee, and the women only stand about him, leaning against the wall. The room below the half-pace hath tables on the sides for the guests that are bidden; who are served with great and comely order; and towards the end of dinner (which in the greatest feasts with them lasteth never above an hour and a half) there is a hymn sung, varied according to the invention of him that composeth it (for they have excellent poesy); but the subject of it is always the praises of Adam, and Noah, and Abraham; whereof the former two peopled the world, and the last was the father of the faithful; concluding ever with a thanksgiving for the nativity of our Saviour, in whose birth the births of all are only blessed.

Dinner being done, the Tirsan retireth again; and having withdrawn himself alone into a place where he maketh some private prayers, he cometh forth the third time to

New Atlantis

give the blessing, with all his descendants, who stand about him as at the first. Then he calleth them forth by one and by one, by name as he pleaseth, though seldom the order of age be inverted. The person that is called (the table being before removed) kneeleth down before the chair, and the father layeth his hand upon his head, or her head, and giveth the blessing in these words: "Son of Bensalem (or daughter of Bensalem), thy father saith it; the man by whom thou hast breath and life speaketh the word; the blessing of the everlasting Father, the Prince of Peace, and the Holy Dove, be upon thee, and make the days of thy prilgrimage good and many." This he saith to every of them; and that done, if there be any of his sons of eminent merit and virtue (so they be not above two), he calleth for them again, and saith, laying his arm over their shoulders, they standing: "Sons, it is well ye are born, give God the praise, and persevere to the end." And withal delivereth to either of them a jewel, made in the figure of an ear of wheat, which they ever after wear in the front of their turban, or hat. This done, they fall to music and dances, and other recreations, after their manner, for the rest of the day. This is the full order of that feast.

By that time six or seven days were spent, I was fallen into strait [56] acquaintance with a merchant of that city, whose name was Joabin. He was a Jew and circumcised;

---

[56] Close.

for they have some few stirps [57] of Jews yet remaining amongst them, whom they leave to their own religion. Which they may the better do, because they are of a far differing disposition from the Jews in other parts. For whereas they hate the name of Christ, and have a secret inbred rancor against the people amongst whom they live, these, contrariwise, give unto our Saviour many high attributes, and love the nation of Bensalem extremely. Surely this man of whom I speak would ever acknowledge that Christ was born of a virgin and that he was more than a man; and he would tell how God made him ruler of the seraphim, which guard his throne; and they call him also the Milken Way, and the Eliah of the Messiah, and many other high names, which though they be inferior to his divine majesty, yet they are far from the language of other Jews.

And for the country of Bensalem, this man would make no end of commending it, being desirous by tradition among the Jews there to have it believed that the people thereof were of the generations of Abraham, by another son, whom they call Nachoran; and that Moses by a secret cabala [58] ordained the laws of Bensalem which they now use; and that when the Messiah should come, and sit in his throne at Jerusalem, the King of Bensalem should sit at his feet, whereas other kings should keep a great distance. But yet setting aside these Jewish dreams, the man

[57] Families. [58] Doctrine.

was a wise man and learned, and of great policy, and excellently seen in the laws and customs of that nation.

Amongst other discourses one day, I told him I was much affected with the relation I had from some of the company of their custom in holding the feast of the family, for that, methought, I had never heard of a solemnity wherein nature did so much preside. And because propagation of families proceedeth from the nuptial copulation, I desired to know of him what laws and customs they had concerning marriage, and whether they kept marriage well, and whether they were tied to one wife. For that where population is so much affected,[59] and such as with them it seemed to be, there is commonly permission of plurality of wives.

To this he said: "You have reason for to commend that excellent institution of the feast of the family; and indeed we have experience that those families that are partakers of the blessings of that feast do flourish and prosper ever after in an extraordinary manner. But hear me now, and I will tell you what I know. You shall understand that there is not under the heavens so chaste a nation as this of Bensalem, nor so free from all pollution or foulness. It is the virgin of the world. I remember I have read in one of your European books of an holy hermit amongst you that desired to see the Spirit of Fornication, and there appeared to him a little foul ugly Aethiop. But if he had

[59] Desired.

desired to see the Spirit of Chastity of Bensalem, it would have appeared to him in the likeness of a fair beautiful Cherubin. For there is nothing amongst mortal men more fair and admirable than the chaste minds of this people. Know therefore that with them there are no stews, no dissolute houses, no courtesans, nor any thing of that kind. Nay they wonder (with detestation) at you in Europe, which permit such things. They say ye have put marriage out of office, for marriage is ordained a remedy for unlawful concupiscence, and natural concupiscence seemeth as a spur to marriage. But when men have at hand a remedy more agreeable to their corrupt will, marriage is almost expulsed. And therefore there are with you seen infinite men that marry not, but chuse rather a libertine and impure single life than to be yoked in marriage; and many that do marry, marry late, when the prime and strength of their years is past. And when they do marry, what is marriage to them but a very bargain, wherein is sought alliance or portion [60] or reputation, with some desire (almost indifferent) of issue, and not the faithful nuptial union of man and wife, that was first instituted. Neither is it possible that those that have cast away so basely so much of their strength should greatly esteem children (being of the same matter) as chaste men do. So likewise during marriage is the case much amended, as it ought to be if those things were tolerated only for neces-

[60] Dowry.

sity? No, but they remain still as a very affront to marriage. The haunting of those dissolute places or resort to courtesans are no more punished in married men than in bachelors. And the depraved custom of change, and the delight in meretricious embracements (where sin is turned into art) maketh marriage a dull thing, and a kind of imposition or tax. They hear you defend these things, as done to avoid greater evils, as advoutries,[61] deflowering of virgins, unnatural lust, and the like. But they say this is a preposterous wisdom, and they call it *Lot's offer*, who to save his guests from abusing, offered his daughters; nay, they say farther that there is little gained in this, for that the same vices and appetites do still remain and abound, unlawful lust being like a furnace, that if you stop the flames altogether, it will quench, but if you give it any vent, it will rage. As for masculine love, they have no touch of it, and yet there are not so faithful and inviolate friendships in the world again as are there; and to speak generally (as I said before) I have not read of any such chastity in any people as theirs. And their usual saying is, *That whosoever is unchaste cannot reverence himself;* and they say, *That the reverence of a man's self is, next religion, the chiefest bridle of all vices.*"

And when he had said this the good Jew paused a little; whereupon I, far more willing to hear him speak on than to speak myself, yet thinking it decent that upon his pause

[61] Adulteries.

of speech I should not be altogether silent, said only this; that I would say to him, as the widow of Sarepta said to Elias,[62] that he was come to bring to memory our sins; and that I confess the righteousness of Bensalem was greater than the righteousness of Europe. At which speech he bowed his head, and went on this manner.

"They have also many wise and excellent laws touching marriage. They allow no polygamy. They have ordained that none do intermarry, or contract, until a month be past from their first interview. Marriage without consent of parents they do not make void, but they mulct[63] it in the inheritors; for the children of such marriages are not admitted to inherit above a third part of their parents' inheritance."

And as we were thus in conference, there came one that seemed to be a messenger, in a rich huke,[64] that spake with the Jew; whereupon he turned to me, and said, "You will pardon me, for I am commanded away in haste." The next morning he came to me again, joyful as it seemed, and said, "There is word come to the Governor of the city, that one of the fathers of Solomon's House will be here this day seven-night; we have seen none of them this dozen years. His coming is in state; but the cause of his coming is secret. I will provide you and your fellows of a good standing[65] to see his entry." I thanked him, and told him I was most glad of the news.

[62] Elijah.
[63] Punish by a fine.
[64] A kind of cape with a hood.
[65] Standing place.

The day being come he made his entry. He was a man of middle stature and age, comely of person, and had an aspect as if he pitied men. He was clothed in a robe of fine black cloth, with wide sleeves, and a cape: his under garment was of excellent white linen down to the foot, girt with a girdle of the same; and a sindon or tippet of the same about his neck. He had gloves that were curious, and set with stone; and shoes of peach-colored velvet. His neck was bare to the shoulders. His hat was like a helmet, or Spanish montero;[66] and his locks curled below it decently: they were of color brown. His beard was cut round and of the same color with his hair, somewhat lighter. He was carried in a rich chariot, without wheels, litter-wise, with two horses at either end, richly trapped in blue velvet embroidered; and two footmen on each side in the like attire. The chariot was all of cedar, gilt, and adorned with crystal; save that the fore-end had panels of sapphires, set in borders of gold, and the hinder-end the like of emeralds of the Peru color. There was also a sun of gold, radiant upon the top, in the midst; and on the top before, a small cherub of gold, with wings displayed. The chariot was covered with cloth of gold tissued upon blue. He had before him fifty attendants, young men all, in white satin loose coats to the midleg; and stockings of white silk, and shoes of blue velvet; and hats of blue velvet with fine plumes of divers colors set round like hat-bands.

[66] A hunter's cap with a flap.

Next before the chariot went two men, bare-headed, in linen garments down to the foot, girt, and shoes of blue velvet, who carried the one a crosier, the other a pastoral staff like a sheep-hook: neither of them of metal, but the crosier of balmwood, the pastoral staff of cedar. Horsemen he had none, neither before nor behind his chariot: as it seemeth, to avoid all tumult and trouble. Behind his chariot went all the officers and principals of the companies [67] of the city. He sat alone, upon cushions, of a kind of excellent plush, blue; and under his foot curious carpets of silk or divers colors, like the Persian, but far finer. He held up his bare hand, as he went, as blessing the people, but in silence. The street was wonderfully well kept; so that there was never any army had their men stand in better battle-array than the people stood. The windows likewise were not crowded, but every one stood in them, as if they had been placed.

When the show was passed, the Jew said to me, "I shall not be able to attend you as I would, in regard of some charge the city hath laid upon me for the entertaining of this great person." Three days after the Jew came to me again, and said, "Ye are happy men; for the father of Solomon's House taketh knowledge of your being here, and commanded me to tell you that he will admit all your company to his presence, and have private conference with one of you that ye shall choose; and for this hath ap-

[67] Guilds.

pointed the next day after tomorrow. And because he meaneth to give you his blessing, he hath appointed it in the forenoon."

We came at our day and hour, and I was chosen by my fellows for the private access. We found him in a fair chamber, richly hanged,[68] and carpeted under foot without any degrees to the state.[69] He was set upon a low throne richly adorned, and a rich cloth of state over his head, of blue satin embroidered. He was alone, save that he had two pages of honor, on either hand one, finely attired in white. His under garments were the like that we saw him wear in the chariot; but instead of his gown, he had on him a mantle with a cape, of the same fine black, fastened about him. When we came in, as we were taught, we bowed low at our first entrance; and when we were come near his chair, he stood up, holding forth his hand ungloved, and in posture of blessing; and we every one of us stooped down, and kissed the hem of his tippet. That done, the rest departed, and I remained. Then he warned the pages forth of the room, and caused me to sit down beside him, and spake to me thus in the Spanish tongue:

"God bless thee, my son; I will give thee the greatest jewel I have. For I will impart unto thee, for the love of God and men, a relation of the true state of Solomon's House. Son, to make you know the true state of Solomon's House, I will keep this order. First, I will set forth unto

[68] Hung with tapestries.   [69] Steps to the canopy.

you the end of our foundation. Secondly, the preparations and instruments we have for our works. Thirdly, the several employments and functions whereto our fellows are assigned. And fourthly, the ordinances and rites which we observe.

"The end of our foundation is the knowledge of causes, and secret motions of things; and the enlarging of the bounds of human empire, to the effecting of all things possible.

"The preparations and instruments are these. We have large and deep caves of several depths; the deepest are sunk six hundred fathoms; and some of them are digged and made under great hills and mountains; so that if you reckon together the depth of the hill, and the depth of the cave, they are, some of them, above three miles deep. For we find that the depth of a hill, and the depth of a cave from the flat, is the same thing; both remote alike from the sun and heaven's beams, and from the open air. These caves we call the lower region, and we use them for all coagulations, indurations, refrigerations, and conservations of bodies.[70] We use them likewise for the imitation of natural mines, and the producing also of new artificial metals, by compositions and materials which we use, and lay there for many years. We use them also sometimes (which may seem strange) for curing of some diseases and for prolongation of life in some hermits that

[70] Thickening, hardening, chilling, and preserving, for scientific research.

New Atlantis

choose to live there, well accommodated of all things necessary, and indeed live very long; by whom also we learn many things.

"We have burials [71] in several earths, where we put divers [72] cements, as the Chinese do their porcelain. But we have them in greater variety, and some of them more fine. We also have great variety of composts and soils, for the making of the earth fruitful.

"We have high towers, the highest about half a mile in height, and some of them likewise set upon high mountains, so that the vantage of the hill, with the tower, is in the highest of them three miles at least. And these places we call the upper region, accounting the air between the high places and the low as a middle region. We use these towers, according to their several heights and situations, for insulation, refrigeration, conservation, and for the view of divers meteors [73]—as winds, rain, snow, hail; and some of the fiery meteors also. And upon them, in some places, are dwellings of hermits, whom we visit sometimes, and instruct what to observe.

"We have great lakes, both salt and fresh, whereof we have use for the fish and fowl. We use them also for burials of some natural bodies, for we find a difference in things buried in earth, or in air below the earth, and things buried in water. We have also pools, of which some do strain fresh water out of salt, and others by art do turn

[71] Burial places.
[72] Various.
[73] Phenomena of weather.

fresh water into salt. We have also some rocks in the midst of the sea, and some bays upon the shore for some works, wherein is required the air and vapor of the sea. We have likewise violent streams and cataracts, which serve us for many motions; and likewise engines for multiplying and enforcing [74] of winds to set also on divers motions.

"We have also a number of artificial wells and fountains, made in imitation of the natural sources and baths, as tincted upon vitriol, sulphur, steel, brass, lead, niter, and other minerals; and again, we have little wells for infusions of many things, where the waters take the virtue quicker and better than in vessels or basins. And amongst them we have a water which we call Water of Paradise, being by that we do to it made very sovereign for health and prolongation of life.

"We have also great and spacious houses, where we imitate and demonstrate meteors—as snow, hail, rain, some artificial rains of bodies, and not of water, thunders, lightnings; also generations of bodies in air—as frogs, flies, and divers others.

"We have also certain chambers, which we call chambers of health, where we qualify the air as we think good and proper for the cure of divers diseases, and preservation of health.

"We have also fair and large baths, of several mixtures, for the cure of diseases and the restoring of man's body

[74] Reinforcing.

from arefaction;[75] and others for the confirming of it in strength of sinews, vital parts, and the very juice and substance of the body.

"We have also large and various orchards and gardens, wherein we do not so much respect beauty as variety of ground and soil, proper for divers trees and herbs, and some very spacious, where trees and berries are set, whereof we make divers kinds of drinks, besides the vineyards. In these we practice likewise all conclusions[76] of grafting and inoculating, as well of wild-trees as fruit-trees, which produceth many effects. And we make by art, in the same orchards and gardens, trees and flowers to come earlier or later than their seasons, and to come up and bear more speedily than by their natural course they do. We make them also by art greater much than their nature; and their fruit greater and sweeter, and of differing taste, smell, color, and figure, from their nature. And many of them we so order as they become of medicinal use.

"We have also means to make divers plants rise by mixtures of earths, without seeds, and likewise to make divers new plants, differing from the vulgar, and to make one tree or plant turn into another.

"We have also parks and enclosures of all sorts of beasts and birds; which we use not only for view or rareness, but likewise for dissections and trials, that thereby we may

[75] Drying up. [76] Experiments.

take light what may be wrought upon the body of man. Wherein we find many strange effects: as continuing life in them, though divers parts, which you account vital, be perished and taken forth; resuscitating of some that seem dead in appearance, and the like. We try also all poisons, and other medicines upon them, as well of chirurgery as physic.[77] By art likewise we make them greater or taller than their kind is, and contrariwise dwarf them and stay their growth; we make them more fruitful and bearing than their kind is, and contrariwise barren and not generative. Also we make them differ in color, shape, activity, many ways. We find means to make commixtures and copulations of divers kinds, which have produced many new kinds, and them not barren, as the general opinion is. We make a number of kinds, of serpents, worms, flies, fishes, of putrefaction,[78] whereof some are advanced (in effect) to be perfect creatures, like beasts or birds, and have sexes, and do propagate. Neither do we this by chance, but we know beforehand of what matter and commixture, what kind of those creatures will arise.

"We have also particular pools where we make trials upon fishes, as we have said before of beasts and birds.

"We have also places for breed and generation of those kinds of worms and flies which are of special use; such as are with you your silkworms and bees.

"I will not hold you long with recounting of our brew-

[77] Of surgery as of medicine.   [78] Rotting matter.

houses, bake-houses, and kitchens, where are made divers drinks, breads, and meats, rare and of special effects. Wines we have of grapes, and drinks of other juice, of fruits, of grains, and of roots, and of mixtures with honey, sugar, manna, and fruits dried and decocted;[79] also of the tears or woundings of trees, and of the pulp of canes. And these drinks are of several ages, some to the age or last[80] of forty years. We have drinks also brewed with several herbs, and roots and spices; yea, with several fleshes and white-meats; whereof some of the drinks are such as they are in effect meat and drink both, so that divers, especially in age, do desire to live with them with little or no meat or bread. And above all we strive to have drinks of extreme thin parts,[81] to insinuate into the body, and yet without all biting, sharpness, or fretting; insomuch as some of them, put upon the back of your hand, will with a little stay pass through to the palm, and taste yet mild to the mouth. We have also waters which we ripen in that fashion, as they become nourishing, so that they are indeed excellent drinks, and many will use no other. Bread we have of several grains, roots, and kernels; yea, and some of flesh, and fish, dried; with divers kinds of leavenings and seasonings; so that some do extremely move appetites, some do nourish so, as divers do live of them, without any other meat, who live very long. So for meats, we have some of them so beaten, and made tender, and mortified,

[79] Condensed.   [80] Duration.   [81] Properties.

yet without all corrupting, as a weak heat of the stomach will turn them into good chilus,[82] as well as a strong heat would meat otherwise prepared. We have some meats also, and breads, and drinks which taken by men enable them to fast long after; and some other that used make the very flesh of men's bodies sensibly more hard and tough, and their strength far greater than otherwise it would be.

"We have dispensatories or shops of medicines; wherein you may easily think, if we have such variety of plants and living creatures, more than you have in Europe (for we know what you have), the simples,[83] drugs and ingredients of medicines, must likewise be in so much the greater variety. We have them likewise of divers ages, and long fermentations. And for their preparations, we have not only all manner of exquisite distillations and separations, and especially by gentle heats, and percolations through divers strainers, yea, and substances; but also exact forms of composition, whereby they incorporate almost as they were natural simples.

"We have also divers mechanical arts which you have not; and stuffs made by them, as papers, linen, silks, tissues, dainty works of feathers of wonderful luster, excellent dyes, and many others: and shops likewise, as well for such as are not brought into vulgar use amongst us, as for those that are. For you must know, that of the things be-

---

[82] Chyle.   [83] Herbs.

fore recited, many of them are grown into use throughout the kingdom, but yet, if they did flow from our invention, we have of them also for patterns and principles.

"We have also furnaces of great diversities, and that keep great diversity of heats: fierce and quick, strong and constant, soft and mild; blown, quiet, dry, moist, and the like. But above all we have heats, in imitation of the sun's and heavenly bodies' heats, that pass divers inequalities, and (as it were) orbs, progresses, and returns, whereby we produce admirable effects. Besides, we have heats of dungs, and of bellies and maws of living creatures and of their bloods and bodies, and of hays and herbs laid up moist, of lime unquenched, and such like. Instruments also which generate heat only by motion. And farther, places for strong insulations; and again, places under the earth, which by nature or art yield heat. These divers heats we use as the nature of the operation which we intend requireth.

"We have also perspective houses, where we make demonstrations of all lights and radiations, and of all colors; and out of things uncolored and transparent, we can represent unto you all several colors, not in rainbows (as it is in gems and prisms), but of themselves single. We represent also all multiplications of light, which we carry to great distance, and make so sharp, as to discern small points and lines. Also all colorations of light; all delusions and deceits of the sight, in figures, magnitudes, motions, colors; all demonstrations of shadows. We find also divers means yet unknown to you of producing of light, originally from divers bodies. We procure means of seeing objects afar off, as in the heaven and remote places; and represent things near as afar off, and things afar off as near; making feigned distances. We have also helps for the sight, far above spectacles and glasses in use. We have also glasses and means to see small and minute bodies perfectly and distinctly; as the shapes and colors of small flies and worms, grains, and flaws in gems which cannot otherwise be seen, observations in urine and blood not otherwise to be seen. We make artificial rainbows, halos, and circles about light. We represent also all manner of reflections, refractions, and multiplications of visual beams of objects.

"We have also precious stones of all kinds, many of them of great beauty and to you unknown; crystals likewise, and glasses of divers kinds; and amongst them some of metals vitrificated,[84] and other materials, besides those of which you make glass. Also a number of fossils and imperfect minerals, which you have not. Likewise loadstones of prodigious virtue: and other rare stones, both natural and artificial.

"We have also sound-houses, where we practice and demonstrate all sounds and their generation. We have harmonies which you have not, of quarter-sounds and lesser slides of sounds. Divers instruments of music likewise to

[84] Turned into glass.

you unknown, some sweeter than any you have; together with bells and rings that are dainty and sweet. We represent small sounds as great and deep; likewise great sounds, extenuate [85] and sharp; we make divers tremblings and warblings of sounds, which in their original are entire. We represent and imitate all articulate sounds and letters, and the voices and notes of beasts and birds. We have certain helps which set to the ear do further the hearing greatly. We have also divers strange and artificial echoes, reflecting the voice many times, and as it were tossing it; and some that give back the voice louder than it came, some shriller and some deeper: yea, some rendering the voice, differing in the letters or articulate sound from that they receive. We have also means to convey sounds in trunks [86] and pipes, in strange lines and distances.

"We have also perfume-houses, wherewith we join also practices of taste. We multiply smells, which may seem strange: we imitate smells, making all smells to breathe out of other mixtures than those that give them. We make divers imitations of taste likewise, so that they will deceive any man's taste. And in this house we contain also a confiture-house, where we make all sweetmeats, dry and moist, and divers pleasant wines, milks, broths, and salads, far in greater variety than you have.

"We have also engine-houses, where are prepared engines and instruments for all sorts of motions. There we

---

[85] Thin.   [86] Tubes.

imitate and practice to make swifter motions than any you have, either out of your muskets or any engine that you have; and to make them and multiply them more easily and with small force, by wheels and other means, and to make them stronger and more violent than yours are, exceeding your greatest cannons and basilisks.[87] We represent also ordnance and instruments of war and engines of all kinds; and likewise new mixtures and compositions of gunpowder, wildfires burning in water and unquenchable, also fireworks of all variety, both for pleasure and use. We imitate also flights of birds; we have some degrees [88] of flying in the air. We have ships and boats for going under water and brooking of seas, also swimming-girdles and supporters. We have divers curious clocks, and other like motions of return, and some perpetual motions. We imitate also motions of living creatures by images of men, beasts, birds, fishes, and serpents; we have also a great number of other various motions, strange for equality, fineness, and subtlety.

"We have also a mathematical-house, where are represented all instruments, as well of geometry as astronomy, exquisitely made.

"We have also houses of deceits of the senses, where we represent all manner of feats of juggling, false apparitions, impostures and illusions, and their fallacies. And surely you will easily believe that we, that have so many

[87] A long cannon.   [88] Of success.

things truly natural which induce admiration, could in a world of particulars deceive the senses if we would disguise those things, and labor to make them seem more miraculous. But we do hate all impostures and lies, insomuch as we have severely forbidden it to all our fellows, under pain of ignominy and fines, that they do not show any natural work or thing adorned or swelling, but only pure as it is, and without all affectation of strangeness.

"These are, my son, the riches of Solomon's House.

"For the several employments and offices of our fellows, we have twelve that sail into foreign countries under the names of other nations (for our own we conceal), who bring us the books and abstracts, and patterns of experiments of all other parts. These we call Merchants of Light.

"We have three that collect the experiments which are in all books. These we call Depredators.

"We have three that collect the experiments of all mechanical arts, and also of liberal sciences, and also of practices which are not brought into arts. These we call Mystery-men.

"We have three that try new experiments, such as themselves think good. These we call Pioneers or Miners.

"We have three that draw the experiments of the former four into titles and tables, to give the better light for the drawing of observations and axioms out of them. These we call Compilers.

"We have three that bend themselves, looking into the

experiments of their fellows, and cast about how to draw out of them things of use and practice for man's life and knowledge, as well for works as for plain demonstration of causes, means of natural divinations, and the easy and clear discovery of the virtues and parts of bodies. These we call Dowry-men or Benefactors.

"Then after divers meetings and consults of our whole number to consider of the former labors and collections, we have three that take care out of them to direct new experiments, of a higher light, more penetrating into nature than the former. These we call Lamps.

"We have three others that do execute the experiments so directed, and report them. These we call Inoculators.

"Lastly, we have three that raise the former discoveries by experiments into greater observations, axioms, and aphorisms. These we call Interpreters of Nature.

"We have also, as you must think, novices and apprentices, that the succession of the former employed men do not fail; besides a great number of servants and attendants, men and women. And this we do also: we have consultations, which of the inventions and experiences which we have discovered shall be published, and which not; and take all an oath of secrecy for the concealing of those which we think fit to keep secret, though some of those we do reveal sometimes to the state, and some not.

"For our ordinances and rites, we have two very long and fair galleries; in one of these we place patterns and samples of all manner of the more rare and excellent inventions; in the other we place the statues of all principal inventors. There we have the statue of your Columbus, that discovered the West Indies; also the inventor of ships; your monk that was the inventor of ordnance and of gunpowder;[89] the inventor of music; the inventor of letters; the inventor of printing; the inventor of observations of astronomy; the inventor of works in metal; the inventor of glass; the inventor of silk of the worm; the inventor of wine; the inventor of corn and bread; the inventor of sugars; and all these by more certain tradition than you have. Then we have divers inventors of our own, of excellent works, which since you have not seen, it were too long to make descriptions of them; and besides, in the right understanding of those descriptions you might easily err. For upon every invention of value we erect a statue to the inventor, and give him a liberal and honorable reward. These statues are some of brass, some of marble and touchstone, some of cedar and other special woods gilt and adorned; some of iron, some of silver, some of gold.

"We have certain hymns and services, which we say daily, of laud and thanks to God for his marvellous works. And forms of prayer, imploring his aid and blessing for the illumination of our labors, and the turning of them into good and holy uses.

"Lastly, we have circuits or visits of divers principal cities of the kingdom; where, as it cometh to pass, we

[89] Roger Bacon.

do publish such new profitable inventions as we think good. And we do also declare natural divinations [90] of diseases, plagues, swarms of hurtful creatures, scarcity, tempests, earthquakes, great inundations, comets, temperature of the year, and divers other things; and we give counsel thereupon, what the people shall do for the prevention and remedy of them."

And when he had said this he stood up; and I, as I had been taught, knelt down; and he laid his right hand upon my head, and said, "God bless thee, my son, and God bless this relation which I have made. I give thee leave to publish it, for the good of other nations; for we here are in God's bosom, a land unknown." And so he left me; having assigned a value of about two thousand ducats for a bounty to me and my fellows. For they give great largesses, where they come, upon all occasions.

[The rest was not perfected]

[90] **Forecast**ing by natural observation.

noblest foundation, as we think, that ever was upon the earth, and the lantern of this kingdom. It is dedicated to the study of the works and creatures of God. Some think it beareth the founder's name a little corrupted, as if it should be Solamona's House. But the records write it as it is spoken. So as I take it to be denominate of the king of the Hebrews, which is famous with you, and no stranger to us; for we have some parts of his works which with you are lost; namely, that Natural History which he wrote of all plants, from the cedar of Libanus [38] to the moss that groweth out of the wall; and of all things that have life and motion. This maketh me think that our king finding himself to symbolize,[39] in many things, with that king of the Hebrews (which lived many years before him) honored him with the title of this foundation. And I am the rather induced to be of this opinion, for that I find in ancient records this order or society is sometimes called Solomon's House, and sometimes the College of the Six Days' Works; whereby I am satisfied that our excellent king had learned from the Hebrews that God had created the world, and all that therein is, within six days: and therefore he instituting that house, for the finding out of the true nature of all things (whereby God mought have the more glory in the workmanship of them, and men the more fruit in the use of them), did give it also that second name.

[38] Lebanon. [39] Agree.

"But now to come to our present purpose. When the king had forbidden to all his people navigation into any part that was not under his crown, he made nevertheless this ordinance: that every twelve years there should be set forth out of this kingdom two ships, appointed to several voyages; that in either of these ships there should be a mission of three of the fellows or brethren of Solomon's House, whose errand was only to give us knowledge of the affairs and state of those countries to which they were designed;[40] and especially of the sciences, arts, manufactures, and inventions of all the world; and withal to bring unto us books, instruments, and patterns in every kind: that the ships, after they had landed the brethren, should return; and that the brethren should stay abroad till the new mission. These ships are not otherwise fraught than with store of victuals, and good quantity of treasure to remain with the brethren, for the buying of such things and rewarding of such persons as they should think fit. Now for me to tell you how the vulgar[41] sort of mariners are contained[42] from being discovered at land, and how they that must be put on shore for any time, color[43] themselves under the names of other nations, and to what places these voyages have been designed, and what places of rendezvous are appointed for the new missions, and the like circumstances of the practice, I may not do it, neither is it much to your desire. But thus you see we

[40] Assigned.
[42] Kept.
[41] Common.
[43] Disguise.

maintain a trade, not for gold, silver, or jewels, nor for silks, nor for spices, nor any other commodity of matter; but only for God's first creature, which was light: to have light, I say, of the growth of [44] all parts of the world."

And when he had said this he was silent, and so were we all; for indeed we were all astonished to hear so strange things so probably told. And he perceiving that we were willing to say somewhat, but had it not ready, in great courtesy took us off, and descended to ask us questions of our voyage and fortunes, and in the end concluded that we mought do well to think with ourselves, what time of stay we would demand of the state, and bade us not to scant [45] ourselves; for he would procure such time as we desired. Whereupon we all rose up and presented ourselves to kiss the skirt of his tippet, but he would not suffer us, and so took his leave. But when it came once amongst our people that the state used [46] to offer conditions to strangers that would stay, we had work enough to get any of our men to look to our ship, and to keep them from going presently to the Governor, to crave conditions; but with much ado we restrained them, till we mought agree what course to take.

We took ourselves now for free men, seeing there was no danger of our utter perdition, and lived most joyfully, going abroad and seeing what was to be seen in the city

---

[44] Of the kind found in.
[45] Stint.
[46] Was accustomed.

and places adjacent, within our tedder;[47] and obtaining acquaintance with many of the city, not of the meanest quality, at whose hands we found such humanity, and such a freedom and desire to take strangers, as it were, into their bosom, as was enough to make us forget all that was dear to us in our own countries; and continually we met with many things, right worthy of observation and relation; as indeed, if there be a mirror in the world worthy to hold men's eyes, it is that country.

One day there were two of our company bidden to a feast of the family, as they call it; a most natural, pious, and reverend custom it is, showing that nation to be compounded of all goodness. This is the manner of it. It is granted to any man that shall live to see thirty persons descended of his body, alive together, and all above three years old, to make this feast, which is done at the cost of the state. The father of the family, whom they call the Tirsan, two days before the feast taketh to him three of such friends as he liketh to choose, and is assisted also by the Governor of the city or place where the feast is celebrated, and all the persons of the family of both sexes are summoned to attend him. These two days the Tirsan sitteth in consultation, concerning the good estate of the family. There, if there be any discord or suits between any of the family, they are compounded[48] and appeased. There, if any of the family be distressed or decayed, order is

[47] Limits; tether. [48] Settled.

taken for their relief, and competent means to live. There, if any be subject to vice or take ill courses, they are reproved and censured. So likewise direction is given touching marriages, and the courses of life which any of them should take, with divers other the like orders and advices. The Governor assisteth,[49] to the end to put in execution by his public authority the decrees and orders of the Tirsan, if they should be disobeyed; though that seldom needeth, such reverence and obedience they give to the order of nature. The Tirsan doth also then ever choose one man from amongst his sons to live in house with him; who is called ever after the Son of the Vine. The reason will hereafter appear.

On the feast day, the father or Tirsan cometh forth after divine service into a large room where the feast is celebrated; which room hath an half-pace [50] at the upper end. Against the wall, in the middle of the half-pace, is a chair placed for him, with a table and carpet before it. Over the chair is a state [51] made round or oval, and it is of ivy; an ivy somewhat whiter than ours, like the leaf of a silver asp, but more shining; for it is green all winter. And the state is curiously wrought with silver and silk of divers colors, broiding or binding in the ivy; and is ever of the work of some of the daughters of the family, and veiled over at the top, with a fine net of silk and silver. But the substance of it is true ivy; whereof, after it is taken

[49] Attends.   [50] Platform.   [51] Canopy.

down, the friends of the family are desirous to have some leaf or sprig to keep.

The Tirsan cometh forth with all his generation or lineage, the males before him, and the females following him; and if there be a mother from whose body the whole lineage is descended, there is a traverse [52] placed in a loft above, on the right hand of the chair, with a privy door, and a carved window of glass, leaded with gold and blue, where she sitteth, but is not seen. When the Tirsan is come forth, he sitteth down in the chair; and all the lineage place themselves against the wall, both at his back, and upon the return [53] of the half-pace, in order of their years, without difference of sex, and stand upon their feet. When he is set, the room being always full of company, but well kept and without disorder, after some pause there cometh in from the lower end of the room a Taratan (which is as much as an herald), and on either side of him two young lads, whereof one carrieth a scroll of their shining yellow parchment and the other a cluster of grapes of gold, with a long foot or stalk. The herald and children are clothed with mantles of sea-water green satin; but the herald's mantle is streamed with gold and hath a train.

Then the herald with three curtsies, or rather inclinations,[54] cometh up as far as the half-pace, and there first taketh into his hand the scroll. This scroll is the king's

[52] Screened compartment.
[53] Sides.   [54] Bows.

charter, containing gift of revenue, and many privileges, exemptions, and points of honor, granted to the father of the family; and it is ever styled and directed. "To such an one, our well-beloved friend and creditor," which is a title proper only to this case. For they say, the king is debtor to no man, but for propagation of his subjects. The seal set to the king's charter is the king's image, embossed or molded in gold; and though such charters be expedited[55] of course, and as of right, yet they are varied by discretion, according to the number and dignity of the family. This charter the herald readeth aloud; and while it is read, the father or Tirsan standeth up, supported by two of his sons, such as he chooseth. Then the herald mounteth the half-pace, and delivereth the charter into his hand; and with that there is an acclamation, by all that are present, in their language, which is thus much, "Happy are the people of Bensalem."

Then the herald taketh into his hand from the other child the cluster of grapes, which is of gold; both the stalk and the grapes. But the grapes are daintily enamelled; and if the males of the family be the greater number, the grapes are enamelled purple, with a little sun set on the top; if the females, then they are enamelled into a greenish yellow, with a crescent on the top. The grapes are in number as many as there are descendants of the family. This golden cluster the herald delivereth also to the Tirsan, who

[55] Granted.

presently delivereth it over to that son that he had formerly chosen to be in house with him; who beareth it before his father, as an ensign of honor, when he goeth in public ever after; and is thereupon called the Son of the Vine.

After this ceremony ended the father or Tirsan retireth; and after some time cometh forth again to dinner, where he sitteth alone under the state as before; and none of his descendants sit with him, of what degree or dignity soever, except he hap to be of Solomon's House. He is served only by his own children, such as are male; who perform unto him all service of the table upon the knee, and the women only stand about him, leaning against the wall. The room below the half-pace hath tables on the sides for the guests that are bidden; who are served with great and comely order; and towards the end of dinner (which in the greatest feasts with them lasteth never above an hour and a half) there is a hymn sung, varied according to the invention of him that composeth it (for they have excellent poesy); but the subject of it is always the praises of Adam, and Noah, and Abraham; whereof the former two peopled the world, and the last was the father of the faithful; concluding ever with a thanksgiving for the nativity of our Saviour, in whose birth the births of all are only blessed.

Dinner being done, the Tirsan retireth again; and having withdrawn himself alone into a place where he maketh some private prayers, he cometh forth the third time to give the blessing, with all his descendants, who stand about him as at the first. Then he calleth them forth by one and by one, by name as he pleaseth, though seldom the order of age be inverted. The person that is called (the table being before removed) kneeleth down before the chair, and the father layeth his hand upon his head, or her head, and giveth the blessing in these words: "Son of Bensalem (or daughter of Bensalem), thy father saith it; the man by whom thou hast breath and life speaketh the word; the blessing of the everlasting Father, the Prince of Peace, and the Holy Dove, be upon thee, and make the days of thy prilgrimage good and many." This he saith to every of them; and that done, if there be any of his sons of eminent merit and virtue (so they be not above two), he calleth for them again, and saith, laying his arm over their shoulders, they standing: "Sons, it is well ye are born, give God the praise, and persevere to the end." And withal delivereth to either of them a jewel, made in the figure of an ear of wheat, which they ever after wear in the front of their turban, or hat. This done, they fall to music and dances, and other recreations, after their manner, for the rest of the day. This is the full order of that feast.

By that time six or seven days were spent, I was fallen into strait [56] acquaintance with a merchant of that city, whose name was Joabin. He was a Jew and circumcised;

[56] Close.

for they have some few stirps [57] of Jews yet remaining amongst them, whom they leave to their own religion. Which they may the better do, because they are of a far differing disposition from the Jews in other parts. For whereas they hate the name of Christ, and have a secret inbred rancor against the people amongst whom they live, these, contrariwise, give unto our Saviour many high attributes, and love the nation of Bensalem extremely. Surely this man of whom I speak would ever acknowledge that Christ was born of a virgin and that he was more than a man; and he would tell how God made him ruler of the seraphim, which guard his throne; and they call him also the Milken Way, and the Eliah of the Messiah, and many other high names, which though they be inferior to his divine majesty, yet they are far from the language of other Jews.

And for the country of Bensalem, this man would make no end of commending it, being desirous by tradition among the Jews there to have it believed that the people thereof were of the generations of Abraham, by another son, whom they call Nachoran; and that Moses by a secret cabala [58] ordained the laws of Bensalem which they now use; and that when the Messiah should come, and sit in his throne at Jerusalem, the King of Bensalem should sit at his feet, whereas other kings should keep a great distance. But yet setting aside these Jewish dreams, the man

[57] Families.   [58] Doctrine.

was a wise man and learned, and of great policy, and excellently seen in the laws and customs of that nation.

Amongst other discourses one day, I told him I was much affected with the relation I had from some of the company of their custom in holding the feast of the family, for that, methought, I had never heard of a solemnity wherein nature did so much preside. And because propagation of families proceedeth from the nuptial copulation, I desired to know of him what laws and customs they had concerning marriage, and whether they kept marriage well, and whether they were tied to one wife. For that where population is so much affected,[59] and such as with them it seemed to be, there is commonly permission of plurality of wives.

To this he said: "You have reason for to commend that excellent institution of the feast of the family; and indeed we have experience that those families that are partakers of the blessings of that feast do flourish and prosper ever after in an extraordinary manner. But hear me now, and I will tell you what I know. You shall understand that there is not under the heavens so chaste a nation as this of Bensalem, nor so free from all pollution or foulness. It is the virgin of the world. I remember I have read in one of your European books of an holy hermit amongst you that desired to see the Spirit of Fornication, and there appeared to him a little foul ugly Aethiop. But if he had

[59] Desired.

desired to see the Spirit of Chastity of Bensalem, it would have appeared to him in the likeness of a fair beautiful Cherubin. For there is nothing amongst mortal men more fair and admirable than the chaste minds of this people. Know therefore that with them there are no stews, no dissolute houses, no courtesans, nor any thing of that kind. Nay they wonder (with detestation) at you in Europe, which permit such things. They say ye have put marriage out of office, for marriage is ordained a remedy for unlawful concupiscence, and natural concupiscence seemeth as a spur to marriage. But when men have at hand a remedy more agreeable to their corrupt will, marriage is almost expulsed. And therefore there are with you seen infinite men that marry not, but chuse rather a libertine and impure single life than to be yoked in marriage; and many that do marry, marry late, when the prime and strength of their years is past. And when they do marry, what is marriage to them but a very bargain, wherein is sought alliance or portion [60] or reputation, with some desire (almost indifferent) of issue, and not the faithful nuptial union of man and wife, that was first instituted. Neither is it possible that those that have cast away so basely so much of their strength should greatly esteem children (being of the same matter) as chaste men do. So likewise during marriage is the case much amended, as it ought to be if those things were tolerated only for neces-

[60] Dowry.

sity? No, but they remain still as a very affront to marriage. The haunting of those dissolute places or resort to courtesans are no more punished in married men than in bachelors. And the depraved custom of change, and the delight in meretricious embracements (where sin is turned into art) maketh marriage a dull thing, and a kind of imposition or tax. They hear you defend these things, as done to avoid greater evils, as advoutries,[61] deflowering of virgins, unnatural lust, and the like. But they say this is a preposterous wisdom, and they call it *Lot's offer*, who to save his guests from abusing, offered his daughters; nay, they say farther that there is little gained in this, for that the same vices and appetites do still remain and abound, unlawful lust being like a furnace, that if you stop the flames altogether, it will quench, but if you give it any vent, it will rage. As for masculine love, they have no touch of it, and yet there are not so faithful and inviolate friendships in the world again as are there; and to speak generally (as I said before) I have not read of any such chastity in any people as theirs. And their usual saying is, *That whosoever is unchaste cannot reverence himself;* and they say, *That the reverence of a man's self is, next religion, the chiefest bridle of all vices.*"

And when he had said this the good Jew paused a little; whereupon I, far more willing to hear him speak on than to speak myself, yet thinking it decent that upon his pause

[61] Adulteries.

of speech I should not be altogether silent, said only this; that I would say to him, as the widow of Sarepta said to Elias,[62] that he was come to bring to memory our sins; and that I confess the righteousness of Bensalem was greater than the righteousness of Europe. At which speech he bowed his head, and went on this manner.

"They have also many wise and excellent laws touching marriage. They allow no polygamy. They have ordained that none do intermarry, or contract, until a month be past from their first interview. Marriage without consent of parents they do not make void, but they mulct[63] it in the inheritors; for the children of such marriages are not admitted to inherit above a third part of their parents' inheritance."

And as we were thus in conference, there came one that seemed to be a messenger, in a rich huke,[64] that spake with the Jew; whereupon he turned to me, and said, "You will pardon me, for I am commanded away in haste." The next morning he came to me again, joyful as it seemed, and said, "There is word come to the Governor of the city, that one of the fathers of Solomon's House will be here this day seven-night; we have seen none of them this dozen years. His coming is in state; but the cause of his coming is secret. I will provide you and your fellows of a good standing[65] to see his entry." I thanked him, and told him I was most glad of the news.

[62] Elijah.
[63] Punish by a fine.
[64] A kind of cape with a hood.
[65] Standing place.

The day being come he made his entry. He was a man of middle stature and age, comely of person, and had an aspect as if he pitied men. He was clothed in a robe of fine black cloth, with wide sleeves, and a cape: his under garment was of excellent white linen down to the foot, girt with a girdle of the same; and a sindon or tippet of the same about his neck. He had gloves that were curious, and set with stone; and shoes of peach-colored velvet. His neck was bare to the shoulders. His hat was like a helmet, or Spanish montero;[66] and his locks curled below it decently: they were of color brown. His beard was cut round and of the same color with his hair, somewhat lighter. He was carried in a rich chariot, without wheels, litter-wise, with two horses at either end, richly trapped in blue velvet embroidered; and two footmen on each side in the like attire. The chariot was all of cedar, gilt, and adorned with crystal; save that the fore-end had panels of sapphires, set in borders of gold, and the hinder-end the like of emeralds of the Peru color. There was also a sun of gold, radiant upon the top, in the midst; and on the top before, a small cherub of gold, with wings displayed. The chariot was covered with cloth of gold tissued upon blue. He had before him fifty attendants, young men all, in white satin loose coats to the midleg; and stockings of white silk, and shoes of blue velvet; and hats of blue velvet with fine plumes of divers colors set round like hat-bands.

[66] A hunter's cap with a flap.

Next before the chariot went two men, bare-headed, in linen garments down to the foot, girt, and shoes of blue velvet, who carried the one a crosier, the other a pastoral staff like a sheep-hook: neither of them of metal, but the crosier of balmwood, the pastoral staff of cedar. Horsemen he had none, neither before nor behind his chariot: as it seemeth, to avoid all tumult and trouble. Behind his chariot went all the officers and principals of the companies [67] of the city. He sat alone, upon cushions, of a kind of excellent plush, blue; and under his foot curious carpets of silk or divers colors, like the Persian, but far finer. He held up his bare hand, as he went, as blessing the people, but in silence. The street was wonderfully well kept; so that there was never any army had their men stand in better battle-array than the people stood. The windows likewise were not crowded, but every one stood in them, as if they had been placed.

When the show was passed, the Jew said to me, "I shall not be able to attend you as I would, in regard of some charge the city hath laid upon me for the entertaining of this great person." Three days after the Jew came to me again, and said, "Ye are happy men; for the father of Solomon's House taketh knowledge of your being here, and commanded me to tell you that he will admit all your company to his presence, and have private conference with one of you that ye shall choose; and for this hath ap-

[67] Guilds.

pointed the next day after tomorrow. And because he meaneth to give you his blessing, he hath appointed it in the forenoon."

We came at our day and hour, and I was chosen by my fellows for the private access. We found him in a fair chamber, richly hanged,[68] and carpeted under foot without any degrees to the state.[69] He was set upon a low throne richly adorned, and a rich cloth of state over his head, of blue satin embroidered. He was alone, save that he had two pages of honor, on either hand one, finely attired in white. His under garments were the like that we saw him wear in the chariot; but instead of his gown, he had on him a mantle with a cape, of the same fine black, fastened about him. When we came in, as we were taught, we bowed low at our first entrance; and when we were come near his chair, he stood up, holding forth his hand ungloved, and in posture of blessing; and we every one of us stooped down, and kissed the hem of his tippet. That done, the rest departed, and I remained. Then he warned the pages forth of the room, and caused me to sit down beside him, and spake to me thus in the Spanish tongue:

"God bless thee, my son; I will give thee the greatest jewel I have. For I will impart unto thee, for the love of God and men, a relation of the true state of Solomon's House. Son, to make you know the true state of Solomon's House, I will keep this order. First, I will set forth unto

[68] Hung with tapestries. [69] Steps to the canopy.

you the end of our foundation. Secondly, the preparations and instruments we have for our works. Thirdly, the several employments and functions whereto our fellows are assigned. And fourthly, the ordinances and rites which we observe.

"The end of our foundation is the knowledge of causes, and secret motions of things; and the enlarging of the bounds of human empire, to the effecting of all things possible.

"The preparations and instruments are these. We have large and deep caves of several depths; the deepest are sunk six hundred fathoms; and some of them are digged and made under great hills and mountains; so that if you reckon together the depth of the hill, and the depth of the cave, they are, some of them, above three miles deep. For we find that the depth of a hill, and the depth of a cave from the flat, is the same thing; both remote alike from the sun and heaven's beams, and from the open air. These caves we call the lower region, and we use them for all coagulations, indurations, refrigerations, and conservations of bodies.[70] We use them likewise for the imitation of natural mines, and the producing also of new artificial metals, by compositions and materials which we use, and lay there for many years. We use them also sometimes (which may seem strange) for curing of some diseases and for prolongation of life in some hermits that

[70] Thickening, hardening, chilling, and preserving, for scientific research.

New Atlantis

choose to live there, well accommodated of all things necessary, and indeed live very long; by whom also we learn many things.

"We have burials [71] in several earths, where we put divers [72] cements, as the Chinese do their porcelain. But we have them in greater variety, and some of them more fine. We also have great variety of composts and soils, for the making of the earth fruitful.

"We have high towers, the highest about half a mile in height, and some of them likewise set upon high mountains, so that the vantage of the hill, with the tower, is in the highest of them three miles at least. And these places we call the upper region, accounting the air between the high places and the low as a middle region. We use these towers, according to their several heights and situations, for insulation, refrigeration, conservation, and for the view of divers meteors [73]—as winds, rain, snow, hail; and some of the fiery meteors also. And upon them, in some places, are dwellings of hermits, whom we visit sometimes, and instruct what to observe.

"We have great lakes, both salt and fresh, whereof we have use for the fish and fowl. We use them also for burials of some natural bodies, for we find a difference in things buried in earth, or in air below the earth, and things buried in water. We have also pools, of which some do strain fresh water out of salt, and others by art do turn

[71] Burial places.
[72] Various.
[73] Phenomena of weather.

fresh water into salt. We have also some rocks in the midst of the sea, and some bays upon the shore for some works, wherein is required the air and vapor of the sea. We have likewise violent streams and cataracts, which serve us for many motions; and likewise engines for multiplying and enforcing [74] of winds to set also on divers motions.

"We have also a number of artificial wells and fountains, made in imitation of the natural sources and baths, as tincted upon vitriol, sulphur, steel, brass, lead, niter, and other minerals; and again, we have little wells for infusions of many things, where the waters take the virtue quicker and better than in vessels or basins. And amongst them we have a water which we call Water of Paradise, being by that we do to it made very sovereign for health and prolongation of life.

"We have also great and spacious houses, where we imitate and demonstrate meteors—as snow, hail, rain, some artificial rains of bodies, and not of water, thunders, lightnings; also generations of bodies in air—as frogs, flies, and divers others.

"We have also certain chambers, which we call chambers of health, where we qualify the air as we think good and proper for the cure of divers diseases, and preservation of health.

"We have also fair and large baths, of several mixtures, for the cure of diseases and the restoring of man's body

[74] Reinforcing.

from arefaction;[75] and others for the confirming of it in strength of sinews, vital parts, and the very juice and substance of the body.

"We have also large and various orchards and gardens, wherein we do not so much respect beauty as variety of ground and soil, proper for divers trees and herbs, and some very spacious, where trees and berries are set, whereof we make divers kinds of drinks, besides the vineyards. In these we practice likewise all conclusions[76] of grafting and inoculating, as well of wild-trees as fruit-trees, which produceth many effects. And we make by art, in the same orchards and gardens, trees and flowers to come earlier or later than their seasons, and to come up and bear more speedily than by their natural course they do. We make them also by art greater much than their nature; and their fruit greater and sweeter, and of differing taste, smell, color, and figure, from their nature. And many of them we so order as they become of medicinal use.

"We have also means to make divers plants rise by mixtures of earths, without seeds, and likewise to make divers new plants, differing from the vulgar, and to make one tree or plant turn into another.

"We have also parks and enclosures of all sorts of beasts and birds; which we use not only for view or rareness, but likewise for dissections and trials, that thereby we may

[75] Drying up. [76] Experiments.

take light what may be wrought upon the body of man. Wherein we find many strange effects: as continuing life in them, though divers parts, which you account vital, be perished and taken forth; resuscitating of some that seem dead in appearance, and the like. We try also all poisons, and other medicines upon them, as well of chirurgery as physic.[77] By art likewise we make them greater or taller than their kind is, and contrariwise dwarf them and stay their growth; we make them more fruitful and bearing than their kind is, and contrariwise barren and not generative. Also we make them differ in color, shape, activity, many ways. We find means to make commixtures and copulations of divers kinds, which have produced many new kinds, and them not barren, as the general opinion is. We make a number of kinds, of serpents, worms, flies, fishes, of putrefaction,[78] whereof some are advanced (in effect) to be perfect creatures, like beasts or birds, and have sexes, and do propagate. Neither do we this by chance, but we know beforehand of what matter and commixture, what kind of those creatures will arise.

"We have also particular pools where we make trials upon fishes, as we have said before of beasts and birds.

"We have also places for breed and generation of those kinds of worms and flies which are of special use; such as are with you your silkworms and bees.

"I will not hold you long with recounting of our brew-

[77] Of surgery as of medicine.   [78] Rotting matter.

New Atlantis

houses, bake-houses, and kitchens, where are made divers drinks, breads, and meats, rare and of special effects. Wines we have of grapes, and drinks of other juice, of fruits, of grains, and of roots, and of mixtures with honey, sugar, manna, and fruits dried and decocted;[79] also of the tears or woundings of trees, and of the pulp of canes. And these drinks are of several ages, some to the age or last[80] of forty years. We have drinks also brewed with several herbs, and roots and spices; yea, with several fleshes and white-meats; whereof some of the drinks are such as they are in effect meat and drink both, so that divers, especially in age, do desire to live with them with little or no meat or bread. And above all we strive to have drinks of extreme thin parts,[81] to insinuate into the body, and yet without all biting, sharpness, or fretting; insomuch as some of them, put upon the back of your hand, will with a little stay pass through to the palm, and taste yet mild to the mouth. We have also waters which we ripen in that fashion, as they become nourishing, so that they are indeed excellent drinks, and many will use no other. Bread we have of several grains, roots, and kernels; yea, and some of flesh, and fish, dried; with divers kinds of leavenings and seasonings; so that some do extremely move appetites, some do nourish so, as divers do live of them, without any other meat, who live very long. So for meats, we have some of them so beaten, and made tender, and mortified,

[79] Condensed. [80] Duration. [81] Properties.

yet without all corrupting, as a weak heat of the stomach will turn them into good chilus,[82] as well as a strong heat would meat otherwise prepared. We have some meats also, and breads, and drinks which taken by men enable them to fast long after; and some other that used make the very flesh of men's bodies sensibly more hard and tough, and their strength far greater than otherwise it would be.

"We have dispensatories or shops of medicines; wherein you may easily think, if we have such variety of plants and living creatures, more than you have in Europe (for we know what you have), the simples,[83] drugs and ingredients of medicines, must likewise be in so much the greater variety. We have them likewise of divers ages, and long fermentations. And for their preparations, we have not only all manner of exquisite distillations and separations, and especially by gentle heats, and percolations through divers strainers, yea, and substances; but also exact forms of composition, whereby they incorporate almost as they were natural simples.

"We have also divers mechanical arts which you have not; and stuffs made by them, as papers, linen, silks, tissues, dainty works of feathers of wonderful luster, excellent dyes, and many others: and shops likewise, as well for such as are not brought into vulgar use amongst us, as for those that are. For you must know, that of the things be-

---

[82] Chyle.   [83] Herbs.

fore recited, many of them are grown into use throughout the kingdom, but yet, if they did flow from our invention, we have of them also for patterns and principles.

"We have also furnaces of great diversities, and that keep great diversity of heats: fierce and quick, strong and constant, soft and mild; blown, quiet, dry, moist, and the like. But above all we have heats, in imitation of the sun's and heavenly bodies' heats, that pass divers inequalities, and (as it were) orbs, progresses, and returns, whereby we produce admirable effects. Besides, we have heats of dungs, and of bellies and maws of living creatures and of their bloods and bodies, and of hays and herbs laid up moist, of lime unquenched, and such like. Instruments also which generate heat only by motion. And farther, places for strong insulations; and again, places under the earth, which by nature or art yield heat. These divers heats we use as the nature of the operation which we intend requireth.

"We have also perspective houses, where we make demonstrations of all lights and radiations, and of all colors; and out of things uncolored and transparent, we can represent unto you all several colors, not in rainbows (as it is in gems and prisms), but of themselves single. We represent also all multiplications of light, which we carry to great distance, and make so sharp, as to discern small points and lines. Also all colorations of light; all delusions and deceits of the sight, in figures, magnitudes, motions, colors; all demonstrations of shadows. We find also divers means yet unknown to you of producing of light, originally from divers bodies. We procure means of seeing objects afar off, as in the heaven and remote places; and represent things near as afar off, and things afar off as near; making feigned distances. We have also helps for the sight, far above spectacles and glasses in use. We have also glasses and means to see small and minute bodies perfectly and distinctly; as the shapes and colors of small flies and worms, grains, and flaws in gems which cannot otherwise be seen, observations in urine and blood not otherwise to be seen. We make artificial rainbows, halos, and circles about light. We represent also all manner of reflections, refractions, and multiplications of visual beams of objects.

"We have also precious stones of all kinds, many of them of great beauty and to you unknown; crystals likewise, and glasses of divers kinds; and amongst them some of metals vitrificated,[84] and other materials, besides those of which you make glass. Also a number of fossils and imperfect minerals, which you have not. Likewise loadstones of prodigious virtue: and other rare stones, both natural and artificial.

"We have also sound-houses, where we practice and demonstrate all sounds and their generation. We have harmonies which you have not, of quarter-sounds and lesser slides of sounds. Divers instruments of music likewise to

[84] Turned into glass.

you unknown, some sweeter than any you have; together with bells and rings that are dainty and sweet. We represent small sounds as great and deep; likewise great sounds, extenuate [85] and sharp; we make divers tremblings and warblings of sounds, which in their original are entire. We represent and imitate all articulate sounds and letters, and the voices and notes of beasts and birds. We have certain helps which set to the ear do further the hearing greatly. We have also divers strange and artificial echoes, reflecting the voice many times, and as it were tossing it; and some that give back the voice louder than it came, some shriller and some deeper: yea, some rendering the voice, differing in the letters or articulate sound from that they receive. We have also means to convey sounds in trunks [86] and pipes, in strange lines and distances.

"We have also perfume-houses, wherewith we join also practices of taste. We multiply smells, which may seem strange: we imitate smells, making all smells to breathe out of other mixtures than those that give them. We make divers imitations of taste likewise, so that they will deceive any man's taste. And in this house we contain also a confiture-house, where we make all sweetmeats, dry and moist, and divers pleasant wines, milks, broths, and salads, far in greater variety than you have.

"We have also engine-houses, where are prepared engines and instruments for all sorts of motions. There we

---

[85] Thin.   [86] Tubes.

imitate and practice to make swifter motions than any you have, either out of your muskets or any engine that you have; and to make them and multiply them more easily and with small force, by wheels and other means, and to make them stronger and more violent than yours are, exceeding your greatest cannons and basilisks.[87] We represent also ordnance and instruments of war and engines of all kinds; and likewise new mixtures and compositions of gunpowder, wildfires burning in water and unquenchable, also fireworks of all variety, both for pleasure and use. We imitate also flights of birds; we have some degrees [88] of flying in the air. We have ships and boats for going under water and brooking of seas, also swimming-girdles and supporters. We have divers curious clocks, and other like motions of return, and some perpetual motions. We imitate also motions of living creatures by images of men, beasts, birds, fishes, and serpents; we have also a great number of other various motions, strange for equality, fineness, and subtlety.

"We have also a mathematical-house, where are represented all instruments, as well of geometry as astronomy, exquisitely made.

"We have also houses of deceits of the senses, where we represent all manner of feats of juggling, false apparitions, impostures and illusions, and their fallacies. And surely you will easily believe that we, that have so many

[87] A long cannon.   [88] Of success.

things truly natural which induce admiration, could in a world of particulars deceive the senses if we would disguise those things, and labor to make them seem more miraculous. But we do hate all impostures and lies, insomuch as we have severely forbidden it to all our fellows, under pain of ignominy and fines, that they do not show any natural work or thing adorned or swelling, but only pure as it is, and without all affectation of strangeness.

"These are, my son, the riches of Solomon's House.

"For the several employments and offices of our fellows, we have twelve that sail into foreign countries under the names of other nations (for our own we conceal), who bring us the books and abstracts, and patterns of experiments of all other parts. These we call Merchants of Light.

"We have three that collect the experiments which are in all books. These we call Depredators.

"We have three that collect the experiments of all mechanical arts, and also of liberal sciences, and also of practices which are not brought into arts. These we call Mystery-men.

"We have three that try new experiments, such as themselves think good. These we call Pioneers or Miners.

"We have three that draw the experiments of the former four into titles and tables, to give the better light for the drawing of observations and axioms out of them. These we call Compilers.

"We have three that bend themselves, looking into the

experiments of their fellows, and cast about how to draw out of them things of use and practice for man's life and knowledge, as well for works as for plain demonstration of causes, means of natural divinations, and the easy and clear discovery of the virtues and parts of bodies. These we call Dowry-men or Benefactors.

"Then after divers meetings and consults of our whole number to consider of the former labors and collections, we have three that take care out of them to direct new experiments, of a higher light, more penetrating into nature than the former. These we call Lamps.

"We have three others that do execute the experiments so directed, and report them. These we call Inoculators.

"Lastly, we have three that raise the former discoveries by experiments into greater observations, axioms, and aphorisms. These we call Interpreters of Nature.

"We have also, as you must think, novices and apprentices, that the succession of the former employed men do not fail; besides a great number of servants and attendants, men and women. And this we do also: we have consultations, which of the inventions and experiences which we have discovered shall be published, and which not; and take all an oath of secrecy for the concealing of those which we think fit to keep secret, though some of those we do reveal sometimes to the state, and some not.

"For our ordinances and rites, we have two very long and fair galleries; in one of these we place patterns and samples of all manner of the more rare and excellent inventions; in the other we place the statues of all principal inventors. There we have the statue of your Columbus, that discovered the West Indies; also the inventor of ships; your monk that was the inventor of ordnance and of gunpowder;[89] the inventor of music; the inventor of letters; the inventor of printing; the inventor of observations of astronomy; the inventor of works in metal; the inventor of glass; the inventor of silk of the worm; the inventor of wine; the inventor of corn and bread; the inventor of sugars; and all these by more certain tradition than you have. Then we have divers inventors of our own, of excellent works, which since you have not seen, it were too long to make descriptions of them; and besides, in the right understanding of those descriptions you might easily err. For upon every invention of value we erect a statue to the inventor, and give him a liberal and honorable reward. These statues are some of brass, some of marble and touchstone, some of cedar and other special woods gilt and adorned; some of iron, some of silver, some of gold.

"We have certain hymns and services, which we say daily, of laud and thanks to God for his marvellous works. And forms of prayer, imploring his aid and blessing for the illumination of our labors, and the turning of them into good and holy uses.

"Lastly, we have circuits or visits of divers principal cities of the kingdom; where, as it cometh to pass, we

[89] Roger Bacon.

do publish such new profitable inventions as we think good. And we do also declare natural divinations [90] of diseases, plagues, swarms of hurtful creatures, scarcity, tempests, earthquakes, great inundations, comets, temperature of the year, and divers other things; and we give counsel thereupon, what the people shall do for the prevention and remedy of them."

And when he had said this he stood up; and I, as I had been taught, knelt down; and he laid his right hand upon my head, and said, "God bless thee, my son, and God bless this relation which I have made. I give thee leave to publish it, for the good of other nations; for we here are in God's bosom, a land unknown." And so he left me; having assigned a value of about two thousand ducats for a bounty to me and my fellows. For they give great largesses, where they come, upon all occasions.

[The rest was not perfected]

[90] **Forecasting** by natural observation.